DONORS

Thomas A. Dodson, M.D.

Dorothy L. Banks-Keas
Polly Black
Robert S. Castro
Shirley Christian
John Crawford
Ryan & Suzanne Dodson
Mr. & Mrs. Louis A. Evans
Joe Fiebig
Charlotte W. Gibbens
Deloris Glenn
In Memory of Polly Hunt
Bari S. Johnson
Bill & Martha King
Gloria Lambert
Mr. & Mrs. Kent Maxwell
Karen A. Pepper Mueller
Dr. & Mrs. Steven A. Mueller
Lacy Saak
Joe M. Sears
Jerry Thompson
Liz & Carlos Tuttle
Dr. & Ms. J. W. Weatherford

JO ANN KESSEL

PIAVINNIA

THE BENT-GUERRIER CONNECTION

Printed in the United States of America

ISBN 978-1-938923-17-3

Library of Congress Catalog Number 2014953988

Designed by Nathan Dunn

Cover Image: "Piavinnia" by Oklahoma City native and award-winning artist Brent Learned, an enrolled member of the Cheyenne and Arapho Tribes of Oklahoma.

Oklahoma Heritage Association

CONTENTS

ACKNOWLEDGMENTS

The research in this book owes much credit to the patient efforts of archivist Phyllis Adams and volunteer Tressie Nealy of the Indian archives section of the Oklahoma Historical Society, under the direction of William D. Welge. Without their good-natured assistance, the task would have been vastly more difficult.

The family of Ann Guerrier Shadlow has been helpful in adding vital information and pictures, especially Charles Pratt and Harvey Pratt. The protagonist herself, Ann Guerrier Shadlow, entered into the spirit of the writing of this book wholeheartedly. She was proud of her grandparents and spoke voluminously about them on tape and recorded interviews, as well as relating the story of her own life.

Many thanks to the Western History Collections of the University of Oklahoma Library for the use of old photographs.

This book could not have been accomplished without the guiding hand and expertise of Max Nichols, former publicity director of the Oklahoma Historical Society. The author gratefully acknowledges his vital role in keeping the author on the straight and narrow path toward integrating a meaningful story. The author also thanks M. J. Van Deventer, author and former editor/publisher of *Persimmon Hill,* a publication of the National Cowboy & Western Heritage Museum.

Most helpful was the input of Dr. William Savage of the history department at the University of Oklahoma, who offered suggestions toward the betterment of the story, doing so with his usual grace and wit.

The writing group at St. Luke's United Methodist Church in Oklahoma City provided weekly impetus to keep on the path. Connie Parker, Virginia Shackford, Helen Murray, Mary Ann Cummins, and Eva Crone all made helpful contributions to the flow of the story.

Finally, thank you to the Oklahoma Heritage Association, Publications Committee Chairman Bob Burke, and Director of Publications and Education Gini Moore Campbell for believing in the project and bringing the finished product to fruition.

This story has been told with the best efforts of the author toward verification of dates and places, recognizing human fallibility and the vagaries of tracing indistinct history. The author employs terms used by Indians themselves, rather than using terms which may be seen as being more politically correct in this century. For instance, the term half-breed rather than mixed blood, and Indian rather than Native American. Another choice is the use of the Cheyenne, rather than Cheyennes.

INTRODUCTION

This is the story of how two half-breed Cheyenne, descended from English (Bent) and French (Guerrier) ancestry, experienced the bloodiest massacre in the history of the government's Indian wars. The wheels of the heavily-laden ox carts of their fathers cut deep ruts in the Santa Fe Trail to and from Westport and St. Louis. The wheels of their own farm wagon and fancy barouche cut ruts in the soil of western Indian Territory and early Oklahoma. The Bent-Guerrier union produced a woman their equal in drive, determination, and life skills who made her mark in the twentieth century, Ann Guerrier Shadlow. The union of these two families followed as a consequence of the monumental Journey of Discovery undertaken by captains William Clark and Meriwether Lewis in 1804 that ended joyfully with their return in 1806.

Lewis and Clark brought back from their trek through the vast unexplored territory to the Pacific Ocean not only specimens of the flora and fauna gathered on the journey but, just as important, their stories. Their tales excited adventurers to cross the great Mississippi River in search of a promised fur trapping business that would supply the world's need for beaver hats, or a career in trading with the many Indian tribes. The Bent brothers and William Guerrier were among those caught up in the excitement and danger dancing before their imaginations, and who left their homes in order to follow their lust for adventure.

The early travelers and explorers trekked toward unknown and unmapped western lands with a passion. This wanderlust, this creativity, this search for new and brighter fields of endeavor infected Americans by the thousands to desert their homes and careers and to travel by wagon, oxcart, horseback, or even by shank's mare in order to seek new lives for themselves in the prairies and mountains. At first, the trickle of humanity was small. The Bents and Guerrier were among the first of the non-native people to lead the way.

The trickle in time became a stream, and then a torrent, the wagon ruts in the soil still visible a century and a half later. The pioneers braved river crossings, endless hot and dry days on the prairie or desert, thirst, hunger, illness, and death on the trail. There were no telephones to report disasters, no automobiles for rapid transit over turnpikes, not even doctors for emergency surgery or patching a wound. They were on their own to make it or not, to survive or perish. And survive they did, to own new lands, to stake their claims and work their lands.

These emigrants left the security of their homes, farms, and jobs in the eastern lands of the United States to seek new lives for themselves and their families in the unknown West. Hearing of the vast lands untilled and the beauty of nature's forests and streams, they piled into their wagons not only the necessities for the journey, but prized family possessions as well. Clocks, rockers, cook stoves, pictures, and even pianos were hauled over the trails to give their new homes a semblance of comfort and family memories. Overloaded, many of the wagons were forced to dump these treasures along the well-worn trails.

But these lands were not uninhabited. Whose lands were these? The many tribes across the country claimed their own lands, lands for hunting purposes, lands for living during the changing seasons, lands to share with an allied tribe. The lands the tribe claimed were not held through deeds registered in courthouses. They were those in which by tradition the tribe lived, moved campsites, hunted game, set up winter quarters, and enjoyed spring grasses for their pony herds. The tribe had no document to flash and no need of one, as the tribal area was known to one and all through tradition and habitual use. The land was communal to the tribe for the benefit of all its members. No land was individually owned by a tribal member. How could he recognize that the white man thought he could own land that the Great Spirit provided for the benefit of all?

The Indians had established their own areas, laws, and customs long before their lands were invaded by hordes of whites seeking their dreams. The Cheyenne was a large and well-established tribe of the central plains, with ownership of the right to sustain themselves through the culture of the buffalo, and with premier horsemanship abilities. Their government, though unwritten, served the tribe well. Their forty-four chiefs kept order in the tribe through respect and reverence for their wisdom, abilities, and generosity toward the tribal members.

The clash of these two cultures was inevitable.

Edmund Returns to the Tribe

1

Young Edmund Guerrier pondered this new thought as he spent a pleasant evening in Louisville, Kansas with his friend John Smith in the spring of 1864. A half-breed Cheyenne, the other half French, Edmund had not seen his Cheyenne relatives since his father took him out of the Cheyenne camps at age eleven and placed him in boarding school at St. Mary's Mission in Kansas, thence to St. Louis University, for his education in the world of the whites. But that was thirteen years ago. Now at age twenty-four, he listened as John Smith urged him to seek out his relatives for a reunion.

John S. Smith[1] was a tailor in St. Louis, born in 1810, who went to the Arkansas River country to trade with the Indians about 1830. There, he married a Cheyenne woman and kept a lodge in the Cheyenne camps for his family, camps that traveled when the tribe moved for hunting, tribal ceremonies, or for the wintering seasons. When Smith was in the camps, he frequently heard inquiries from Edmund's relatives about him. They wondered where he was, how he was. In Smith's opinion, Edmund should seek out his relatives for a visit, to ease their minds about him. After all, he had disappeared from their midst in 1851, long ago. They remembered Hawk, Edmund's Cheyenne name, and were concerned for his welfare.

Edmund thought about it. He had been busy with his own affairs in the white world, mainly working for the government. He had whacked bulls on the trail from Fort Leavenworth, convoyed a thousand horses from the same fort, and transported Apache prisoners of war to Kit Carson's garrison at Fort Sumner, before being hired as a sutler at Fort Riley. Now he was planning a trading expedition with another trader, John Stickler, into the Indian country of Colorado and Kansas. This might be the ideal time to find his relatives.

But his feelings about a possible reunion were mixed. He remembered his early days in the tribe, his loving mother, his extended Cheyenne family, and his old playmates in the Indian camp. He grew up as a free-roaming Cheyenne boy. Recalled his youth, he felt a strong urge to revisit those halcyon days, those doting relatives. But, he wondered how he would be accepted back into the tribe. How would they greet him, his sisters, half-brother, and cousins, after so long an absence? His Cheyenne mother, Tah-tah-tois-neh, and his father, William Guerrier, were both dead. With some misgivings, he nevertheless made a decision. He would see his relatives as soon as unfolding life events would allow.

His first task was to meet up with Stickler. United, the pair then traveled to Fort Lyon on the Arkansas River in southern Colorado, trading along the way. At Fort Lyon, they learned that William Bent was escorting a large body of Cheyenne to Fort Larned for a meeting with the post commander, where Bent sought a pact of peace between the tribe and the army.

The name of William Bent was a familiar one to Edmund Guerrier. Although he had never met the famous man, he had heard many stories from his father about this pioneer of the Santa Fe Trail, owner of the largest and earliest of the trading posts in southern Colorado. Edmund's father, William Guerrier, had been a trader who worked for William Bent and his Bent, St. Vrain and Company outfit during the 1840s. Edmund knew the stories of Bent's friendly association with the Cheyenne who often camped near the fort to trade their pelts at the post. He knew that Bent had married Owl Woman, the eldest daughter of the revered medicine man and Keeper of the Sacred Arrows, White Thunder,[2] and his wife, Tail Woman. And, he knew that William Bent was regarded highly as a peacemaker among the Indians he dealt with, primarily the Cheyenne and its allied tribe, the Arapaho. And now, Bent was traveling with the tribe in yet another effort toward the goal of enticing the Cheyenne into peaceful behavior. The tribe was angry and upset, spoiling to avenge its recent abusive treatment and several recent unprovoked attacks from volunteer cavalry units.

Edmund Guerrier and John Stickler left Fort Lyon headed east toward their destination of Fort Larned, a government fort on the Santa Fe Trail northeast of Fort Dodge in eastern Kansas. There, the pair hoped to trade with the Cheyenne while the tribe assembled around the fort during the meeting between Bent, the post commandant, and the Indians. Edmund's other purpose was to meet with his relatives. He wondered whether or not they would be able to understand each other. As he had spoken English for the past thirteen years, he remembered only a few words in Cheyenne, the rest only a vague memory. But with apprehension yet longing, he pushed forward toward Fort Larned, scared but eager. Fate, however, provided a dangerous delay on the route, which could have meant death to Edmund and his trading companion.

Camped one afternoon along the trail for a siesta and respite, Edmund and Stickler were surprised by a visit from two friendly Cheyenne, who ventured out to kill a buffalo for an evening meal for the foursome to share. The party was soon joined by several Arapaho, who advised them that the Kiowa, Comanche, and Arapaho were "out," meaning that war parties were spoiling for a fight or some loot. When the group bedded for the night, a Kiowa war party sneaked into their camp and alerted the Arapaho that they were there, and to get away quickly. The Arapaho then crawled to warn their allies the Cheyenne, who awakened Stickler whose wife was Cheyenne, and Edmund who was himself Cheyenne. Talking to the Kiowa, the Cheyenne pointed to Edmund, saying that he was Cheyenne by blood and urged the Kiowa to let them go. "There are lots of white men traveling along the Santa Fe road you can get," one of the Cheyenne told the Kiowa.[3] Luckily, the Kiowa agreed with the

Cheyenne to let Edmund and Stickler live and go on their way.

The party split up. Stickler rode on toward Fort Larned and was able to reach it without further incident to himself, although he lost all his ponies to thievery on that trip. Edmund opted to stay with the two Cheyenne visitors. He felt this was a good time to greet his relatives. But when he reached the new Cheyenne camp, he found the people in an uproar.

The tribe had just moved its camp away from Fort Larned and was in an agitated and vengeful mood, as the peace talks at Fort Larned had failed miserably. Bent had arrived with the tribe as planned, but he and the tribal leaders soon learned that nothing could be accomplished within a fort governed by drunken Indian-haters. Bent, small in stature at 5'6", had a way with him, ordinarily. With a handsome yet rugged face, he was soft spoken but deliberate in his speech and knew the ways of conciliation between antagonists. This time, however, there was no hope. The camp commandant was a drunk and allowed his soldiers to drink freely and to treat the Indians with disdain. The Cheyenne, who had arrived to discuss peace at the behest of William Bent, went away angry. They moved camp, as the talks were useless. Bent himself was disgusted at the outcome.

This was the condition of the tribe[4] when Edmund reached the Cheyenne camp seeking a reunion with his relatives. There, he saw firsthand what it meant for a tribe to be "all out," to view an Indian war on the plains.

All seemed to be in a state of confusion in the Cheyenne camp, with people milling about. But Edmund remembered that this was not the case at all, as each person had his responsibilities when the tribe moved to a new location. The women were busy setting up the family lodges, unhooking the tepee poles from the travois, erecting them, then covering the poles with buffalo skins. The younger men had charge of herding the camp's ponies onto fresh grass nearby. The warriors staked their prize war ponies near each lodge and stashed their arms and weapons conveniently within the lodge. They did this out of long habit and prudence, lest they be unprepared when a surprise attack from an enemy tribe or an army unit should occur.

Edmund found his family. He was greeted warmly with hugs, cries of delight, and soft handshakes, contrary to his apprehensions. No need to fear. He was totally accepted by his relatives and the larger tribe. Although a half-breed, he was one of them. His family greeted him by using his Indian name of Hawk, the name he was given as a child living in the Indian camps with his Cheyenne relatives. Hearing the name Hawk rolling off the tongues of his people took Edmund by surprise, as he had nearly forgotten the comforting sound of his Indian name during the many years he was away attending white schools in the East, where that name was never spoken.

As he greeted his family, Hawk's eye caught in the distance the figure of a young girl walking rapidly on a mission of her own. Petite in size, she wore a gleaming soft-white buckskin beaded dress. Her dark hair was plaited, then tied with buckskin thongs. Edmund's throat caught as he took in her beauty. Click. His mind photographed the image of this Cheyenne girl, of her deliberate walk and her graceful bearing. He planned to inquire about her.

Unmarried, Edmund had not been looking for an attachment. He had been too busy. Before his hiring as a post sutler at Fort Riley, he had convoyed hundreds of horses for the government, as well as transported Apache prisoners of war to Kit Carson's garrison at Fort Sumner. On the trails or in government posts, he had no time to look for a sweetheart. Certainly, he could have attracted the young girls. At 5'6", he was of average height for that era in America, but he was also trim, well-built and athletic. With dark hazel eyes, French aquiline nose, and wavy dark auburn hair with golden glints worn in the French style, loose to his shoulders, he was handsome. An eligible bachelor dressed in fancy white man's clothes, wearing beaded moccasins. Before, he had not been interested in a long-term attachment.

But this time, it was different. He could not let this go without trying to see her again. Who was she? When his relatives insisted that he join them over the summer to become reacquainted and to honor them with a visit, the presence of this girl was a large measure of his decision to accept their invitation.

Two days later as he walked with his younger half-brother Henry in the Cheyenne camp, Edmund spotted her again and inquired of her to Henry. Henry followed the direction of Edmund's lips as he twisted them to the side in the polite Cheyenne way which resisted pointing directly. Henry said she was Julia, Walking Woman, youngest daughter of William Bent and his wife Owl Woman, who died following Julia's birth. Bent then married Yellow Woman, later known as Slow Smoking, sister of Owl Woman, who produced Bent's next child, Charles, born about 1849.

Edmund recalled an early friendship with George Bent, William Bent's son and Julia's older brother, a young man near his own age. That was it. That was the entrée he needed to meet Julia. He would renew his acquaintance with George and request an introduction to his sister, the lovely Walking Woman.

But there was not time to pursue his interest in becoming acquainted with Julia. The camp was in an uproar. George Bent was in a hurry, rushing in and out of camp, always busy. The Cheyenne rightfully felt slighted and demeaned following the failed peace talks at Fort Larned, where they had traveled in good faith at the behest of their friend William Bent. With Bent's help, the tribe wanted to present its case for peaceful treatment from the government. Now, the peace talks were useless and nothing was accomplished, except further angering the Indians and driving them toward war.

Up to this abortive meeting, the tribe had been agitated and uneasy, as their camps and hunting parties had been attacked indiscriminately by volunteer Colorado cavalry units without regard to the tribe's peaceful intentions and behavior. Black Kettle, a chief of the Cheyenne, was a peace chief, had been in Washington, D. C., and was well-known for his efforts toward making peace with the government forces. But the Colorado volunteers were hell-bent on killing Indians, any and all of them.

Major T. I. McKenny, inspector general of the Department

of Kansas, reported to General Samuel R. Curtis: "I think that if great caution is not exercised on our part there will be a bloody war. It should be our policy to conciliate them, guard our mails and trains well to prevent theft, and stop these scouting parties that are roaming over the country, who do not know one tribe from another, and who will kill anything in the shape of an Indian. It will require but a few more murders on the part of our troops to unite all these warlike tribes."[5]

Major Henry D. Wallen, commanding officer at Fort Sumner, agreed. He telegraphed his superiors in Washington that the Colorado volunteers should be stopped at once, to prevent an all-out Indian war.[6] This was not done, and when the Colorado volunteers continued their attacks with abandon, the predictions were proved correct. The plains Indians went to war fulltime.

By his own choice, Edmund was not a combatant. He thought of himself as French, and American, having for half his life lost sight of his Cheyenne roots. He had been living in the white world since leaving for his schooling at the age of eleven and had no taste for revenge and depredations against the white man. Therefore he was not personally engaged in the raiding. But he was present in the Cheyenne camp and witnessed the warriors' preparations for battle and their return to camp with spoils from the raids. He knew the warriors were raiding heavily along the stage lines, into ranches and trading posts, and up and down the emigrant trails.

In the melee of the camp during the weeks of these raids, Edmund had glimpsed at Julia occasionally but failed to find the right moment to meet her properly. And, he knew that the honor of the Cheyenne maidens was fiercely guarded by their families. Of all the plains tribes, it was well known that the Cheyenne girls were the most closely watched. He remembered the tradition that he would need approval of his intentions to court Julia from a family member. Her father William Bent was not present, having left the peace meeting following the failure of the talks. Her older brother George, active in the raiding, frequently was out of camp. Or, if returned from a raid, George was involved in distributing the spoils or dancing the scalp and victory dances each evening. Edmund reckoned this was not the proper time to go courting, as the tribe was in the midst of an all-out war.

Edmund's erudite description of the scenes in the Cheyenne camp was recorded, "No man in these days can realize what happens in camp when a big Indian tribe is on the warpath," said Guerrier. "Day and night came plunder from wagon trains, trading posts, and the homes of settlers—scalps, red with dry blood, and some fresh and moist; captive women and children; horses and mules, sugar, coffee, dry goods, money, letters, guns, ammunition, whiskey; in fact, a man could hardly recount the innumerable things that were piled in the tepees. Scouts were coming and going, war parties arriving and departing, and at night there were war dances, scalp dances, and the incantations of the 'medicine man.'"[7]

Two white women and several children captives were understandably frightened. Edmund tried to reassure them, telling them that because they had not been killed initially upon capture, they probably would be allowed to live. But he was less successful in assuaging their hunger, as there was no food in camp besides the buffalo meat that the Indians preferred, but which the captives were unable to eat.

The Indians were raiding along the stage lines in Colorado, killing and looting where they struck. As a seasoned warrior of twenty-one years with a military background from his service in the army of the Confederate States of America, George Bent was involved in this raiding, as were his brothers Robert and young Charles. The warriors left their camp in the full array of all their battle finery.

The morning of their departure, each man took the time to paint his face and body with colors and designs chosen as his personal symbols. He donned his headdress of eagle feathers, banded on the forehead with Cheyenne beadwork, and adorned on the sides with the tails of the white ermine. Some headdresses had eagle feather trailers that skimmed the ground on either side of the horse he rode, so long were they. Other warriors wore their plaited hair wrapped in leather thongs or adorned with various furs. A few warriors used the entire head of the wolf or the bear as their own bonnets. Each was guided in the choice of dress through his personal visions, denoting his power.

Their costumes were complete with the addition of leather leggings, breech clout, and beaded moccasins. The warriors further adorned themselves with copper or bone or metal earrings and bracelets. After donning his special attire, each man reached for his bois d'arc bow, quiver of handmade arrows with metal tips, lance adorned with pendant feathers, and at last picked up his uniquely decorated skin shield that told of his personal power through its symbols. At that time in 1864, most warriors also owned guns, protected in deerskin gun cases adorned with beadwork.

The warrior now was prepared. He stepped outside his lodge and unhooked the rope of his warhorse tethered outside the tepee, and prepared his special horse for their day together at war. He tied the horse's tail up short and added feathers to a thong around the horse's tail, then painted designs on the horse. Perhaps a circle around one eye, perhaps a zigzag of a lightning streak down one leg for fleetness of foot, perhaps the warrior's hand print on the flank. Each symbol had meaning and was special to the horse's owner.

He and his mount were ready. Each felt the excitement of the chase. Each had blood in his eye. Beautiful as they were, the horse and rider provided a spectacular scene, frightening and foreboding danger. As they joined the other mounted warriors, order was kept through the admonitions of the warrior society to keep ranks and act for the benefit of the whole war party until the fight actually began.

The wanton plundering enacted during the raids at this time was enormous. Julia's brother and the eldest son of William Bent, Robert Bent was one of those who returned from a raid with spoils. As he rode back into the circle of the Cheyenne camp, he called to an elderly woman watching from the sidelines.

"Heya, grandmother," he said. "Do you want some jewelry?"

"Yes. I'll take it," she replied.

Robert tossed her an arm, the arm of a Mexican woman, severed at the elbow, the arm still holding the bracelets and rings of the unfortunate senora.[8]

As a result of these depredations by the tribes, the main stage roads in Colorado leading to Denver were closed to traffic of any kind. Food goods necessarily became scarce. Prices of the food still available in Denver skyrocketed, alarming the citizens who clamored to Colorado Governor John Evans to do something to stop the raids. Evans set the gears in motion, authorizing Colonel J. M. Chivington to gather a band of volunteers together into an army to fight the Indians. His volunteer band eventually became a nearly one-thousand strong rabble of men, Indian haters.

Colonel Chivington was an enormous man, over 6' tall and broad in frame. A Methodist elder, he nevertheless had no qualms about his task. In fact, he relished it. He joined in league with Major Scott Anthony, the commandant at Fort Lyon, a stern hardliner in his attitude toward the Indians. Indeed, at a meal with his officers on November 24, Chivington remarked, "Well, I long to be wading in gore."[9] A few months before in April, he and his troops fought three major battles, burned four Cheyenne villages, and killed several Cheyenne, including the peaceful chief, Lean Bear.[10]

Meanwhile, in August, some of the Cheyenne and Arapaho peace chiefs went to educated half-breeds Edmund Guerrier and George Bent to enlist their services in writing a letter to the forces at Fort Lyon, the army's fort on the Arkansas River in southeastern Colorado. Dated August 29, 1864, at the Cheyenne village, the letter was marked for history.

"We received a letter from Bent, wishing us to make peace. We held a council in regard to it; all came to the conclusion to make peace with you, providing you make peace with the Kiowas, Comanches, Arapahos, Apaches, and Sioux. We are going to send a messenger to the Kiowas and to the other nations about our going to make peace with you. We heard that you have some prisoners at Denver; we have some prisoners of yours which we are willing to give up, providing you give up yours. There are three war parties out yet, and two of Arapahos; they have been out some time and are expected in soon. When we held this council there were a few Arapahos and Sioux present. We want news from you in return. (That is, a letter)." Signed: Black Kettle and other chiefs.[11]

Black Kettle was at the time the principal peace chief of the Cheyenne tribe, and was held in reverence by his tribe and the whites alike. A handsome man with erect carriage, long dark hair, and a kindly expression on his countenance, he commanded respect. Major Edward Wynkoop described him in an address to the United States Indian Commission.

"... by means of his administrative ability and wisdom, rather than by deeds of prowess in the field, he became a great chieftain. He was not only regarded as the ruling spirit of his tribe, but was also looked upon by all nomadic tribes of the plains as a superior, one who word was law, who advice was heeded. His innate dignity and lofty bearing, combined with his sagacity and intelligence, had that moral effect which placed him in the position of a potentate.

The whole force of his nature was concentrated in the one idea of how best to act for the good of his race … and his utmost endeavors used to preserve peace and friendship between his race and their oppressors."[12]

Black Kettle was the son of Swift Hawk Lying Down, and was born in 1801. He was a member of the Suhtai tribe, that Cheyenne branch from the northeast who spoke a different dialect from the main body of Cheyennes.[13] In 1848, Black Kettle led a war party against the Ute. By mistake, the Cheyennes ran into the Ute camp without warning and were surprised to be suddenly in the midst of a battle. Black Kettle's wife was thrown from her horse and captured. He later married a Wotap woman and, by custom, went to live with her people. He was elected chief of that band when the old chief, Bear with Feathers, died.[14] From that time up to the writing of his letter to Fort Lyon, he sought peace for his tribe, as was his duty and responsibility as a peace chief.

Following their letter to Fort Lyon, Black Kettle and other chiefs were invited to the fort to discuss the situation with Major Wynkoop, who then persuaded the chiefs to meet with Governor John Evans at a place near Denver.

"… these braves who are with me are all willing to do what I say," Black Kettle told Evans. "I want you to give all the chiefs of the soldiers here to understand that we are for peace, and that we have made peace, that we may not be mistaken for our enemies."[15]

Evans was agitated and made no decision to end the war. Instead, he was angry and accusatory. The chiefs left, then went to see Major Anthony, the hostile replacement for the more conciliatory Wynkoop. Anthony told the chiefs to stay in their camps and gave permission for them to conduct a buffalo hunt, as they had nothing to fear from the troops.

The Cheyenne and Arapaho seeking peace were uneasy and dispersed. Black Kettle's Cheyenne made camp on Sand Creek, about forty miles north of Fort Lyon, and were joined there by Arapaho chief, Left Hand, and his band. Because all was peaceful and his hope for the future seemed to be nearing fruition, William Bent allowed his family to join Black Kettle on Sand Creek. William's wife Slow Smoking, and his children George, Julia, and Charles, were there. And, Edmund Guerrier was there in the lodge of his relatives.

Edmund as yet had not made himself known to the one person who held his interest, the teenage beauty Julia Bent. He had been involved with the affairs of the tribe, interpreting for Black Kettle followed by the move to Sand Creek. But now that the tribe had settled into a winter camp near Fort Lyon, having been assured by Major Wynkoop and Major Anthony of their safety from attack by government troops, Edmund felt that he could comfortably relax his vigilance. Always a practical man, next in order in his life's plan was to formulate a way to meet and court Julia, openly, with approval from herself and her family. He might arrange to meet her on her trip to the river to fill her family's water vessels. He could hope that she would join him as his partner in an evening social dance around the central fire. Possibly she might join him in a rendezvous wrapped together in his robe, should he open the robe and invite her in, a traditional manner of courting within the tribe. The robe offered some protection from prying eyes and ears, a certain privacy within a crowd of people, as the couple was still visible to relatives concerned about a daughter's chastity and reputation.

That night of November 28, 1864, after pondering his method of introduction, he decided to begin his siege of love the next day, then lapsed into a satisfied sleep.

Edmund was fooled again, by a completely unexpected catastrophe.

Sand Creek

2

Early in the morning of November 29, 1864, Edmund Guerrier was awakened in Black Kettle's camp by a group of early-rising women who discerned troops in the distance. "Heya!' Heya! Soldiers!" they cried. Guerrier sounded the alarm to the rest of the camp, then ran to John Smith's lodge. The two of them, both with past associations with the government, thought that the soldiers must be making a mistake in charging the camp. This was, after all, the camp of Black Kettle who had recently met with Governor John Evans and Colonel E. M. Wynkoop and expressed his desire for peace. What Guerrier and Smith did not know was that Colonel Chivington had sent dragoons to William Bent's stockade, surrounded it so that Bent could not warn the Indians, and forced Bent's son, Robert, to lead the troops to Sand Creek by force of gunpoint.

Robert grudgingly led Chivington to a site on level land two miles east of the Indian village where he knew the mounted troops could be seen in the grey dawn by the Indians in camp, who would then have some time to prepare themselves to hide, run, or do battle, if necessary. As Chivington approached, he directed one body of horsemen to cut off the pony herd to the east, and another unit to cut off the southern herd in order to prevent the Indians' escape by horseback. Captain Silas Soule refused his orders.

The village was located in a bend of Sand Creek where it flowed from the northwest, then turned east, its south bank having tall willow trees below a high bluff. Chivington stopped his horse atop that bluff to sit and watch as he sent the main body of his troops down the banks to begin their slaughter. Black Kettle's camp lay directly below the bluff.

When Guerrier and Smith dashed toward the soldiers to warn them off the peaceful and sleeping camp, Smith waved his hat to get their attention. It worked. They were seen. The soldiers spied Guerrier and Smith, dismounted, and began firing at them.[1]

"It seems incredible that we were not killed," said Guerrier. "As a matter of fact, we were not touched, though the bullets fairly rained upon us. It may be easy to a man who never tried it, but you simply couldn't keep your feet on the ground. When a bullet struck close to your toes, you certainly jerked your foot up."[2] Actually, Edmund was hit, but with his adrenalin pumping through excitement and fear did not realize it at the time.

George Bent reported on the disgraceful affair:

"I looked toward the chief's lodge and saw Black Kettle had a large American flag tied to the end of a long lodge pole and was standing in front of his lodge holding the pole … I heard him call to the people not to be afraid, that the soldiers would not hurt them; then the troops opened fire."[3]

Young Charles Bent, age fifteen, rushed from his lodge and quickly was whacked over the head by a trooper's saber. He was about to be shot when some Mexican men who were riding with the troopers recognized Charles as William Bent's son and begged to have his life spared. The Mexican men were the sons of the old trapper Charlie Autobeas with whom William Bent had partnered on a trapping trip early in his first visit to beaver country. Fortunately, Charles' life was spared. He was captured instead and imprisoned at Fort Lyon.[4] His young friend, Jack Smith, son of the trader John S. Smith, was not so lucky. When he rushed back into his lodge for weapons, he was deliberately hunted down and shot, on orders from the officers. Soule, horrified, continued to defy Chivington's orders and held his troops back.

When Charles saw the carnage and slaughter of his people, he vowed never to rest in the pursuit of his vengeance against the whites. He lived to carry out that threat until his death.

Peace Chief White Antelope cried, "Soldiers no hurt me," crossed his arms and sang his death song before being cut down in a hail of bullets. White Antelope suffered the indignity of having his genitals and ears cut off, the scrotum to be made into a tobacco pouch.[5] Chivington's gang of ruffians shot, stabbed, mutilated, and scalped their victims mercilessly, unborn children cut from their mother's womb, babies killed in their mother's arms, women's genitals gouged out and displayed on sticks, fingers and ears chopped off to be made into necklaces.

William Bent's former wife, Yellow Woman (Slow Smoking) proved her bravery in defending her people and her camp from the attackers. "She went gravely to the rifle pits ... where other women who could shoot the guns and bows were waiting."[6] Here, her husband Old Bachelor and their two young sons were killed.[7]

George Bent and other men ran west after horses, found none, then pursued by soldiers, raced toward Dry Creek where the group jumped into the riverbed under five-foot banks and joined a larger group, including Black Kettle, downstream. They were digging trenches with their bare hands into the sand banks for protection from the bullets. Just as he reached Black Kettle's trench, George was knocked down with a bullet in his hip. Soon the troops moved their cannons up the stream and were firing on the Indians. Thankfully, the day of Chivington's gore was winding down, and night fell as the troops made fires within their hollow square on the tribe's campground amid the dead and dying and debris from the lodges.

Black Kettle was determined to find his wife, whom he knew to have been shot and fallen. That night, by starlight, he padded softly down the creek bed into camp and found Ar-no-ho-wok alive but shot several times. He slung her onto his back and returned to the protection of the bed of Dry Creek.[8]

According to Craig Moore, USPS ranger at the Sand Creek Massacre site in southeastern Colorado, most of the Indians killed by Chivington's troops that day were those who had run northwest up

Black Kettle's camp was located below the bluff. The view is looking north at the Sand Creek Massacre site. *Courtesy Author's Collection.*

the creek beds two to three miles and finally were overtaken there.[9]

Edmund, realizing the troops were bent on annihilation, took off running to the northeast in search of the band's horses. After an exhausting run of five miles, he eventually met one of his cousins, a daughter of White Antelope, who was driving a small herd of horses toward the Cheyenne camps on the Smoky Hill. She and Edmund were able to catch horses and then raced toward those camps, seeking safety as well as sounding the alarm about the massacre. Their fellow tribesmen needed help desperately and quickly.

While Chivington's troops finished killing the wounded and ransacking the village for trophies, the pitiful few who escaped the carnage straggled on toward the gathering place under cover of darkness. "That was the worst night I ever went through," said George Bent.[10] The survivors were wounded, half-naked, bereft of

Arbor and marker at Sand Creek Massacre site, southern Colorado, 2011. *Courtesy Author's Collection.*

Atop bluff overlooking site of Sand Creek Massacre site in 2011. The view is northeast along the creek where survivors hid in the creek bank. *Courtesy Author's Collection.*

A view from the bluff over the Sand Creek Massacre site in 2011, facing east, from which Col. John M. Chivington and troops emerged. *Courtesy Author's Collection.*

clothing and blankets on a freezing windswept night on the open plain. Edmund Guerrier reported 148 killed. George Bent said 137 slain, mostly women and children. The distraught survivors of the dead and missing mutilated themselves, in the Indian way of grief for dead loved ones, by gashing their arms until the blood flowed and cutting their hair.[11]

The next day, having heard of the plight of their relatives, the Cheyenne camped on the Smoky Hill River rushed food, blankets and clothing to the survivors, nearly frozen from their night on the open plain. They brought plenty of spare horses in order to transport the people back to their camp. George's hip wound was so severe that he could not mount a horse and had to be assisted atop the pony. Edmund's battle wound was not so threatening. He suffered the graze from a bullet on his upper right arm that, when healed, left a scar. The two men were fortunate to have escaped with their lives.[12]

After several days of rest and healing in the Smoky Hill camp, Edmund and George decided to seek the safety and shelter of William Bent's stockade and began a leisurely trip toward it. On two of the camp's horses, they were forced to proceed slowly because of George's painful wound. As the pair rode near to Fort Lyon and saw the soldier's tents nearby, Edmund was concerned that their little party would be discovered before reaching Bent's stockade and decided to take his chances by surrendering to the army rather than being killed by them. He knew he had experienced enough blood and slaughter. As he rode on toward Fort Lyon and surrender, George slipped behind the lines of soldiers and was able to make his way to his father's home, there to complete his recuperation in safety, in the company of his father, stepmother, sister Mary and her husband, and brother Robert.

Julia reached the haven of the Cheyenne camp on the Smoky Hill frightened and distraught, but unhurt.

Chivington and his men, meanwhile, sped to Denver where they were feted with a hero's welcome. They paraded in the streets and filled the lecture halls with eager audiences waiting to hear of their victory and view the Indian trophies of goods from the lodge, body parts and scalps. Soule, however, was shot and killed on the streets of Denver.

For his part, Edmund intended to see more of the young Cheyenne girl who had taken his fancy. He had not experienced the sort of meeting he had planned for them. Not at all. For now, however, he was in internment in the custody of the army. His hopes and plans were on hold.

Memorial Marker in 2011 at the site of the Sand Creek Massacre on November 29 and 30, 1864 in southern Colorado. Note the many honorary gifts and tokens left by visitors. *Courtesy Author's Collection.*

The Estimable Bents

3

To start at the beginning, this tale unfolds with the history of the two important families it follows—Bent and Guerrier—through its children Julia and Edmund; both families were peopled with adventurous individuals who pursued their goals with drive and wit.

The story of the Bent brothers, who were involved in the settlement of the American West and pacification of the Plains Indian tribes, is well known to those readers interested in the nineteenth century westward movement.

Historically, however, the name of Bent traces back even further in the history of the United States. The first Bent to reach these shores was John Bent, who in 1638 fled England aboard the ship *Covenant* to avoid British taxes. John Bent founded Sudbury, Massachusetts with the other escaping settlers and, with his son Peter, platted Marlboro, Massachusetts.[1]

A later descendant, Captain Silas Bent, the family obviously still disliking British taxes, was a leader in the famous Boston Tea Party affair in which dissidents dressed as Indians boarded the king's ships in Boston harbor and dumped cartons of highly-prized imported tea into the harbor in protest of the British parliament's tax on the product. Captain Bent also served in the Revolutionary War as a Minuteman and became a lieutenant colonel in the 7th Regiment of militia.

Silas Bent II, the son of Captain Silas Bent, moved in his twenties to Wheeling, now West Virginia, where he studied for the bar and married Martha Kerr. They moved to Charleston and opened a store. Their first child, a son they named Charles, was born there on November 11, 1799.

Silas Bent II became a judge of the Court of Common Pleas in Charleston. In 1805, he was appointed deputy surveyor for Washington County, Ohio. His next prestigious appointment was as deputy surveyor for the new Louisiana Territory. He moved his family to St. Louis in 1806. He went on to be appointed presiding judge of the Court of Common Pleas of the Territory of Missouri from 1817 to 1821, with Lucas and Augustus Choteau his associate judges. Silas II died in St. Louis on November 20, 1827, after serving for six years as Clerk of the St. Louis County Court.

Silas Bent II left a large family of eleven children, seven boys and four girls. After the birth of Charles on November 11, 1799, the children of Silas II and Martha were Juliannah (July 18, 1801), John (May 31, 1803), Lucy (March 8, 1805), Dorcas (March 12, 1807),

William (May 23, 1809), Mary (June 25, 1811), George (April 13, 1814), Robert (February 23, 1816), Edward (September 12, 1818), and Silas III (October 10, 1820).[2] Edward was the only child who died in childhood, in 1824 at the age of six.

Many of the Bent children impacted the lives not only of their siblings through their devotion and assistance to one another, but they affected the course of the settlement of St. Louis, the trans-Mississippi lands west of St. Louis, and even the far waters of the Pacific Ocean in Japan.

As a teenager, the eldest daughter, Juliannah, was certain she knew what she wanted. Her suitor was persuasive. She was agreeable. Lilburn Boggs observed the time-honored custom of the day by seeking an audience with his prospective bride's father, Silas II. As her parents were agreeable to the match, Juliannah then wed a young man who was to make his mark in the history of the state of Missouri. Soon after their marriage, Lilburn and Juliannah rushed to a land boom up the Missouri River, where their first child, Angus, was born. Lilburn's store there failed, but he stayed on and became deputy factor and Indian agent. Juliannah bore him a second son, Henry, born at Fort Osage. But very quickly tragedy struck; one month later, Juliannah died while on a visit to her parental home in St. Louis.[3] One of her sons, Angus Boggs, later was hired by the Bent brothers to manage the company's farm southwest of Westport.

Lilburn Boggs[4] went on to father ten more children by his second wife, Panthea, granddaughter of Daniel Boone. Of these children, the sons Tom Boggs and William Boggs later joined their uncles, Charles and William Bent, as employees, trading with the Indians for the Bent, St. Vrain and Company. Lilburn's son by Panthea, Tom Boggs, married while in the West. He chose as his wife the fourteen-year-old stepdaughter of Charles Bent, Rumalda Luna,[5] and thereby forged another connection with his Uncle Charles.

The second daughter, Lucy Bent, married James Russell of Oak Hill, in southwest St. Louis. This Russell family had migrated west from Virginia. One son, William Russell, bought the 432-acre property called Oak Hill in 1805, and his brother James purchased it from William in 1811. It was a coal-producing land and prosperous, providing income for the family. Later a tile and chimney plant made with the clay on the property began. James Russell and Lucy Bent married in 1826, the year before her father's death. She was the second wife for James and younger by twenty years. They named one son Bent Russell. Another son, Charles Silas Russell, married Mary Elizabeth Mead, and that pair produced a son who was to achieve fame nationally as a western artist, primarily self-taught. He was Charles Marion Russell, born March 19, 1864. It was reported that "Charlie Russell's mother was a natural storyteller and from her he inherited a gift of wit and gab."[6] But Charles' parents had to concede defeat in their attempts at providing a formal education for him, as he wanted only to sketch and mold models. After he fared so poorly at an eastern military school, they allowed him to travel to Montana to try out life on a ranch belonging to a friend of his father, that of Pike Miller.[7] Charles worked on several ranches in Montana for eleven years, mostly as a night rider, as he preferred his days free to sketch and paint. Charles Russell grew up on the plantation, Oak Hill, bought by his grandfather, James Russell. But he was drawn to the West and made his artistic name in western art. After all, he was the grandnephew of Charles and William Bent, and as such, would have heard many stories of their exploits from his family.

Silas Bent entered naval service as a midshipman in 1839 and became a noted hydrographer of naval fame. He was Commodore Matthew Perry's flag lieutenant on the ship *Mississippi* on Perry's first journey to Japan to open trade with that country in 1852 and 1854. Silas was found in San Francisco in 1850 by fellow St. Louisan William Clark Kennerly when Kennerly stopped to share a meal with him as he headed toward the California gold fields. The pair dined aboard Bent's ship, the *Preble*, anchored in San Francisco Bay.[8]

Over dinner, Kennerly heard Silas' adventures at sea on the *Preble*, including the rescue of eighteen shipwrecked American sailors held prisoner by the Japanese at Nagasaki just the year before in 1849, while Bent caught up on news from St. Louis. Bent made hydrographic surveys of Japanese waters, published by the government, later lecturing on his discoveries.[9]

John Bent became a noted St. Louis attorney and was elected to the state legislature. He met his death in an unfortunate carriage accident at the age of 42 on May 18, 1845.

Dorcas Bent married a prominent St. Louis jurist, Judge William Chiles Carr, and proved her mettle as a society hostess for her husband's friends.[10] In 1842, Judge Carr donated land known as Carr Square to the city. This family also provided a home for her brother William's children when they attended Webster College in St. Louis.

Four of the Bent sons would seek their fortune in the West. They were Charles, William, George, and Robert.

The oldest son, Charles, was seven years old when his family migrated to the small waterfront town of St. Louis on the great Mississippi River. The town since its founding in 1763 had been primarily French, as it had been established by the French entrepreneur Pierre Laclede of New Orleans for use as a base for the fur trading grant that Laclede and his partner Gilbert Maxent had received for exclusive trade with the Indians of the Missouri River and the western side of the Mississippi River.[11] Laclede chose the site for its rocky shelf over the bluffs for protection from the river and its easy access to the river near the foot of present-day Market Street. Laclede set Auguste Chouteau, his fourteen-year-old stepson by Madame Marie Therese Chouteau, to work on building cabins, a fur warehouse, and a stockade. Pierre Laclede built a large one-story Louisiana-style galleried home for Madame Chouteau and their family.

After Laclede's death, Auguste Chouteau enlarged the house by adding a second story and painting the structure white. Their home became the center of the arts and culture and was the seat of power in the early days of St. Louis.

Comprised of not more than a few hundred inhabitants, it was as active in the trapping and trading business as the other Mississippi River towns of Kaskaskia and Cahokia. There were one hundred traders operating out of St. Louis and St. Genevieve who sold their goods downriver to Kaskaskia and Cahokia and made a substantial profit from the $6,000 annual purchases, as the trade was not taxed.[12] Small as it was, however, St. Louis sported two billiard halls to cater to the favorite pastime of the French. The wooden houses fronting the street had galleried facades in the French fashion, with all manner of fanciful tilting windows and turrets that gave it a Gallic charm.

The idyllic underpopulation of the river village changed rapidly after 1804, however, when the territory became American. On March 9 of that year, the Spanish flag was lowered and the French flag raised. The next day on March 10, the French flag was lowered and the American flag was raised. The emperor Napoleon Bonaparte sold the vast Louisiana Territory to the United States, an act that doubled the country's land base by one stroke of President Thomas Jefferson's pen. Jefferson sent his secretary Meriwether Lewis, along with Lewis' friend from army days, William Clark, on a scouting and mapping expedition across the country to the Pacific Ocean and back, in order to seek a water path to the western shore.

Because of the purchase of this vast land, therefore, the United States chose the already-established and orderly town of St. Louis as the site to set up offices to govern the new Louisiana Territory. Government officials were appointed. When Silas Bent II was appointed in 1806 as deputy surveyor and moved his family to St. Louis, they arrived only a few days before the Lewis and Clark party was heard shooting their guns from their boats as they sped down the Mississippi River toward their first home port in two years. All St. Louis turned out to welcome the wayfarers back, as the entire country had despaired of their fate, as well as a despondent Jefferson. The pair arrived with their travel diaries, their hides, and pelts that they immediately stored in the Chouteau fur warehouse, and their stories. Young Charles Bent was jumping up and down with excitement as he watched their arrival from the dock.

The fame of these two men was unparalleled. All St. Louis was giddy with the news of their return. They were feted, wined, and dined in the homes of every major family in the town. Meriwether Lewis was appointed Territorial Governor of the Louisiana Territory and William Clark was named Indian agent for the new land and its inhabitants. After the long round of welcoming festivities following their return, Lewis was designated to take their travel journals to President Jefferson in Washington, D.C., left St. Louis on a boat, stopped to take the Natchez Trace on his journey eastward, and was found dead in a mysterious manner in a private home where he had chanced to spend the night. He had been shot, his death a suspected suicide. Lewis had begun to drink heavily following his return from the celebrated Journey of Discovery, and compounded that insult to his already precarious emotional stability by adding the use of laudanum, leading to erratic and paranoid behavior prior to his departure for Washington. Because of his premature death, Lewis therefore never gave a full report to President Jefferson on their journey nor completed the journals that he and Clark began on the trip. Some were skeptical of the suicide theory, however, and opined that foul play, in the form of a conspiracy, was to blame.[13] [14]

Clark, on the other hand, led a full and distinguished life in St. Louis following his appointment as General of the Militia and Indian Agent for the new territory.

The red-haired Clark settled down in St. Louis following his marriage to Julia Hancock, daughter of Colonel George Hancock, who was a member of Washington's Fourth Congress. The Clarks rented a house at Main and Pine streets at first, and William busied himself tending to his Indian charges.

In 1806, the few narrow streets were a mere thirty-five feet across, barely allowing room for ox-drawn carts to pass. They were always muddy. There were two confectionery stores that served ice cream and cake, the two billiard halls, two hotels, and a theater for plays. Duels, then fashionable, were held on Bloody Island in the Mississippi. As more Americans moved to St. Louis, the prominent names became Ashley, Bent, Pratte, Clark, Chouteau, McKnight, and Hunt.

William Clark built a two-story brick home at the southeast corner of Main and Vine in 1818, his property a half-block long and ran down to the river. William attached to his house a grand council hall measuring 100 feet long by 35 feet wide, appointed with large chandeliers suspended from the high ceiling. This was his chamber to meet with delegations of visiting Indians under his care. He decorated the hall with all manner of Indian goods, both from his travels and from gifts bestowed on him by the visiting tribal members. "There were feather headdresses, canoes, arms, shields, beds, clothes, ornaments, cooking utensils, agricultural and musical instruments, headgear, war bonnets, snow shoes, infants' clothing, cradles, and a rare Roman coin found by an Indian on the bank of the River des Peres and presented to Clark."[15]

This remarkable museum of General Clark was visited by the children and adults of St. Louis, as well as by visiting dignitaries such as Marquis de Lafayette, George Catlin, Henry Clay, Daniel Webster, Washington Irving, and Samuel Clement. All were fascinated by the display. But, ah, the stories were spellbinding. The young men felt their blood rising when told of the myriad beaver, bear, buffalo, deer, and antelope inhabiting those mountains and plains, so eager were they to take the road west and make their fortunes in the fur trade. One of these was Charles Bent. Silas Bent II said it best: "All parties have joined here in expressing their high sense of the great merit of the Gentlemen."[16]

There were other diversions in St. Louis to entertain and amuse the growing Bent children. The Bent family, an illustrious name in the early annals of the Americanized St. Louis, was among the cream of St. Louis society and as such, joined in the fashionable activities of the town: the theater; racing horses; hunting deer, quail, and partridges in the nearby woods; sleighing on the frozen Mississippi River in winter; a Thespian society; lectures at the St. Louis Lyceum; concerts; and parties.

Most of the parties were given in the host's home. One ball given by William Clark and his second wife, Harriet Kennerly

Radford Clark, (his dear Julia having died in 1821), occurred in January 1827 and was attended by two hundred of the leading families in St. Louis. When the guests assembled at 8:00 in the evening, there appeared "taste and elegance of costume, graceful dances, gay uniforms, excellent music, brilliant lights, good humor and politeness of the guests."[17] At 1:30 in the morning, a seated supper provided every luxury, and afterward the guests danced until dawn.

Charles Bent, however, was not swayed by the riches of St. Louis life. He spent his time listening to the stories of William Clark, visiting the council house museum, and on the waterfront observing all the activities of the bustling trapping and trading business. He knew what he wanted to do. His decision to seek his fortune in the west was made at an early age. He wanted to see for himself the myriad beaver, bear, buffalo, deer, and antelope inhabiting the mountains and the plains.

Charles Bent was the first of the Bent brothers who dared to travel west of the mighty river in search of his life's career. His pioneering adventure led the way for three of his brothers to join him there. What they would find would be excitement, travail, heartache, and death.[18]

A Fort on the Arkansas River

4

After attending Jefferson College in Canonsburg, Pennsylvania, though falling short of graduating, Charles Bent began working for Manuel Lisa's Missouri Fur Company as a trapper on the Missouri River.[1] When Lisa died suddenly in 1820, Joshua Pilcher assumed management of the company, keeping Charles busy as a clerk, trapper, and Missouri River man. Five years later, Charles, with a little extra money on hand, embarked on his first commercial venture and invested in the company, becoming a partner in the Pilcher and Company firm, which was issued a license by the well-known William Clark. William Bent joined his older brother on the river trapping and trading, when he was about age sixteen. Although both Charles at 5'7" and William at 5'6" were small men, they were stockily built and had no trouble keeping up with the voyagers and other trappers on the river.

The brothers followed the trapping trade until Charles, as the leader and older of the pair, began to despair of earning a living through the diminishing trade in pelts. Because so many groups of trappers had invaded the best hunting grounds, the animals were harder to find. At the same time that the beaver were thinning from overharvesting, the beaver hat rage was waning due to the growing popularity of silk hats. Thus, the demand and price for pelts plummeted. Charles began to look elsewhere for a comfortable living. He thought of trading. After all, he knew the country, had experience in fending for himself and others, and had the temperament required for the job.

When Charles was age thirty, he was elected as wagon master to lead a caravan of thirty-eight wagons to Santa Fe in Mexican territory. In May of 1829, the wagons rendezvoused at Council Grove for the westward trip. The captain of a wagon train, by necessity, was forced into many tedious roles and responsibilities. Besides directing the route, he was charged with keeping the train moving and prodding stragglers into line; sending scouts ahead to locate camping grounds and watering holes for the men and cattle; other scouts to search for Indian signs; protecting the train from natural and manmade disasters, such as Indian attacks; and keeping the peace and settling disagreements, of which there were plenty. And yet, by the age of thirty and with ten years of travel and trapping under his belt, Charles had gathered the maturity and travel experience to accomplish these tasks. The wagons in his train were trade wagons, loaded with goods to sell or barter, with their merchants or delegates guarding their wares from the wagons' benches. Excitement was high, as it was the first large trading venture into northern Mexico, and all hoped for its success. The caravan set out from Council Grove with the wagons spaced four abreast by Charles,[2] for strength in numbers. Safety was of paramount importance, both for the men and for the trade goods.

President Andrew Jackson had ordered four companies of infantry from Fort Leavenworth, led by Major Benet Riley, to accompany this important wagon train that was embarked on early trade with the capital of Mexico in the north, Santa Fe. Charles Bent was especially impressed with the stamina and reliability of the oxen used to haul Major Riley's supply wagons, and determined to use them himself on any future trips to the west. The oxen stood the journey better than horses or even mules. But there was a catch in Charles' comfort in being accompanied by federal forces on this dangerous journey, as Major Riley's orders were to accompany the train only as far as the Arkansas River, the northern boundary of Mexican territory, there to wait for the wagons to return from Santa Fe on their homeward journey.[3]

Charles Bent was astonished at the government's lack of concern over the safety of the men and merchandise in the train. And, he had invited his younger brother, William, to come along and therefore was responsible for William's life and safety.

When the wagon train reached the Arkansas River, Charles had a talk with Major Riley, who had held up and proceeded no farther. Charles advised Major Riley of the reports of large groups of Indians along the line of the wagon train's travel. He urged Riley to reconsider halting his troops at the Arkansas River, due to his concern about the danger to the men and their goods in case of an attack. This was, he argued, the first large wagon train into Mexico and the United States government was quite properly concerned about its safe conduct. But, Riley was adamant. He was a soldier who followed orders, and his orders were to halt his march at the river.

With no other choice, reluctantly the wagons left the soldiers back at the Arkansas. Very shortly, however, they were wishing for the protection the soldiers provided. They were attacked. Young William Bent, out on a foray on his mule, was startled by a group of Indians. He fired one shot, then raced toward the wagons only to see that the three-man advance party that included his brother Charles was being attacked by another group of Indians. The brothers yelled at one another, then teamed up, charged directly at the attacks with guns blazing, and halted the Indians' attack long enough for the wagons to corral and rifle pits to be dug. Volunteers hurried back to the river to alert Major Riley, whose troops raced to the scene and dispersed the Indians, but Riley again refused to stay with the wagon train and returned to his camp across the Arkansas. The traders despaired. This time, lady luck stepped in and saved Charles' wagon train from further misfortunes. One hundred Mexican buffalo hunters appeared and begged to join the procession, for their own protection. The caravan continued slowly, and was overjoyed when another one hundred mountain men and volunteers, heaving heard of the traders' plight on the trail, hurried out from Santa Fe to escort the wagons the rest of the way.

It was in Santa Fe, in an exuberant holiday at the end of their journey, that young William first encountered Kit Carson, another small man of his own age. Thus was forged a life-long friendship for the pair.[4]

Financially, the trip was a huge success and the merchandise was sold quickly. Santa Fe was so far an outreach from the Mexican capitol in Mexico City that few needed supplies arrived on a timely basis. Charles saw that supplying Santa Fe and its neighbor to the north, Taos, could provide him with a lucrative business.

William Bent, however, in his youthful exuberance at age twenty, saw an opportunity for something different. He wanted to strike out on his own, away from the watchful eye of his older brother. One evening in Santa Fe, he thought of a way to approach his brother about his idea.

William caught Charles in a jovial mood, then introduced his plan to remain in New Mexico when Charlie returned to St. Louis with the trade goods. He explained that he wanted to trek up into the mountains with old Charlie Autobeas and other trappers for a winter of trapping for beaver. They would do some trading with the Indians as well. Charles was concerned. He realized that William, a young man of 20 years, wanted adventures and wealth of his own. He was ready to step out from behind his older brother's protection. Charles acquiesced gracefully, wishing his brother good luck and Godspeed on his journey.

Thus, the brothers parted, and William struck out by himself, without the guidance of his older brother, Charles. After all, he was a grown man by then, and had lived through four years of trapping on the Missouri River, followed by a hair-raising adventure on the Santa Fe road. He wanted to seek his fortune on his own.

William's group pushed north, and decided to set up for the winter on the Arkansas River near Fountain Creek, at the site of present-day Pueblo, Colorado. They set up a camp and surrounded it with a stockade fence. Soon, a party of Cheyenne appeared on their way west to harass the Utes, their enemies. Two Cheyenne stayed behind when the main party left on its mission. The pair of Cheyenne wanted to gawk at William's trade wares, items they had never seen before. Much to their consternation, a war party of Comanche roared into camp, another enemy of the Cheyenne. William quickly hid the Cheyenne in his tent and allayed the suspicions of the Comanche, sending them on their way.[5] The Cheyenne were indebted to William Bent for their lives and spread the story to their tribe, cementing the beginning of a trust and reliance on the man they eventually named "Little White Man," Wa-si-cha-chieschi-la.

William soon had another adventure with the Indians, this time in Arizona where he had traveled to trap pelts. His party's horses were stolen and the camp attacked. But worse was the pitiful haul of furs he had for all his trouble.[6] William then decided that trading with the Indians was safer and more lucrative than trapping. From then on, trading was his main concern and industry.

His brother Charles, meanwhile, was ferrying goods back and forth from Independence, Missouri to Santa Fe. Charles had a similar thought as William. He wanted to concentrate on trading, and decided a partnership with another young trader from St. Louis was just the thing to facilitate business. Ceran St. Vrain, from a distinguished French St. Louis family,[7] would do the trading and operate the mercantile in Santa Fe, while Charles brought the goods back and forth over the trail. Thus, the Bent, St. Vrain and Company, with Charles, Ceran and William as the major partners, was established. The date was 1830 or 1831.

William Bent soon moved back to his stockade near Pueblo, and renewed his trading activities with the groups of Indians who traversed the area. One day, a Cheyenne named Yellow Wolf[8] came to trade with William and wanted to talk. He wondered why William had built his trading post so far away from the traditional Cheyenne hunting and camping grounds. Here at this place, it was inconvenient for the Cheyenne to trade with the post. William, always with a keen ear turned toward the best trading circumstances, asked if Yellow Wolf had a better site in mind. Yellow Wolf did.

Yellow Wolf recommended an area east of the present post called the Big Timbers, where the Cheyenne often camped. He described a large grove of cottonwoods for shelter, plenty of available water, and frequent herds of buffalo nearby. There, the Cheyenne could exchange their buffalo robs for the goods stocked by William at the trading post.

William decided to move his post to the east but chose, instead, a site on the north side of the Arkansas River about seven miles east of present La Junta, Colorado. Years later, William would admit that Yellow Wolf was right all along, and built a stockade in the Big Timbers.

But in 1832, William was well enough satisfied with the site chosen to begin building a large adobe fort for use in trading with the tribes of nearby Indians, as well as a supply base for trading on the Santa Fe Trail. The younger brothers, George at 18 and Robert at 16, received reluctant permission from their mother to go west to live with their older brothers and arrived in time to help erect this trading post.[9]

Charles and William laid out an area for the building at 137 feet by 178 feet. They hired masons from Mexico to make adobe bricks for the walls, which were fourteen feet high and thirty inches thick. Twenty-five rooms outlined a central court and were shaded by a veranda. The rooms were ample size, about fifteen by twenty feet, with dirt floors. Towers were placed strategically on two corners, for defense. There was a small cannon, although this was not a warlike fort and was not heavily fortified. The guns were mainly rifles that were used for trading purposes. Essentially two stories, the second tier contained quarters for the owners, as well as for visitors. The fort boasted food storage rooms, a kitchen, dining hall, blacksmith shop, rooms for tailoring and carpentry, and a large trade room. The fort could accommodate guests and could house up to 200 men and 300 to 400 hundred animals. There was a large corral behind the fort that protected the company's animals with its eight-foot walls, topped with desert cactus to discourage thieves.

The trade room was stocked with all manner of supplies for trading with the Indians, soldiers, mountain men, and Mexicans.

There was a meeting room for Indian councils, and a magazine room. The fort owned a robe press for baling buffalo robes. The fort originally was named Fort William in honor of its builder and prime mover, but that was altered later to simply Bent's Fort by the common usage of the mountain men.[10] For an exotic effect and to amaze guests, George even stocked the fort with goats and peacocks, and had a billiards table hauled in from Independence.

When Lewis Garrard visited the fort in 1846, he found in the clerk's office "a first rate spy-glass with which I viewed the caballada coming from the grazing ground seven miles up the river. In the belfry, two eagles, of the American bald species, look from their prison."[11] From the telescope, he could see "a good view of the Spanish peaks … apparently fifteen miles distant— in reality one hundred and twenty."[12]

Eighteen-year-old Susan Magoffin, pregnant and jostled incessantly in her wagon over the trail, straggled into Bent's Fort toward the end of her pregnancy, relieved to find unexpected amenities awaiting her. She reported about the fort at length. "There are no chairs but a cushion next to the wall on two sides, so the company set all round in a circle. There is no other furniture than a table on which stands a bucket of water free to all. Any water that may be left in the cup after drinking is unceremoniously tossed onto the floor."[13] Amenities were there, no doubt, but civilized manners were lacking in this concentration of western adventurers. She was pleased, however, to be greeted upon her arrival with a mint julep and to have the dirt floor of her room sprinkled with water several times a day to keep down dust. Her guestroom was outfitted with a bed, table and chairs, and a washbasin.[14] Susan, unfortunately, lost her baby at the fort, buried outside the walls.

Masterminding this construction fell to William, and he had his hands full. Although he could count on the usual good relations with the Cheyenne tribe, the Cheyenne also had traditional enemies who might appear on the scene to cause trouble. Once while the fort was being built, Bent's friend and employee Kit Carson was given a task that took him outside the fort's walls. Kit was overseeing a group of twelve white men and two Cheyenne who were cutting timber nearby for use in the fort's construction. Meanwhile, a group of Crow Indians staged a surprise raid and ran off all the fort's horses, leaving Carson and the twelve white men afoot. Carson and his crew attacked the Crow as quickly as they could and killed two of them, while the two Cheyenne, who were still in possession of their mounts, rounded up all the fort's stolen horses. Carson's quick maneuver saved the fort from what could have been an embarrassing and vital loss.[15]

Charles was on the road trading in Santa Fe and Taos where he happened to meet the beautiful young widow, the Spanish-speaking Maria Ignacia Jaramillo. Her deceased husband had left her with one daughter, Rumalda Luna, a child of four years. Smitten with her, Charles Bent married Maria Ignacia in 1835 or early 1836, and provided a house for the three of them one block north of the plaza in Taos. It was a modest establishment, a duplex, as it shared a wall with the adjoining house, but it was a house that would see the scene of a massacre, with that separating wall playing a large part in the story. But here, Ignacia learned English, dressed in American clothes, and bore Charles five children. For Charles, Taos became his home.

The partners Charles and William Bent and Ceran St. Vrain soon had a decision to make with regard to the delegation of responsibilities. They must decide who would oversee the operation of this large fort and be the active agent in the management of its personnel.

The Beautiful Owl Woman

5

In 1832, the decision was made. William Bent was the brother who would manage the fort. While Charles kept to the trail hauling goods to the various stores and forts, William was content to stick with trade. He was the proprietor of Bent's Fort, a large operation. A short dark-haired man with a pleasant expression, he was known for his benevolence and courtesies with the many pilgrims who passed by the fort or who stopped there for a while. His friendship with the Cheyenne tribe led many bands of that tribe to move south and make their home camps nearby the fort, leading to a permanent split in the tribe. Henceforth, those who moved south were to be known as the Southern Cheyenne, their Montana relatives who stayed in the north as the Northern Cheyenne.

Along with the Cheyenne who trusted him, and the traders and trappers who dealt with him, government officials came to rely on William both as a reporter of the various tribes' locations and moods, and as an interpreter. He was a busy man who dealt with a myriad of employees as well. Among regular fort personnel were Indian women and at least one Negro woman, a cook, a blacksmith and wheelwright, stock drovers, a few clerks and bookkeepers, and hunters who were expected to keep the fort supplied with fresh meat.[1] The fort could employ more than 100 men at times, including many traders.

By 1834, William had completed the work of erecting, stocking with robes and wares, and manning his large fort on the Arkansas River. The hectic times of construction were over, and his life settled into the day-to-day routines of business that he quickly mastered. He began to reflect upon his life, and realized that something was missing. He was then twenty-six years old. Unmarried, and with no sweetheart, he looked for one—discreetly.

When the large Cheyenne tribe camped nearby to trade with the fort in exchange for buffalo robes, William was impressed with the tribe's holy man, White Thunder, and began to visit White Thunder in his lodge. White Thunder had beautiful daughters. The children of White Thunder and his wife Tail Woman were daughters Owl Woman, Slow Smoking (known in the literature as Yellow Woman), Island, and a son Pushing Bear. [2]

The older daughter Owl Woman possessed the grace of movement and calmness of demeanor that William so admired, and soon he could not take his eyes off her. Smitten with her beauty and charm, he wanted her for his wife. He discussed the situation with his older brother Charles, visiting the fort from home in Taos. Charles recognized White Thunder, No-pi-no-nomie, and Keeper of the Sacred Arrows, as a stalwart fellow, much respected by the tribe, and approved William's plan. They both knew this marriage would solidify the bond between the Bent, St. Vrain and Company trading post and the Cheyenne, a most positive step toward future benefits. What actually happened was that this marriage into the family of White Thunder caused that part of the tribe who followed White Thunder to decide to stay in the area around Bent's Fort to be with their religious leader and his family. This was a second powerful reason for the southern Cheyenne to cluster around Bent's Fort, besides their wish to trade at the fort.

And so it was done. William married Mes-ta-me-ist, Owl Woman, by the Indian tradition, providing many gifts to her family and hosting a feast for the tribe. William kept a lodge for Owl Woman and his expected family in the Big Timbers camp of White Thunder, a two-day trip from the fort of about thirty miles. He also carved out a suite of rooms at the fort for them. Owl Woman was free to stay at the fort with all the hustle and bustle of traders, mountain men, Mexicans, Indians, and Army personnel who came and went, or she could join her Cheyenne family in their lodges if she wished to participate in the life of her Indian relatives. Her first three children were Mary in 1838, Robert in 1840, and George in 1843. They were exposed to both the Indian and white worlds, and this arrangement suited William and Owl Woman for a period of twelve years. The Indians called William "Little White Man," and he became a member of the tribe due to his marriage to Owl Woman.

Bill Boggs described Owl Woman as "a most estimable woman of much good influence."[3] She was a gracious and caring wife to William and ministered to him and their children. When William became ill with a seriously inflamed throat infection and could not eat or drink fluids, she sent for the tribal medicine man, Lean Bear. After one look at William's throat, Lean Bear went out of the tepee and gathered a handful of sand burrs. He attached each sand burr to a length of sinew, coated each with marrow fat, then pushed the mass of burrs down William's throat several times, drawing out the diseased matter with each retrieval. Soon, William was able to accept the broth that Owl Woman breathed down his mouth from her own mouth in a quill. In a few days, he was healed.[4] Bent thereafter relied on Lean Bear to treat his entire family.[5]

On a trip to Bent's Fort for the United States topographical engineers Lieutenant James W. Abert sketched Owl Woman, describing her as a handsome woman with small delicate hands, fine wavy hair, dressed in a beaded buckskin dress and beaded moccasins with matching attached beaded leggings.[6]

About this time, the Cheyenne were in a state of anger, demanding retribution against the Kiowa. The tribe learned that forty-two of their young men on a raid of the Kiowa camps had been slaughtered by their enemy, and they were in the mood for revenge. Porcupine Bear, leader of the Dog Soldiers, ran to the Sioux and Arapaho camps with the war pipe, to induce those tribes to join a large war party against the Kiowa. When the entire tribe moved against the enemy, the sacred Medicine Arrows moved with the people. However, seldom were those totems taken into battle. But Porcupine Bear insisted to White Thunder that the sacred Medicine Arrows be joined against the Kiowa. When he arrived at the Northern Cheyenne camp, a trader was there, dispensing whiskey. A drunken brawl ensued in which Porcupine Bear knifed and killed his cousin, Little Creek. By tribal custom and law, Porcupine Bear, his family, and the Dog Soldiers who accompanied him were exiled from the tribe as outlaws.

In the ensuing battle with the Kiowa, doomed as White Thunder knew it would be, he was killed. Tail Woman took charge of the Medicine Arrows on the trip back to their camp above Bent's Fort until the succeeding Arrow Keeper, Lame Medicine Man, was chosen. Fortunately, the Apaches, Kiowa and Comanche wished for peace. This was accomplished in the summer of 1840 at Two Butte Creek, followed by the tribes camping together on both sides of the Arkansas River at Bent's Fort, with much celebration, exchanges of gifts and feasts, horse races, and other games. The feud was ended. [7] Peace reigned among these tribes.[8]

William recovered from his throat infection slowly. But he was impatient to return to his duties as manager of wide-ranging activities at the fort. He had need of a constant supply of hunters to bring in game to feed his hungry employees, and employed a number of traders as well. These traders brought in supplies from the east over the trail, and sought out the Indians in their camps in order to barter trade goods for pelts.

The hunters and traders were important men, essential to the operation and maintenance of the fort. Some of them gained their modicum of fame; others were to become more important in the affairs of the West.

One of the hunters was Jean Baptiste Charbonneau. His early life was an exciting adventure for the toddler, as he was the youngest adventurer who started west from St. Louis to cross the country to the Pacific Ocean and back as a member of the Lewis and Clark Journey of Discovery. When he was an infant, the child of the French voyageur Toussaint Charbonneau and his teenage wife Sacagawea, Lewis and Clark hired his father as a member of the expedition, and in a stunning move, allowed Sacagawea and their child along on the trip. The captains conjectured that a traveling party that included an Indian woman and her child would reassure the various tribes they might encounter that their mission was a peaceful one. Their decision was based on another premise as well. As she was a member of the horse-rich Shoshone tribe, they were hopeful that their act of delivering their chief's daughter to her homeland would persuade the tribe to sell or trade their precious horses so that the Journey of Discovery could park their boats and travel across the mountains with greater ease.

Their hope of horses from the Shoshone was fulfilled. When the captains entered the Shoshone country and met the tribe's chief, they were astonished when Sacagawea rushed to him with tears in her eyes and hugged the chief, her brother. She had not seen him since her abduction by a marauding tribe years before. Sacagawea and her son made the entire trip with the expedition, during which Captain Clark doted on Baptiste, nicknamed him "Pomp," and promised to provide him with an education in St. Louis, should his parents agree. A few years later, Pomp traveled to St. Louis and was educated and protected by Captain William Clark, according to his promise. Now Baptiste returned to the West as a hunter of game for the Bent, St. Vrain and Company at Bent's Fort. His services were much praised, as he was known as the best man on foot in the mountains at that time. And, he spoke several languages, as William Clark had also sent him to Europe for part of his education.

The names of a few of Bent, St. Vrain and Company's traders became legendary as well. There was Lewis Garrard, who penned in 1850 his exciting memoir entitled *Wah-toyah and the Taos Trail*, recounting his trading trip across the mountains into Taos with the company.

Another trader was William Boggs, the son of Missouri Governor Lilburn Boggs and his second wife Panthea Boone, and Thomas Boggs, William Boggs' brother.

There was John Smith, a St. Louis youth who went west to trade for the company, married a Cheyenne woman, and ran his own lodge in the Cheyenne camp. Smith began trading for the company in 1838. An accomplished linguist, he spoke French and Spanish, as well as that of the Cheyenne, Sioux and other tribes. Following his marriage into the Cheyenne tribe, he lived with them most of the year. He was described by biographer Stan Hoig:

> He could be both mean and kind, rough and gracious, savage and civilized. He was a proven friend to the Indians, yet it was not beyond him to assist (Indian agent S.G.) Colley in trading the Indians their own annuity goods. He was a close friend to Black Kettle and son-in-law to Yellow Wolf, yet he aided the army in campaigns against the warring Dog Soldiers.[9]

It was John Smith who later, along with Edmund Guerrier, tried to stop Chivington's volunteer unit from attacking Black Kettle's sleeping village at Sand Creek, where the pair was repulsed by flying bullets, and where his half-Cheyenne son Jack was shot to death by the volunteers.

Another famous trader for the company was Kit Carson, who worked intermittently for Bent, St. Vrain and Company as a hunter from 1831 until 1845. A good friend of the Bents, Kit later became an explorer, Indian agent, lieutenant colonel in the Civil War, and Indian fighter. In about 1841, Kit married the relative of Owl Woman, Making Out Road, who was sixteen at the time. This allowed Kit Carson and William Bent to be known as related by marriage, as well as employer and employee. Kit's marriage was unfavorable from the beginning, however, as the pair argued and fought constantly. After their first baby died, they separated permanently.[10]

And then there was William Guerrier, a French trader from St. Louis. Guerrier would play an important role in the succession of the Bent and Guerrier families. Guerrier traveled, trapped, and traded in the reaches of the Upper Missouri River, into northern Mexico and along the rivers of eastern Indian Territory in what is now the state of Oklahoma before beginning his association with the Bent, St. Vrain and Company circa 1839.

A French Trapper Heads West

6

A direct descendant of early St. Louis inhabitants, and whose maternal grandfather accompanied Pierre LaClede and Auguste Chouteau on a trip up the Mississippi River for the founding of the village in 1763, William Guerrier was born as Guillaume Le Guerrier in St. Louis on January 4, 1812 to Charles Le Guerrier, Sr. and Felicité Ortes (Hortiz).[1]

His father Charles Le Guerrier, Sr. was born in Cahokia, Illinois, an earlier French trapping and trading village on the east side of the river, but he subsequently moved to St. Louis where he was baptized in 1787 at age nine. Charles, Sr. was the son of Francis Benoit (1737-1787) who died in the year of his son's baptism, and whose French "dit" name was Le Guerrier, the dit a French custom used as a second name, or "also known as" reference.[2]

It appears that Charles Le Guerrier,

Sr. was apprenticed to a carpenter following his father's death, as he became a leading carpenter in the early life of St. Louis when the territory was still under the dominion of Catholic Spain. And in March 1806 he married Felicité, the 19-year-old daughter of Jean Baptiste Ortes and Elizabeth Barada Ortes, in King of France Cathedral. Of the three Ortes daughters—Florence, Marie Louise, and Felicité— Felicité was the youngest.[3]

Felicité's father, Jean Baptiste Ortes, ten years younger than Pierre LaClede, was LaClede's friend in their home province of Bearn in southern France near the Pyrenees and emigrated with LaClede to New Orleans. When LaClede and his business partner Maxent received the trapping and trading license for the upper Missouri region from the Spanish government in New Orleans, Ortes accompanied LaClede up the Mississippi River in December 1763 when the site for the company's trading post and fur warehouse was chosen.

From the beginning of St. Louis, Ortes was important in the early life as a carpenter and joiner. He and his partner Jean Baptiste Cambas built two houses and a barn on their grant of Block 56 between Myrtle and Almond, but Ortes sold his half interest in the property to Cambas in 1773 and bought a frame house elsewhere. He built houses for Francois Cottin and Joseph Robidoux, a barn for himself, a roof for Louis Vige's billiard parlor. Busy and well known in the community, he was godfather at baptisms, witness to marriages, and petitioned for and signed the final contract for a new cathedral in 1778. He loved to attend auctions, one purchase being a pair of crimson velvet breeches. He also turned to farming with the help of one slave, and was a member of the First Company of militia when St. Louis was attacked by Indians. In all, a productive life.

And, on August 20, 1782, he married at the age of forty-five a fourteen-year-old girl from Vincennes, Elizabeth Barada.

Five years after Felicité Ortes' marriage to Charles Le Guerrier, Sr., the eldest daughter Florence and her husband Joseph Philibert recorded a deed giving a Main Street lot to Felicité and her children, excluding the husband Charles Le Guerrier any rights to it, not an uncommon French family procedure. One sister's gift to the other. Block 12, on the waterfront.[4] This property was undoubtedly where Guillaume Le Guerrier (William Guerrier) was born in 1812.

Then in 1818, this Block 12 property was exchanged for Block 29, between Vine and Locust and First and Second streets, where the LeGuerriers lived and Charles Sr. practiced his carpentry and building skills, and the family produced eight children. His residence was listed as 99 Church Street; two blocks from the Mississippi River waterfront. Guillaume was at the time six years old.

When Felicité died in 1832, this property flowed through to her seven remaining children, son Jean Baptiste having died at age three. The living children were Marie Claire, Charles, Jr., Victoire Eulalie, Guillaume, Isabelle "Elizabeth," Felicité, and Marie Julia.[5] [6]

When the block 29 property was divided into seven legal interests, six siblings signed quit claims to Charles Le Guerrier, Jr. their brother. Thus, after 1840, William Guerrier had no legal interest in any family property in St. Louis. His father Charles Le Guerrier,

Sr. moved to Westport in Jackson County, Missouri to live with his daughter Marie Claire Philibert and her husband Gabriel, who was the blacksmith/gunsmith to the Kaw Indian tribe for many years.

The first glimpse of William in the West occurred in 1824 when Guerrier and a St. Vrain son, Ceran, formed a trading partnership. They filled their wagons with trading goods and journeyed to Taos to trade with the Taos Indians and the Mexicans in the village, and to buy furs from the hunters and trappers in the area to sell in St. Louis. This trip was unsuccessful for Guerrier as, for various unstated reasons, St. Vrain dissolved his partnership with Guerrier and paid him off in Taos. St. Vrain wrote to B. Pratte that he paid Guerrier $100 and two mules for his part in the venture, and asked Pratte to return Guerrier's pre-paid account to him when he returned to St. Louis. St. Vrain then hoped to sell his trading stock to Provoe and Le Clerc for their business and to continue on to Sonora for more trading.[7] Apparently, a difference of opinion had developed between the pair, their Taos trade business was unsuccessful, or other reasons St. Vrain found "too tedious to mention" in his letter.

Strangely, this partnership occurred when William Guerrier was only twelve years old, if the account of his birth date is correct. St. Vrain's date of April 27, 1824 on his letter to Pratte leaves no room for doubt of its correctness. This, then, is the first acknowledgement of him as the trader William Guerrier, rather than Guillaume Le Guerrier.

Guerrier family lore next places William in the employ of the Chouteau family, probably in their trading post on the Grand

River, where he possibly fathered Indian children. This claim has not been established as yet. However, when Auguste Pierre Chouteau died suddenly at Fort Gibson in Indian Territory on Christmas day in 1839, and the trading post on the Grand River was sold to Lewis Ross, brother of Cherokee Chief John Ross, the company's trappers and traders were forced to disperse. Guerrier appeared that very year farther west.

He found work as a trader in 1939 with Bent, St. Vrain and Company at Bent's Fort on the Santa Fe road from Westport to Santa Fe, northern Mexico. Guerrier knew the Bents and St. Vrain from their association in St. Louis, suggesting a comfortable work relationship.

A lusty man, Guerrier wanted a woman in his life. Besides, he knew that in order to be successful, a trader found it to be important to his business to have a wife in the tribe he dealt with.[8] So, shortly after he ventured into Cheyenne lands as a trader with Bent's Fort, Guerrier married by Indian custom a Cheyenne woman. She was a member of the southern branch of the Cheyenne, those who split from the northern branch in order to trade at Bent's Fort and to hunt buffalo in Colorado and Kansas.

Guerrier chose the maiden Tah-tah-tois-neh, who bore him a son in a Cheyenne camp on the Smoky Hill River in central Kansas on January 16, 1840.[9] Guerrier thought of his old friends the Chouteaus when he named his son, Edmund Gasseau Chouteau Guerrier, in honor of Francois Gesseau Chouteau of the Westport warehouses and his son Edmund Francois Chouteau.

William Guerrier's patrimonial largesse in bestowing the Chouteau names on his newborn son was striking. Obviously, he not only knew the father-son Chouteau, but respected them as well. Francois Gesseau was the eldest son of Pierre Chouteau and his second wife, Brigitte Saucier. Francois Gesseau, known as Gesseau, was born February 7, 1797 and was fifteen years older than William Guerrier. William Guerrier would have known him not only in their hometown of St. Louis, but also as an Indian trader and dealer in furs and peltries of Chouteau's Landing, the future Westport and Kansas City. Gesseau and his wife, Thérèse Bérenice, were hospitable people who showed kindness to travelers.

At that time, Edmund Francois, their son, born January 6, 1821 in St. Louis, was eight years old, living with his parents at Chouteau's Landing when not in school in St. Louis. Gesseau died suddenly April 18, 1838 of a heart attack at the age of forty-one, nearly two years before the birth of William Guerrier's son.

Gesseau's son, Edmund Francois Chouteau, after attending the St. Louis College (later St. Louis University) where Edmund Guerrier later studied, began work for the Chouteau firm in St. Louis. He later served as lieutenant in the army. William Guerrier would have encountered this young man again, as Edmund Chouteau was an official witness in the Treaty of Laramie in 1851. William Guerrier at that time was a trader in partnership with Seth Ward, who was post sutler at Fort Laramie at the time of the treaty.[10]

Guerrier fathered three sisters to Edmund, two of them by Tah-tah-tois-neh.[11] These daughters were Rosa and Julia.[12] And,

William Bent's home is the center two-story brick structure with pillars and center fireplace chimney. It contained four rooms. Following Bent's death, Seth Ward purchased the home and attached a larger two-story brick home, shown left. Right, in 1915, new owners attached a grand red brick structure to the original Bent and Ward homes. *Courtesy Shirley Christian.*

Guerrier sired another son by a Sioux woman following the death of Tah-tah-tois-neh in 1849, who became half-brother to Edmund. Guerrier named him Henry, born in 1854, who was eventually adopted by the Cheyenne. [13] The third sister was Florence, probably a daughter of the Sioux woman. Florence was not listed as a survivor of the Sand Creek Massacre nor was she given land in the Treaty of the Little Arkansas as were Edmund, Rosa, and Julia. [14]

As an infant in 1840, Edmund was carried in his mother's arms gently, but after three months, he was lashed into a carefully beaded cradle board for safekeeping while his mother went about her daily tasks. When in camp, she leaned the cradle board against a tree or lodge pole where she could keep a check on him, and when moving camp, she hung his cradle board from her saddle so he could watch the passing activities or sleep if he felt like it. Typically, he was never spanked by his Cheyenne relatives. Rather, as he grew, his pride and ambition were stressed. He was urged to act in a way that would be to his advantage, by earning the respect of the older people. He learned to ride early, and at the age of six was able to ride an Indian pony bareback. With other boys his age, he went out hunting birds with a small bow and sharpened sticks for arrows, and became proficient at killing birds and rabbits, which he always brought back to his lodge for his mother to cook for supper. He became a good swimmer and enjoyed romping in the streams. With his friends, he learned to play "war," riding a stick as his horse. He built forts and Indian camps in the dirt and molded clay figures for the people and the animals. He was growing up as a typical Cheyenne boy. And, in a special naming ceremony, he was given his Cheyenne name, Hawk. Edmund would be known as Hawk in all his days by his people, the Cheyenne. The choice of this name, Hawk, was prophetic, as Edmund later was to fulfill the talents of the high-flying, sharp-eyed raptor.

While Edmund prospered as a growing child with Tah-tah-tois-neh, her Cheyenne relatives and his sisters, William Guerrier spent his days on the trails to Indian encampments as a trader for Bent's Fort. His adventures in the west of his dreams continued to inspire him to work diligently at his career.

Governor Charles Bent Murdered

7

A traveler named Field stopped at Bent's Fort for a rest on his journey. He was met in the fort by Robert Bent, who hosted and entertained him during his brief respite. The Bents were hospitable to travelers along their trail, always offering accommodations and food to the visitors. Field noticed with delight that the fort was stocked with cattle, sheep, goats, three buffalo calves, and chickens free-ranging in the courtyard. He noticed a few prairie critters that had been caught and tamed as well.[1] Yet, he could not help bemoan that the land around the fort had been drastically stripped of timber to supply the cook stoves and fireplaces of needed fuel. After six years of deforestation around the fort, William Bent was forced to send his hunters and wood gatherers farther afield to restock his meat supply and his wood piles.

The partners decided to expand their enterprises in order to trade with other tribes and increase their inventory for sale in Westport. Ceran St. Vrain and the Bent brothers in the firm gathered in council to discuss their next projects.

By 1840, when Edmund Guerrier was born on the Smoky Hill River, the Bent, St. Vrain and Company had established the company's management hierarchy to oversee its far-flung business enterprises.

When the company decided to build a second fort north of Denver, George Bent was instrumental in masterminding its construction. Named Fort St. Vrain, it was smaller in size than Bent's Fort, but nevertheless measured 130 feet by 60 feet. This trading post was staffed by Marcellin St. Vrain, Ceran's brother.

A third trading post was added, called Adobe Walls, in the Texas Panhandle for use in trading with the more southern tribes of Kiowa, Comanche, and Apache. All three forts were built of adobe.

Robert Bent, the youngest and reportedly the most handsome of the Bent brothers who went west, was called Green Bird by the Cheyenne. Robert never became a partner in the company. He worked for the business as a trapper, trader, trail boss and hunter. Robert married a Cheyenne woman and lived with her at the fort. In October of 1841, Robert was assigned to take a wagon train out from the fort for trading purposes. Traveling along the trail beside the Arkansas River, Robert left his wagon train to scout into the interior in order to kill a buffalo to provision the train's meat supply. To the great dismay of his family, he was sighted by Comanche on the prowl and was killed and scalped by them. Robert's body was carried back to the fort and was buried outside the walls. Charles, William and George bewailed the loss of their younger brother at the young age of twenty-eight. He was the first of the brothers to be buried in alien land, away from his homeland of St. Louis.

George Bent was very active in the company's affairs and became a partner in Bent, St. Vrain and Company. Besides helping build all three adobe forts, George traveled the trails with trade goods, was in charge of the fort when William was gone, led wagon trains, and greeted visitors such as John Charles Fremont on his way to California and Oregon-bound Marcus Whitman. In fact, George experienced all of the assignments and dangers of his older brother, William. The Cheyenne named him Little Beaver. George married a Mexican woman, and because he was back and forth on the road to Taos and Santa Fe with trade goods from the fort, he decided to settle his home in Taos. [2] There, he and his wife began a family. [3]

William, of course, was the overall manager of the main post at Bent's Fort and of all its trading activities. He developed a rhythmical time pattern with regard to trade. As it took three or four months to make the round trip from Bent's Fort to Missouri, twenty-five to thirty wagons set out from the fort each spring, drawn by twelve oxen in spans per wagon. The wagons were packed with buffalo hides for shipment from Westport to St.

Louis. Behind them, horses, mules and oxen were herded forward, for sale in the East. The wagons were used at night as corrals for the stock, to prevent plundering. The wagon masters were accustomed to pacing the trip to hit all the grass and water for the stock at the right times. William hired Mexicans as drovers, and Shawnee or Delaware Indians as hunters to supply the train with meat during the journey. The wagons returned in August with trade goods for use in bartering with the various tribes.[4] All in all, a good plan, as everyone knew his special job and what was expected of him.

William was even-handed in his dealings with Indians, and made a hard and fast rule of conduct with them. He would not interfere or take sides in any of their disputes or battles. The fort was occasionally attacked, but never while William was in residence. The Indians respected William for his neutrality in the matter.

William was also busy with his own growing family at Bent's Fort. Owl Woman had given birth to three children: Mary on January 22, 1838; Robert in 1840; and George on July 7, 1843. Owl Woman divided her time taking the children between the fort and the lodges William had provided for them in the camp of her Cheyenne relatives.

It was hard for William to get away from the fort, unless George could fill in for him, as the many traders employed by the company kept him occupied stocking their wagons with trade wares. William Guerrier was one of these traders. Guerrier set out on a trip to trade with the Cheyenne at the Big Timbers, about thirty miles from Bent's Fort. He was accompanied by young Bill Boggs, son of Panthea and Lilburn Boggs. Boggs wrote later about his trip with Guerrier. "Guerrier wore a hooded capote and leggings of white blanket around his trousers," wrote Boggs, "He was so illiterate he had to use sticks to count, but few men knew the Cheyenne any better."[5]

Bill Boggs, in his youth in the wilderness, may not have known yet about the counting system the traders used in transacting sales of furs from the Indians. The furs were first divided into separate piles according to skin variety and condition of the pelt. The Indian received wooden sticks that were grooved from one to ten, indicating the numbers of beaver in his credit. Then he could trade these sticks for kettles, knives, guns, dress attire, or alcoholic spirits, according to the stick value of the article he desired, although the Bent, St. Vrain and Company did not provide alcohol to its Indian customers as did other trading companies. These sticks were called owing sticks, each stick counting for a certain number of pelts.[6]

Thus, William Guerrier was only transacting business in the usual manner when he used counting sticks with the Indians. In addition, Guerrier possessed another asset which came in handy on more than one occasion. He learned Indian languages, and was skillful as an interpreter. That ability was put to use during one crisis when a group of Delaware Indians were causing trouble for the Cheyenne and a fight was about to erupt between these two enemy tribes. William Bent sent Guerrier as an interpreter to mediate the dispute between the tribes, and Guerrier's skills brought about a peaceful settlement of the issue.

Guerrier's services as interpreter were called upon at another time on August 9, 1845 when he interpreted for Lieutenant James W. Abert for a council with the Indians, held at Bent's Fort. Abert wrote of him, "A white, familiarly known as Bill Garey [sp], acted as Cheyenne interpreter. A long residence among them had enabled him to repeat all their graceful and expressive gestures, which add the poetry of motion to the music of their language, of which gestures form an important part."[7] Of course, Guerrier had been among the Cheyenne for several years and knew not only the Cheyenne language, but sign language as well.

Guerrier eventually left the employ of William Bent at Bent's Fort and moved farther east to Pueblo, where he showed up in the diary of Alexander Barclay beginning in November 1846.[8] There is no documented reason or purpose for this move. He continued to trade with the Indians, collecting furs and pelts in trade. He was a jack-of-all-trades, delivering mules and oxen to other traders, making a fly wheel for his partner Alexander Barclay's corn mill, and joining in the raucous revelry afforded in the hardscrabble area of Pueblo. On at least two occasions, he was found by Barclay at "The Houses," two miles upstream from the fort at Pueblo, idling his time, drinking and playing cards. He formed a partnership with Joseph Doyle during the summer of 1848 for a six-wagon trip to St. Louis with trade goods. Shortly after the completion of this trip, he went into partnership with Seth Ward, and the pair set out for Wyoming country. William Bent would not see him for awhile.

William Bent was always gratified when he could bring about tranquility in the tribes and worked diligently toward that goal when problems arose. He often left the fort to trade with the Indians in their camps, but when in residence, William was the official greeter of all new arrivals. Surprisingly, there were many. One day, an unexpected wagon train arrived. Out of a wagon stepped a stranger, a thin young man who appeared wan and in need of nourishment. He sought out William Bent and introduced himself. He was Frank Blair, Jr., son of Francis Preston Blair of Washington, an advisor to President Andrew Jackson and co-publisher of the administration's newspaper, *The Globe*.[9]

Frank was ill and had been sent west by his family to repair his broken health. When Frank met the Bent brother, George, an immediate bond formed between them. George and Frank became life-long bosom buddies and had many high times together. The pair was in Taos to visit George's family when Frank imbibed too much whiskey during an all-night party, and was being escorted across the plaza by George. The plaza happened to be filled with a large group of cohorts of Padre Martinez, the Catholic priest who hated Charles Bent because of various legal issues affecting both of them regarding a land grant. These Mexicans on the plaza attacked and severely beat George and Frank before friends rescued them. Charles tried, but was unsuccessful in having these hoodlums prosecuted.

Charles Bent, meanwhile, had married the attractive Mexican widow Ignacia Jaramillo Luna and provided a home for her and her young daughter, Rumalda Luna, just off the square in Taos. The couple lost two children in infancy, George and Virginia, but were blessed with children Alfredo and, in 1842, Teresina.[10] When Kit Carson visited Charles and his family on a trading trip to Taos, he spied Ignacia's sister. Equally as attractive as Ignacia, Maria Josefa had the same creamy skin, thick black wavy hair, and flashing black eyes. Kit fell hard for Maria Josefa, and married her in a swirl of celebration in Taos on February 6, 1843.[11] Thus, Charles Bent and Kit Carson became brothers-in-law, as Kit and William Bent had been when they married the so-called "sisters" Owl Woman and Making Out Road.

Bent, St. Vrain and Company had opened stores both in Taos and in Santa Fe, which Charles tended while William operated Bent's Fort. From trading in Santa Fe over a period of years, Charles was knowledgeable about the ways of doing business in that northern Mexican capitol. He was well acquainted with the policies of the Mexican government, but more importantly, he knew the military strength of the Mexican forces there. When Charles reported to the American government in 1846, he gave his estimation of the relative weakness of the Mexican troops in the area. He also warned that the Mexican governor expected reinforcements from the south to arrive soon. The United States coveted that land for the westward expansion of its Manifest

Destiny policy, and quickly dispatched Colonel Stephen W. Kearny and his forces to Bent's Fort in order to follow up on the lead that Charles had given.

The troops soon arrived at the fort, with the colonel in the lead. He dismounted and searched for Charles Bent, but met William instead. Introducing himself, he first asked permission of Bent to garrison his troops' tents outside the walls of the fort, across from the large wooden entrance gates. Bent granted Kearny's wish. Bent then learned that Kearny had been sent by the government to go into Mexico in order to take over the territory with his troops. He was counting on obtaining current information from Charles Bent about the Mexican troop deployment in the northern Mexican capitol of Santa Fe. Upon learning that Charles was not at the fort right then, Kearny, wishing to carry out his orders as quickly as possible, then asked William to go to Santa Fe to scout the situation. If additional Mexican soldiers had arrived in the capitol, he needed that information in order to plan his tactics. William was agreeable to being of service to the government and knew that his appearance in Santa Fe on the business of his trading company would arouse no suspicion. He gathered a few men for the journey. But before he left, already disgusted with the trash and litter of the soldiers camping on his doorstep, he asked Colonel Kearny to have his men move their quarters farther away from the fort. The troops picked up their trash and moved.

Bent returned to the fort from Santa Fe, and gave his report. His answer was no. No reinforcements had arrived in Santa

Fe from the south. Immediately, a relieved Kearny marched his army into the sleepy Mexican capitol and took the village of Santa Fe without firing a shot, on August 18, 1846. Thus, New Mexico expeditiously became a United States Territory, and Taos trader Charles Bent was appointed its first territorial governor. One of his first appointments was that of Frank Blair as his Attorney General.

However, the appointment of Charles Bent to head the new territory became a mixed blessing to Charles, his immediate family, and the entirety of the Bent clan. At first, there was pride in the appointment and much rejoicing. Surely, there was no one more knowledgeable about the ways of the Spanish people in the territory, and of business dealings in the region. Charles had been trading there for fourteen years, made his home in Taos, and married the daughter of a prominent Spanish family. But Taos had been a hot bed of dissension for some time and the town was boiling with flared tempers. Only five months following his appointment, the life of Charles Bent was to end in a massacre on January 19, 1847.

Early that morning, a group of angry Mexicans and Taos Pueblo Indians rioted and marched to Governor Bent's home, a duplex, one block from the village square. Charles quickly arose and met them in the doorway of his home. In an effort to quiet them and to quell their anger, he reminded them that he had helped their families in time of need and had doctored their wives and children when ill, his medical skills often sought in the village.

But this was a mob that was not to be dissuaded. They shouted their unhappiness at being governed by the Americans and began to shoot at him with rifles and arrows. Charles was hit in the head by Indian arrows. He wife Ignacia called to him, urging him to flee on a horse corralled behind the house, but he refused, not wanting to leave his family in time of danger. "If they want to kill me, they can kill me here with my family," he said.[12]

Meanwhile, Ignacia's sister, Mrs. Kit (Josefa) Carson, Mrs. Boggs and an "Indian slave"[13] had dug a hole through the wall between the houses for an escape route. Charles pushed the children through the wall first, then Mrs. Carson and Mrs. Boggs. Ignacia insisted that he precede her through the wall, but the arrows he had in his head hurt so that he pulled them out and crushed them against the wall before going through the hole to the next house.[14] Stepping in front of Ignacia, the Indian slave woman took the bullet meant for Mrs. Bent as she entered the hole. The mob followed Charles into the next room where they shot and scalped him, then stripped his clothes, with his family watching fearfully. Out of sentiment for the women and children, they were spared.

Also killed in this bloody uprising were the Sheriff Luis Estavan Lee, Provost Judge Lawyer Leal, Narcizo Beaubien, Ignacia's brother Pablo Jaramillo, and her uncle Cornelio Vigil. When the riot reached Arroyo Hondo, Mr. Turley, the owner of the distillery, and seven of his workers also were killed.[15]

The remaining family of Charles Bent stayed with

sympathetic friends until February 3, when the army arrived to fight the insurgents. Two hundred fifty Taos Indians were killed at their pueblo and six Mexicans were hung in the plaza in retribution.

George Bent was appointed foreman of the grand jury investigating the killings of his brother and the others on that fateful day. Ignacia Bent testified at the trial, having lost a husband, brother, and uncle in the slaughter. The trial lasted fifteen days, and fifteen men were sentenced to death. Charles' brother William was present when, the following April, the murderers of his brother were hanged in Taos.[16]

William was heartsick over the murder of his beloved brother, Charles. Charles had been the leader, the guide post, the older man who led young William over the trail toward his destiny in the West, at Bent's Fort. William had now lost two brothers, both murdered and scalped. He had now only one brother left in proximity, George, who lived in Taos but was back and forth visiting when he could. He tried to be thankful, but his heart was hurting.

An old friend of William was appointed for the Upper Platte and Arkansas tribes as Indian agent. This was Tom Fitzpatrick, a trapper, trader, and guide, who settled in to operate out of his Bent's Fort station. George arrived at the fort in the fall of 1847 and planned to accompany Tom Fitzpatrick to the

North Platte for the winter, trapping for fur. Tragedy struck, again. George never left for that trip, as he became ill and died, in spite of William's frantic ministrations. In October, George was buried outside the walls alongside his brother Robert.[17]

Could William's heart recover? Before he had time to grieve the loss of his two beloved brothers in one year, fate smacked him anew with a death even closer to his heart and life, that of his good wife, Owl Woman. Owl Woman gave birth to her fourth child, a girl William named Julia after his sister Juliannah. Then, Owl Woman died. The family life and bliss of William Bent and Owl Woman came to a tragic end. What, then, was William to do with four children, one of them an infant, when he had a business to operate and one hundred employees to supervise? He made an appropriate choice.[18]

Bent's Fort Blown Up

8

During the marriage of William and Owl Woman, her younger sisters were welcome in William's lodgings, both at the fort and in the Cheyenne camps. Slow Smoking and Island were cared for as William's own family. Then, following the death of Owl Woman in 1847, Island and Slow Smoking became his wives.

It was traditional with the Indians that a man could have as many wives as he felt he could care for. Also not uncommon was the custom of marrying the deceased wife's sister. Both of these young women had lived with William for many years. So, William merely followed the path of his wife's people by marrying her sisters. He was, after all, considered a great white chief of the trading post and a member of the tribe.

Island and Slow Smoking inherited their sister's children. This would have been expected and welcomed by the children as well as by the tribe. In the Cheyenne family, a child's mother's female relatives were also called "Mother" and were as equally responsible for that child's care and nurturing as the birth mother.

William, however, wished to keep his newborn daughter, Julia, near him at the fort during her infancy. He invited an older Cheyenne couple to take up lodgings at the fort and care for Julia within his supervision. The patriarch of this family was a medicine man, a holy man, from the Suhtai branch of Cheyenne. This family had joined the Cheyenne when they traveled from their northern homeland to trade with William Bent and to live part of the year near his trading post on the Arkansas River. But the holy man was not a northern Cheyenne from the larger tribe. He and his family had migrated south from the upper Missouri River band of Cheyenne who spoke a different dialect, distinct from the larger main tribe who called themselves the Buffalo Hair Rope People, and who spoke the major dialect.[1] From this family, Julia learned to speak the dialect of her Suhtai foster parents, and always spoke that language.

While William had settled the problem of a second marriage and had placed Julia with her Suhtai foster parents for care, he was beset with a business dilemma equally as profound in his life as his family matters. All was not well with William's association with the only company partner still alive, Ceran St. Vrain. The Bent, St. Vrain and Company firm, held together by Charles Bent and then George Bent, encountered difficulties after their deaths. Ceran St. Vrain and William Bent, the last two officers in the firm, could not agree on business practices. Ceran, without authorization from William, offered Bent's Fort to the army. The offer was rejected. Ceran predicted the demise of the buffalo robe business, but William was for too long drawn to his trading business on the Arkansas River to consider moving to Taos or Santa Fe to become a shopkeeper in the company's stores. Finally, Ceran left the firm, and was probably paid a settlement by his partner for his share of the firm. William wondered what he should do. At last, the War Department offered William a sum for the fort, reportedly between $12,000 and $50,000. William refused the offer, disgusted.[2]

During this time when Julia was a toddling two year old, she lived with her stepmothers Slow Smoking and Island at Bent's Fort and in the Indian camps, as well as with her foster parents in the lodge. Slow Smoking was pregnant. And in 1849, she presented William with his fifth and last child, a son he named Charles in honor of his beloved older brother who had been murdered.[3] Soon after Charles' birth, William delivered twenty wagons of robes to St. Louis, accompanied this time by his son Robert, age eight. While he was gone, Island and Slow Smoking took their mother Tail Woman and Bent's other children to a great meeting of tribes on a Cimarron feeder. The purpose of the gathering was to attend a Sun Dance and to trade. As they gathered, people began to sicken and fall over with cramps. A warrior shouted from astride his pony, "If I could see this thing [the cholera], if I knew where it was, I would go there and kill it." Just then, Little Old Man fell from his horse and died in his wife's arms.

The sisters loaded their ill mother and the children on a travois and moved out rapidly toward the fort. But too late.[4]

Tail Woman died on the trail, and was buried on a scaffold.[5] The mourning family finally reached Bent's Fort and safety, finding Bent already back from his journey.[6]

However, William was more than a little miffed when Slow Smoking showed up at the fort, sensing that she may have brought cholera to the fort when she returned. Although no cholera outbreak was reported at Bent's Fort, William soon made a very strange decision, historically undecipherable. He destroyed the old fort he had built sixteen years before, the primary trading post on the Santa Fe Trail, and his home with Owl Woman and their children.

William packed his trade goods into twenty wagons, had them driven away from the fort, then rode back and placed kegs of gun powder along the walls and fired the fort. It blew up![7] There is no known record of his reasoning.[8] He was disappointed with the army's offered price for the fort he had slaved over with his sweat and hard work for so many years. And after all, he had spent fourteen years with his wife and children at this home. The fort had been the home of Robert, Charles and George until the latter two brothers had married and moved to Taos. Robert had died in 1841.Charles and George had died two years before, as well as the beautiful Owl Woman. Ceran St. Vrain had quit the company. Perhaps there were too many memories associated with the fort.[9]

William then took his family north, away from the Arkansas, to Fort St. Vrain, thence later to Fort Laramie. His purpose was to build up trade with the Sioux, Northern Arapaho and Northern Cheyenne. Having accomplished this, he decided to return to the

Arkansas country.[10]

Whatever the reason for his moves, William then built and settled into a stockade on the Purgatoire River for a few brief years. He built three log cabins, arranged in a U-shape facing the river, with a stockade guarding the front entrance, and began to experience a large rise in business there in the Big Timbers. He recalled ruefully that this was the place the Cheyenne Yellow Wolf had recommended to him years before. Finally, he was there. The stockade was set amidst large cottonwood trees, thinly scattered over an area three-fourths mile wide and three or four miles long, a safe and inviting place for the Indians to winter where their ponies had cottonwood bark for forage in the bitter winters when there was no grass.

Meanwhile, William had lost one of his wives, apparently to wanderlust. Slow Smoking was a restless person who frequently moved locations and married and separated as often. She left Bent's lodge and married Pain in Legs, with whom she had a daughter named Scout Woman. But she left Pain in Legs prior to 1864 and married another man, Old Bachelor, and bore him two sons.[11]

The Guerrier family meanwhile had its own disaster. Even as Slow Smoking lost her mother to cholera, Edmund Guerrier lost his mother Tah-tah-tois-neh and his newborn baby brother to the same disease in 1849, just after her delivery of the child.[12] Edmund was an orphan at age nine, just as William Bent's oldest four children had been orphaned by the death of Owl Woman. Edmund's Cheyenne relatives cared for him for the next two years.

William Guerrier was not present in camp when Tah-tah-tois-neh and her new baby died. William and Seth Ward were reported as having met the traveling party of the Cherokee-Evans Company from eastern Indian Territory on the Santa Fe Trail on June 4, 1849. The Cherokee-Evans Company was on its way to California goldfields to try its luck staking claims, while the Guerrier-Ward train was on its path to Independence with a load of peltries for sale, taking along the letters of the gold-seekers to forward home to the families worried about the fates of their loved ones.[13] They also noted in their diaries that when passing the William Bent stockade on the trail, they could see that it had burned down.

After Guerrier left Bent's employ and his subsequent activities at Pueblo, he set upon a new trading relationship by forming a partnership with Seth Ward in Wyoming country. Guerrier became post sutler and Indian trader at Fort Laramie.[14] Indian agent Tutt wrote to Major John Dougherty in 1853 that Ward and Guerrier were not having a very good year in trading with the Indians. But Tutt thought their business might pick up if they had a good trade with the Kiowas and Comanches for mules. At the time, however, Guerrier operated another business at the fort. He built boats, in company with Bissonette and Sebille.[15] Very likely, he learned the boat-building business from Auguste Pierre Chouteau while he was on the Grand River prior to 1839.

The Fort Laramie post commander, Richard Garnett, hired Guerrier and Ward to build a bridge across the Laramie River to replace the poorly constructed one that had washed away.[16] And, the partners were given permission to exact a toll for its use, further adding to their income, $5 for each wagon and $1 for a draft animal. They set up a trading post at the site that also served food for the travelers. Their business was lucrative, producing a good income for the pair.

The partners also built up a cattle business that was credited as the first cattle ranching operation in Wyoming, and they did it in an unusual way, without having to drive their own cattle. As their trading post was on the Oregon Trail, many emigrants reached that point in their travels with spent or lame oxen, and were desperate to continue their journey. Guerrier and Ward traded the travelers one good ox for two or three lame ones, thereby building a substantial herd for themselves. Their post also kept a stock of mules for sale or trade, and supplied J. M. Hockaday, who operated the first mail route to Salt Lake City.[17]

Guerrier was busy with his new enterprises, but he had not forgotten his Cheyenne son Edmund whom he had left in the care of Cheyenne relatives back in Colorado. In 1851, he traveled to find Edmund, snatched him from the Cheyenne camp, and took him to St. Mary's Mission in Kansas to begin his education. As uneducated as William was reported to be, he vowed that his son would suffer no such handicap. Edmund, at age eleven, knew nothing of the world but the ways of the Cheyenne. William planned to remedy that deficit. How did Edmund feel about this abrupt change in his environment and lifestyle? He applied himself to the tasks he was bidden. What else could he do? He was Cheyenne. Brave.

Education at St. Mary's was just what Edmund needed at that

time of his life to prepare him for his role in the larger society of the white man, where his skills would be called upon. Founded in 1838 by the Belgian priest Pierre-Jean De Smet for the religious schooling of the Pottawatomi Tribe, by 1848 the school accepted boys and girls in two schools, the girls' school run by the Sacred Heart order.[18] And, of course, Edmund became Catholic, as was his French father. He settled into his education with a will. At St. Mary's he learned reading, writing, and numbers, as well as the manners and customs of the white men. The practical arts of agriculture and horticulture were taught, as well as singing the mass in the choir.[19] An apt pupil, intelligent and adaptable, Edmund learned quickly. Hawk deserved his name. Over the next years living full time at St. Mary's, he used his innate strength to develop coping skills for his life ahead.

Meanwhile, his father and Seth Ward prospered at their trading post at Ash Point, near Torrington, Wyoming. They bought the post in 1851 from John Richard of the American Fur Company, but later moved to Sand Point, nine miles from Fort Laramie on the North Platte. A traveler described camping on the river bank under two fine trees one mile from the post, which consisted of three buildings, one of which was an unfinished stone structure.

As Guerrier prospered in Wyoming, William Bent was becoming restless on the Purgatoire River in Colorado. His stockade had burned, and he needed a place to conduct business.[20] Bent soon began dreaming about his old fort and missing the size and feel of it. The old days. Could he bring them back? He decided to try, but on a smaller scale this time. His brothers dead, Ceran St. Vrain no longer in the company, William's needs were less. Still, he wanted the glory of another fort like the one he blew up. So, in 1853, he began again, by building Bent's New Fort on the north side of the Arkansas River, thirty-eight miles from his stockade. His daughter Julia reminisced about her new home in later years:

> This fort was not built of adobe, like the first one. I saw the clay walls of the first fort, crumbling with the weather. The old fort was much larger. But the new fort, where I grew up, was smaller and it was built of stone. My father brought in workmen from Mexico to dig the stones and haul them to the site. But it was a fine enough fort, and a good home for me. It had about twelve rooms, some for living quarters for the family, some for guests, a dining hall, kitchen, but what I remember most is the large trade room. It was busy all the time with people coming and going, to the traders bringing in goods and unpacking all the cartons, the trappers bringing in their skins and swapping them for supplies and ammunition, the Indians hauling in their buffalo robes and trading them for kettles, blankets, and beads. For a child my age, it was a fascinating place to be. Father placed the two small cannon on the roof, but we never had to use them. It was built on the north side of the Arkansas River, about thirty eight miles from the old stockade in the Big Timbers, where we spent a lot of time too. I

lived at the new fort for many years.[21]

Julia was fascinated with the many appealing features in her home at the fort, but her father William was having second thoughts again. Only Island was with him and the children at the fort.

Bent soon began to realize the futility of trying to recreate the past and relive old glories. The new fort just was not the same. He tried to sell it but the deal fell through so he decided to stay there, reluctantly.[22] Another of his decisions would be more felicitous, he hoped. He was concerned about the education of his children. After all, the children of his brothers had been sent east to Missouri for their education. His own children surely deserved the same consideration. He spoke to his wife about his plans, and Island agreed, supportive of him in this matter concerning their children.

Because Bent was Indian agent for the several tribes and made frequent trips to Westport to pick up annuity goods for distribution to them, he took Mary, George and Robert with him on his next trip east. Bent and Island would be able to visit with the children each time they made that trip to Westport. Bent left the two younger children, Julia and Charles, at the fort, but placed the three older ones under the guardianship of Albert Boone in Westport in 1853.[23] There they attended their first organized school in the white world.

With Bent back and forth from the stockade to Westport at least twice a year on his trips to restock his wares in Colorado and to deposit his pelts in Westport, he could see the children in school there and keep track of their health and school efforts. And, he was pleased that Island could visit with her stepchildren.

Always alert to business needs, William realized that he needed a large operation at the Westport end of his journey and decided to buy a farm south of town. He first set his nephew Angus Boggs to work as its manager,[24] later hiring his new son-in-law, Robison M. Moore, for the position.[25] Son George spent his summers at the farm, away from school, and in the 1860 U.S. Census, was listed with the family of Robison and Mary Moore there on Bent's 400-acre farm. The farm was used in various ways. It was a staging station, storing goods from Westport and St. Louis that were waiting to be transported to Bent's Colorado and other trading bases, a place to house cattle and other livestock until sold, as well as a maintenance facility for the wagons.

With some of their children in school and themselves conducting business in their long-established but separate paths, Bent and Guerrier carried on peacefully in their careers. The serenity of William Guerrier and his son Edmund was not to last, however. Fate had a blow in store.[26]

A Tragic End for William Guerrier

9

The three years following 1853 passed peacefully enough. William Bent's three oldest children were attending school in Westport. William was able to visit them on the frequent trips from Bent's Fort to pick up trade goods for his fort's business.

Bent's old French employee, trader William Guerrier, was now the prosperous co-owner of a trading post on the Laramie River near Fort Laramie and was the sutler of the fort. Guerrier was busy with his cattle and boat-building businesses. But Guerrier never forgot his son Edmund, who was completing his studies at St. Mary's school in Kansas. In 1856, William Guerrier recalled that Edmund had attended St. Mary's for five years and was now sixteen years old. William Guerrier decided that Edmund was ready for college. As Edmund's father, he must attend to transferring him to an institution of higher learning. William decided on St. Louis University, in a town where William knew many of the residents and where Edmund might feel more comfortable. He traveled to St. Mary's where he picked up Edmund, then went on to Collinsville to introduce Edmund to his guardian while he was in school there, a prosperous farmer named Henry F. Mayer. Then father and son went on to St. Louis, where Edmund enrolled in the university.

After five years at St. Mary's school, Edmund was wise to the ways of the white world, was knowledgeable in his studies, and had learned to write and speak English thoroughly. Realizing that his son was smart, William Guerrier thought that Edmund was prepared both for a university setting and a larger town.

It was at St. Louis University that Edmund studied pharmacy and played football,[1] all 5'6" of him. Though small in stature, Edmund was well-built and kept his body trim. He was strong, and quietly fearless. He was a good-looking man with dark hazel eyes and wavy auburn hair with golden glints, and generally wore a gentle expression on his handsome face. Edmund thought of himself as French, although he had the ruddier skin of his Cheyenne parents. He wore his hair in the style of the French, hanging loosely to his shoulders, rather than the long braids of his Cheyenne kinsmen. But, on his feet for all of his life he wore only Cheyenne moccasins.

Upon his return to Wyoming after depositing Edmund in St. Louis, William Guerrier was issued a license to trade with the Sioux, Cheyenne and Arapaho tribes in a large territory encompassing parts of Colorado, Wyoming and South Dakota.[2] His partnership with Ward also supplied the government's orders for Indian annuities that year, those annuities such as flour and sugar the government had promised the tribes in various treaties in exchange for their land. Of the pair, Ward preferred to tend the trading post at Laramie, while Guerrier preferred his long-accustomed role as Indian trader on the road. The partners were very successful.

An incident occurred the following year that sent the traders scurrying, however. Lieutenant John L. Grattan from Fort Laramie arrested an Indian following the supposed theft of a cow, which the Indians denied having taken. This led to Lieutenant Grattan and his entire command of twenty-eight men being slain by the Sioux. Commandant General William S. Harney issued a general alarm and ordered all traders into the fort in 1857. Ward and Guerrier were forced to move their trading post to the Laramie River.[3]

Edmund, in St. Louis, knew nothing of this. But he did hear of his father's successful trading year later that fall, as there was a newspaper article about it in a Kansas City paper in August of 1857.

> The Fort Laramie trains arrived the present week, with 12,000 buffalo robes, besides furs, peltries, etc. The trains belonged to Messrs. Ward and Geary, extensive traders in the mountains, and filled the streets into town … The wagons looked like immense elephants, being filled high above the beds and tightly covered with tarpaulins. This is the richest received at any one time the present season.[4]

The next news that Edmund heard about his father shocked him. He couldn't believe it. His father was dead!

His father was trading with the Indians on the Niobrara River, near present Lusk, Wyoming, in February of 1858. Standing in his wagon swapping his trade goods for hides and pelts, he stepped up on the tongue of his wagon with a lighted pipe in his mouth when a spark dropped into a bag of gunpowder below him. In a flash, William's life was over. William's mistake was one an experienced trader dreads. A moment of carelessness, a live spark, and a bag of gunpowder. His employees had neglected to cover the bag of gun powder.[5]

When his father died in the gunpowder explosion, Edmund's university life came to a sudden halt. He had reached his majority at the same time, in January. Unsure of his next step, he decided to travel to Collinsville to seek the advice of his guardian Henry F. Mayer, a farmer and also the post sutler at Fort Lyon, about future possibilities open to him.

Mayer had given Edmund's future his gravest thoughts before his arrival, as he liked the boy and wished him well. The elder Guerrier's estate still had an amount of $1,900 remaining, enough to give his son a start in his career. Therefore, Mayer gave Edmund his fairest views on the matter.

> Take this money, Edmund, and travel as widely in the west as your means will allow. When you are broke – you'll get broke, all right – come back and we'll talk it over. My purpose is that you shall learn the ways of the world, and be cheated and robbed before you engage in business for yourself. You will recover from your losses, but if you should engage in business without this knowledge, and then lose your property, you might

never be able to retrieve your bad fortune.[6]

Mayer's advice was worldly-wise, Edmund could see. He decided to act on the recommendation of the older man, following the precepts he had learned in his life with the Cheyenne, that a young man should listen to the teachings of his elders.

Edmund was respectful of the elder Henry Mayer, but Mayer was equally impressed with his young ward. "I know him to be an upright, intelligent, correct young man," said Mayer. "He is entirely reliable. I trust every word he says."[7] Mayer's confidence helped boost Edmund's determination to meet the world as an orphan with the best of his abilities.

Edmund gratefully received his $1,900 inheritance from Mayer, and began his journey. His first stop seeking employment was at Fort Leavenworth in Kansas, where he was hired as a bullwhacker for Irvin and Jackman, government freighters there. His assignment was with a train headed from Fort Leavenworth to Fort Union in New Mexico.

In his youthful vanity, Edmund arrayed himself in the finery of the time, and became something of a clotheshorse. Unmarried, he spent his earnings on decking himself out in fine breeches, shirts, and vests. And, he adopted two personal dress idiosyncrasies that he followed all the rest of his life. He wore Cheyenne moccasins on his feet and a kerchief around his head tied under his chin like a babushka to keep his shoulder-length hair under control in the prairie winds.[8] And, he never failed to find employment.

William Bent was fully occupied with his own affairs, about to become even more difficult.

Bent's Fort

Bent's Old Fort National Historic Site, located 8 miles east of La Junta, Colorado on State Highway 194, features a reconstructed 1840s adobe fur trading post on the mountain branch of the Santa Fe Trail where traders, trappers, travelers, and the Cheyenne and Arapaho tribes came together in peaceful terms for trade. Today, living historians recreate the sights, sounds, and smells of the past with guided tours, demonstrations, and special events.

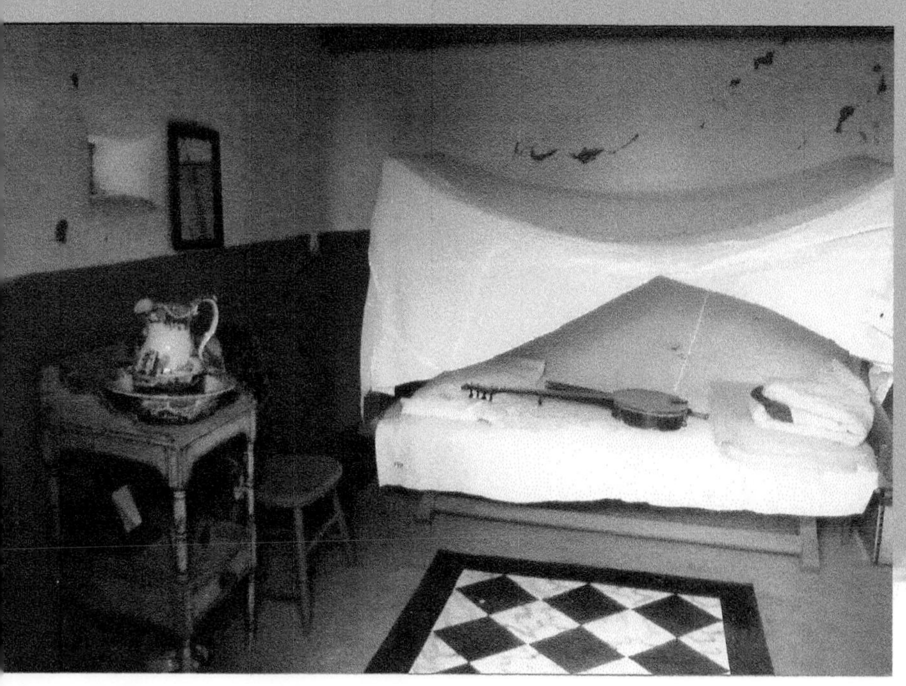

Bent Pleads for Prairie Peace

10

The late 1850s were busy years for the Bents. William decided to have a home in Kansas City as living quarters for him and Island during their trips there for restocking the fort with trade goods. In April of 1858, he established residence at 1032 West 55th Street,[1] a two-story brick home with two rooms down and two rooms upstairs, a porch over the lower floor and a center staircase. Here, he could use the home as a gathering place for his scattered family and be able to check personally on the activities at his farm operation. Julia and Charles accompanied their parents on some of these trips. And, the three Bent children at school in St. Louis under the supervision of William's sister, Dorcas Carr, would be able to gather at William's Kansas City home during school vacations.

Bent, at an unknown date, also placed his younger children, Julia and Charles, in the Westport boarding school. In order to do this, Bent gave Roman Nose a fine sorrel horse along with his bidden task of retrieving Julia from the Indian camp and bringing her to her father. Julia had been living with the Indians, but William wanted to educate her in the white man's schools. That accomplished, she and Charles were taken to Westport for schooling.[2]

Bent placed these two younger children in the home of Albert Boone, three blocks from Boone's general store. Now, Boone had the care of all five of the Bent children. Bent's relative by marriage, Boone was a large affable man who was glad to accommodate his friend for the care of his family's educational needs. All of Bent's family and in-laws were on the best of amicable and loving terms.

William's old friend Kit Carson was himself busy with his children. He and Maria Josefa had their twenty-four-day-old son, Christopher, baptized in Taos on July 6, 1858.[3]

Island accompanied William and the children on this trip, but demanded that she would only live in a tepee in the Boone's yard. She felt out of place in a house, and especially on a white man's bed. The women of Westport were astonished at seeing Island astride a horse in her skirt, with the skirt tails tucked up around her legs. The men in town grew accustomed to hearing the hoof clops of her finely matched pair of mules pulling her carriage.[4]

Charles followed his older siblings peacefully by settling down to his studies at the Western Academy in Westport, led by Reverend Nathan Scarritt. Not so for his sister Julia. She discovered very quickly that life in Westport with the Boone family and her studies at the Western Academy were not for her. At some point, she ran away. She was not persuaded at any time to return to the white man's studies. She was Cheyenne. She wanted to live with the Indians.

Bent, however, was only briefly involved with house building and children. His main concerns were his trade business, and especially, the conditions of his beloved Cheyenne. He made a report to the government in 1858. He said the Cheyenne and Arapaho were "very uneasy and restless about their country, the whites coming into it, making large and extensive settlements and laying off and building towns all over the best part."[5]

Bent and his Indians were right to be disturbed about the number of whites coming into their territory, as the Colorado gold rush had begun. Someone had seen a goose quill of gold in the hands of the Delaware Indian Fall Leaf, and the story spread. On Bent's trip to Kansas City that July, he was besieged with questions about the gold speculation. He traveled on to St. Louis to visit his children for two months, then returned to Kansas City where he was interviewed by a reporter from the *Journal of Commerce* on September 15. At the docks where Bent was restocking his wagons for the return trip to Colorado, the reporter asked him about the stories of gold in his territory.

"Col. William Bent has been trading in the vicinity of the country for many years," wrote the reporter. "He says the existence of gold has been known to the Indians ever since his residence among them. He made inquiries after the discovery of gold in California and ever since has been satisfied of its existence. The Indians, however, have always remonstrated against the knowledge being made known to the whites … As one old chief told Bent, if the white men ever found the gold they would surely take from them their 'best and last home.'"[6]

When towns began to spring up in Colorado, the Indians realized that they were losing their way of life, and did not mind if their own lives were lost along with it. To die a warrior in defense of his homeland is to die a glorious death. Bent, however, was able to settle them down.

Because of his reports to Washington and his obvious concern for the welfare of the Indians, Bent was named Indian agent for the Upper Arkansas Agency in April 1859. That position alone could keep a man busy. In the most recent census, the agency listed 3,150 Cheyenne on the South Platte and Arkansas rivers, with 900 warriors of that number living in 30 lodges and owning 17,000 horses. This did not count the Arapaho, Comanche and Kiowa under his jurisdiction. Bent was charged with keeping track of these Indians and supplying them with government annuities, as well as his usual business of trading with the tribe. He decided to enlist the services of a helper, one of his own family.

Bent allowed his eldest son Robert, then seventeen to contract for hauling the Indians' annuity goods, and even lent Robert sufficient wagons to perform this job. Robert's first commercial enterprise fell on hard times, however, when he reached the Upper Platte distribution point and found only a few lodges of Indians gathered. Robert had to sit it out until all the Indians arrived many days later, all the while paying his hired hands their daily wages.[7]

Bent immediately wrote a report to Washington:

> The Cheyans and Arrapahos have took my advice to them last winter and this past spring. I am proud to say they have behaved themselves exceedingly well … have

> passed theair laws amongst themselves that they will do anything I may advise. After I deliver the Indians their goods I intend … to have a conversation with the Kioways and Commanches. I suppose that will be purtay saucy – but as I have bin appointed agent I fell it my dutay to see all of the Indians under my agency – if they sculp me … you Must excuse my bad Spelling as I have bin so long in the Wild Waste I have almost forgotten how to Spell.[8]

His next report was more polished:

> A smothered passion for revenge agitates these Indians, perpetually fomented by the failure of food, the encircling encroachments of the white population, and the exasperating sense of decay and impending extinction with which they are surrounded … A desperate war of starvation and extinction is imminent and inevitable, unless prompt measures shall prevent it..[9]

Bent's concern for the welfare and future of his Indians is patently obvious. But he was soon to become concerned about the future of his own daughter, Mary, who had fallen in love with twenty-seven year old Robison M. Moore.[10] Bent traveled to Westport to check out Mary's suitor, lent his approval to the young man, and provided Mary and Robison a splendid wedding on April 3, 1860. He even lent Moore money for a start in the mercantile business, generous to a fault, as always, with his family.

While Bent continually listened for the sound of war drums to begin around the Arkansas River, he was aware that the entire country was pacing itself into a general conflagration. The southern states, incensed about the perceived lack of consideration for their way of life emanating from Washington, were seceding from the Union. Back on the Arkansas, Bent had no notion that one of his sons would soon be engaged in the country's War Between the States.

In 1861, three months before the outbreak of America's civil war, the Cheyenne agreed to a new treaty, at the behest of the newly appointed Indian agent Albert Boone and William Bent, who had resigned and recommended Boone. Known as the Fort Wise Treaty, signed by President Abraham Lincoln on December 15, 1861, the agreement limited the Cheyenne to a small area of the Arkansas River in southern Colorado, in return for $450,000 over fifteen years plus money for vocational pursuits. But only a few of the peace chiefs were induced to sign it. The warring bands and the Dog Soldiers refused to come to the fort to sign it and were angry that their former lands had been ceded without their consent.

William Bent made sure that his half-breed son Robert received 640 acres of land along the Arkansas River, as did John Smith's son Jack. This governmental largess was a boon for the Bent family, then blessed with a large chunk of Colorado territory.

The majority of the tribe, however, the non-signers, continued their unrest about the injustice imposed on them.

While William Bent's sons, George and Charles, were attending St. Louis Academy in St. Louis and in the care of their aunt Dorcas Carr, they visited their father's new family home in Westport during summer vacations. Westport was a town of southern sympathizers and the boys heard this talk. When they learned about the firing on Fort Sumter and the outbreak of the country's Civil War, George enlisted in Colonel Martin E. Green's regiment, though he was only seventeen. Charles tried to enlist, but was turned away as too young. George was ready for a little action and a good fight, after his confinement in academic studies. His regiment was in the 2nd Brigade of Bowen's Division of General Earl Van Dorn's army, and saw many battles. George took part in the Battle of Wilson's Creek where General Nathaniel Lyon, the Union commander, was killed. Next, he fought in the Battle of Pea Ridge in Arkansas where the Confederates were defeated.[11] He was present at the siege of Corinth, Mississippi in 1862, deserted Captain John C. Landis' horse artillery unit, and was captured when the Union cavalry isolated and surrounded a large group of Confederates.[12]

George was marched back through Missouri and down the streets of St. Louis on his way to a Union prison. A former classmate happened to see the passing parade of captured rebels and recognized George Bent among the prisoners. The classmate hailed George in the street and asked where he was going. To a Yankee prison, was the answer. His classmate quickly ran to find Robert Bent, George's brother.

Robert Bent, in St. Louis attending to some business for his father, ran to find George's St. Louis guardian, Robert Campbell, who in turn hurried to his friend Bernard G. Farrar, the District Provost Marshall. Farrar secured George's release on his own recognizance if he signed an Oath of Allegiance to the United States and promised to fight no more.[13]

George would fight again, but not in the Civil War. His father William tried to keep George busy with trading activities and luxurious gifts. On a trip to Denver, William outfitted George with a fine new suit, expensive field glasses, and a sorrel race horse costing $500.[14] But George had other ideas. He was weary of taunts and long looks from Union sympathizers and army personnel who frequented his father's stockade. George felt that he had his own war to fight. In spite of his father's efforts to keep him peaceful, George left his father and the white man's ways in the spring of 1863 in order to join the Cheyenne in their camp. He joined a soldier society within the tribe, the Crooked Lance society, urged by his mentor Black Kettle who was a member, as well as Roman Nose. This group had as a totem four crooked lances wrapped in otter skin, festooned with eagle feathers and capped with a snake-shaped elk horn. They were known as the boldest of the society men and were allowed to wear government uniforms in battle. George Bent, when he was fighting General P. E. Connor's troops on the Powder River, wore a U.S. Army major's uniform he found while ransacking Julesburg station.[15]

As for William Bent and his wife, Island, their life continued as it had over the years, with William making his trips back and forth to Westport to continue his trading career in spite of the Civil War raging in the East. He had become more disillusioned with his new stone fort, and tried to sell it to the army but the government decided that he had no clear title to the land and declined to deal with him. Finally, he cleared out of Bent's New Fort, enlarged his stockade, and allowed the army to use the stone fort as a storage facility with the understanding that he would be paid for its lease. The army on September 9 signed a lease agreement for $65 per month.[16]

The army occupied the stone fort in 1860, renaming it Fort Wise before it was changed to Fort Lyon in 1861. The army set about building five large stables, six buildings for the company's quarters and twelve for the officers, as well as a hospital, guardhouse, bake house, and laundry. In 1864, Major Wynkoop had his men build an enclosing wall for defense of the fort. The army's land was expanded to 38,000 acres.[17]

Bent's enlarged stockade comprised a square structure, 100 feet long on each side, surrounding an inner courtyard. With all rooms sixteen by twenty feet, it had Bent's quarters along with rooms for employees, storage and stables. Moats were dug around the walls to provide dirt for the earthen roof, which also provided safety in case of attack. Bent felt his family was safe, but was distressed about the temper of the Indians.

Hostilities between the whites and the Indians, never far below the surface, boiled again. Lieutenant George Eayres was sent by the army to kill Indians as punishment for the theft of cattle, which the Indians denied having taken. Eayres attacked and killed the Cheyenne Chief Lean Bear, who was coming toward him unarmed and alone, in a gesture of friendship. The fight began. Eayres pursued and killed Cheyenne as he found them. Furious, the Cheyenne raided at Walnut Creek. The war was on again.

Back at his stockade, William Bent found that he had his own little bit of excitement, this time in his own household. In August of 1864, Island was seized with a sudden passion and left William for another man. William reported his "old squaw ran off a few days ago, or rather went off with Jo Barraldo, as she like him better than she did me. If I ever get sight of the young man, it will go hard with him." William was fifty-five that year, Barraldo much younger. William had a right to see a rival in that younger man.[18]

Slow Smoking, ever an adventurous and wandering soul, who had left William Bent after the birth of their son Charlie, was able to escape death during the massacre at Sand Creek, but her husband Old Bachelor and their two sons were killed.[19]

During these early years of the 1860s, Edmund Guerrier, now a young adult, had kept busy working for the government in various capacities, as his work ethic was commendable and trusted by the authorities. Following his first assignment as a bullwhacker for Irvin and Jackman at Fort Leavenworth, his next job was a little easier but just as dusty and physically tiring. He convoyed one thousand horses again from Fort Leavenworth to Fort Union, a long journey for men and animals. Although a tremendous herd, the horses were gentle and did not mind much being tied to a wagon in bunches of fifty to sixty each. Even so, there would have been at least twenty wagons, leading horses that needed forage and water at intervals, not a simple task to accomplish.

Another government job that Edmund tackled was to help transport five hundred Mescalero Apaches, prisoners of war rounded up by Kit Carson, from Fort Stanton to the garrison at Fort Sumter. Here, Edmund most likely met the famed frontiersman Carson, so closely joined to the Bent family. Weary from travel and hard work, Guerrier then took a year's departure from government work in order to while away some time in Kansas with Lucien Dagenette, an old school chum. Following this lapse, he accepted a position as sutler under his former guardian, Henry F. Mayer, who was then post sutler at Fort Riley.

While Edmund kept busy honing his employment skills and work ethic, he was also meeting some of the important and instrumental figures of the West who would see his potential and further his career. When he decided to undertake a trading venture with John Stickler to Fort Lyon and then to Fort Larned, he had no inkling that he would soon find himself camping with the Cheyenne during one of the bloodiest massacres perpetrated during the Indian wars on the plain.

November 29, 1864 was the date of the massacre at Sand Creek in southern Colorado which began the story of the Bents and Guerriers, many of whom were in the Cheyenne camp when it was viciously attacked without warning by Major Chivington and his band of volunteers. Yellow Woman (Slow Smoking), William Bent's former wife and mother of his son Charles, George Bent, Julia Bent, and Edmund Guerrier were present. Robert Bent was forced by Chivington to lead the troops to the site.

While in prison following his surrender to the Army and as his arm healed from a gunshot wound, he had time to think about his future. He knew that he would not be held long in custody. What was he to do upon release? He was a grown man, but he had no job or source of income. He needed employment. That was a necessity if he wanted to continue thinking about Julia in his future.[20]

Guerrier with Hancock and Custer

11

When Edmund was released from custody at Fort Lyon, he sought employment as he needed an income for clothing and supplies, all his goods having been ravaged during the sacking of the village by Chivington's men at Sand Creek. He found a position suited to his talents at Fort Larned acting as a courier and interpreter for Colonel Jesse Leavenworth, who was Indian agent for the Kiowa and Comanche tribes. Leavenworth was asked to mediate a truce with the Cheyenne and Arapaho. Bent and Carson were known as westerners who knew more about the Indians than anyone.

But Bent had his own definite views about securing peace. "If the matter were left up to me," William said, "I guarantee with my life that in three months I could have all the Indians along the Arkansas at peace without the expense of war."[1]

Fine words. Lofty ideals. Years of experience and practice in dealing with the Indians. But almost as he spoke those words, General Connor of Paiute Indian fame was on the prowl looking for Indians to kill, one of those Bent's own wife.

The problem was a basic rupture of administrative goals within the government, as the Interior Department sought to solve the Indian problem through peace treaties, while the War Department advocated for punishment and complete submission of the Indians and often thwarted efforts toward peace.

While Leavenworth negotiated with the Kiowa, Kiowa-Apache, Comanche and Big Mouth of the Arapaho and a truce was signed at the mouth of the Little Arkansas on August 18, at the same time General Connor's Pawnee and Delaware scouts picked up the trail of a Cheyenne war party that had been raiding. Island and four warriors were leading a travois and pack animals loaded with plunder, ahead of the main body of raiders, when they fell for a ruse. General Connor's Pawnee scouts spied the small party, showed themselves and beckoned to them in the Cheyenne way to come closer. When within range, a larger body of Pawnee and Delaware scouts along with the cavalry fell upon the group, killing Island and her warrior companions. She died August 16, 1865. The Pawnee celebrated with a scalp dance.[2]

Although Island had deserted William Bent for Jo Barraldo, who subsequently left her, she had decided to rejoin her tribe and participate in raiding against the whites. The Bent family mourned the loss of a wife and stepmother, no one more so than George

Bent, who was especially fond of Island. Julia was nearing eighteen when her stepmother was killed, Charles sixteen.

While William Bent pursued his dream of peace for the tribes, his sons George and Charles pursued the ways of war. They were involved in an attack on a government train near Pumpkin Creek. Colonel Henry Sawyer and his troops were accompanying a party of wagon trains whose purpose was to open up a road to the Montana mines. When the train reached the Powder River area near Pumpkin Buttes in August 1865, they were attacked by the Cheyenne and Sioux, who fought a battle with the troops for four days. George Bent was easily recognizable, as he wore a government-issued staff officer's uniform that he had taken from the storeroom in Julesburg. At Pumpkin Buttes, three Cheyenne were killed and five Sioux were wounded, two of whom died later.[3]

But William Bent would not give up. He finally was instrumental in persuading several bands of Cheyenne, Arapaho, and Kiowa-Apache to meet with government agents. The site chosen would later become Wichita, Kansas, at the mouth of the Little Arkansas River where Leavenworth earlier had hosted the truce signatories.

Where the steel grey river sliced through groves of trees, the Indian camps arrived and formed circles of teepees. Black Kettle, a principal chief of his tribe and advocate for peace, was there. He raised his well-tempered voice in protest at being asked to sign another treaty, under the circumstances. There were only eighty lodges of Cheyenne present for the meeting, while two hundred more lodges were still in the north. He knew that his tribe was not well represented as so few of the Cheyenne were present.

"All my friends – the Indians that are holding back," said Black Kettle, "they are afraid to come in; are afraid they will be betrayed as I have been. I am not afraid of white men, but come and take you by the hand, and am glad to have the opportunity of doing so. These lands that you propose to give us I know nothing about. There is but a handful here now of the Cheyenne nation, and I would rather defer making any permanent treaty until the others come."[4]

But in the end, those Cheyenne present were persuaded to sign the Treaty of the Little Arkansas. They would agree to cede their lands between the Arkansas and Platte rivers and to accept in return a reserve south of the Arkansas. They were not to venture within ten miles of the main traveled road, post or station without permission. The government could build roads and military posts on their reserve, if necessary.

In this October 14, 1865 treaty, brought about through the efforts of William Bent, the government repudiated "the gross and wanton outrages perpetrated against certain bands of Cheyenne and Arapaho Indians … at Sand Creek … while said Indians were at peace with the United States and under its flag." In compensation, chiefs Black Kettle, Seven Bulls, Little Robe, and Black White Man were each given three hundred twenty acres, plus sums of money for their destroyed property.

Certain persons related to the Cheyenne and Arapaho by

blood were each awarded a section of land amounting to six hundred forty acres. Included in these were William Bent's daughter Mary Bent Moore and her children Ada, William, and George. And, more names: Edmund Guerrier, Rosa Guerrier, and Julia Guerrier, [5] the latter two his sisters. Edmund's half-brother Henry was not included.

During the treaty negotiations in the tent of General William S. Harney, chief Black Kettle was invited to tell his side of the story of Sand Creek. Black Kettle eloquently told of having requested peace during his meeting with Colorado Governor Evans and of being assured of his tribe's safety by the commander of Fort Lyon. When attacked, he held up an American flag and a white flag of truce to announce his peaceful status, to no avail. He told of his wife's nine serious wounds from the battle and showed General Harney her many scars. General Harney regretted Black Kettle's losses and his wife's near death at the hands of the Colorado volunteers. As a gesture of his good will, General Harney presented Black Kettle with a fine bay horse from his own stable as a gift. Black Kettle accepted the gift.

After the treaty was signed and Black Kettle moved with his band to the south as the document bade, George Bent went to him with a proposal. George spoke to the older man of his wish for the hand of Black Kettle's niece, Magpie, his beloved daughter. The chief welcomed George as a prospective member of his family, realizing that George's place as her husband would be in the lodge of her parents, Black Kettle and his wife.

With gifts of ponies and other goods, George married Black

Kettle's niece. As a wedding present, Black Kettle presented George the fine bay horse that he had received from General Harney. The newlyweds stayed with the chief that summer, while George acted as a trader for David Butterfield.

Shrewd old Black Kettle had been right, however, in his reluctance to sign the treaty without concurrence of the rest of the tribe. Of the larger bands of Cheyenne still in the north, some were at peace and others were pursuing warfare. The Dog Soldiers were particularly incensed. They did not want to give up their lands on the Smoky Hill, as ordered in the treaty. The Cheyenne Dog Soldiers were a warrior society and therefore became more important during these times when raids were going on and there was war between the tribe and the government. These Dog Soldiers in the north had joined with a few bands of Sioux of like persuasion, and had separated from the main body of Cheyenne, forming nearly a separate tribe. They were important men, holding great power on the plains. The Dog Soldiers therefore had to be consulted.

Edmund Guerrier, having stopped in the Cheyenne camp of Little Robe south of Fort Dodge, was persuaded by Little Robe to accompany him on a trip to search out both the peaceful and the warring Cheyenne camps farther north who were unaware that the Cheyenne in the south were at peace. On the trip to find them, the pair were forced to share Edmund's little Mexican mule as Little Robe's horse gave out. To accomplish this, each person would ride a few miles ahead then strike out on foot, leaving the mule to graze until the other man could catch the mule and ride ahead of the one on foot. This plan worked for four or five days, but left each man's feet sore and blistered.[6] For food, they killed a buffalo. One of Edmund's positive traits was that he was able to use his wits to save himself and others during a crisis. A reliable and trustworthy companion.

Having persuaded some of the Indians to start toward their peaceful brothers in the south, Edmund and Little Robe returned to Fort Dodge and sold for $120 the twelve head of oxen they discovered on their way back, a lucky find.

Hired by Colonel Wynkoop in 1866 as an interpreter, Edmund was sent out to bring in the Dog Soldiers[7] to parley with the government about their support for the recent treaty. William Bent was at the time trading with the dissidents on the Smoky Hill road when his son Charles went berserk. Charles, a Dog Solder, by that time was an influential Cheyenne leader. But during Guerrier's negotiations with the Dog Soldiers, Charles became drunk on trader's whiskey and threatened to kill his father and his brother George.[8] William, saddened, gave up and left camp. Alcohol was a destroyer to the Indians.

Charles Bent, in his fury, continued his attacks on the trails. Charles was the leader of a large band of three hundred Indians who attacked a caravan of religious leaders near the Colorado-Kansas territorial line on May 22, 1867, and came close to causing the death of the new bishop of Santa Fe, John B. Lamy. Bishop Lamy was escorting a group of Jesuit priests, Lorettine Sisters, and seminarians to Santa Fe as his diocesan helpers when the Indians appeared and surrounded them. During the two-hour battle, Charles Bent's white horse was killed under him before the Indians finally dispersed across Arkansas River. The caravan was saved.[9]

While Charles Bent led his Dog Soldiers on raids that spring, his father looked toward his own comfort. William Bent took a new wife two years after the death of Island. In 1867, he married Adalina Harvey, the half-breed daughter of a Blackfoot woman and an especially raucous fur trader named Alexander Harvey, whom William knew from their fur trapping days together on the Upper Missouri River.[10] Five years younger than George Bent, George nevertheless knew her as they both were the wards of Robert Campbell when George attended Webster College in St. Louis. George learned from his father's black servant that William was drunk at the time of their marriage. Pregnant, she soon left Bent's stockade for the safety and security of the Bent's house in Westport for her delivery.[11]

Edmund Guerrier, as well, kept plenty busy. He remained in the Indian camps for a year and worked for various traders and as an interpreter for Colonel Wynkoop, until Wynkoop recommended him as an interpreter to General Hancock. Hancock, who arrived in the spring of 1867, was ready for an all-out war of extermination of the Indians. Guerrier was used by the government sometimes as an interpreter, sometimes as a scout, and sometimes both simultaneously. As it happened, Guerrier was a great friend of the Cheyenne warrior Roman Nose, whose wife was a cousin of Guerrier.[12] This relationship was prelude to what happened next in

Guerrier's role as government interpreter.

When General Hancock arrived in the spring of 1867, ready to make peace with the Indians or exterminate them, he came prepared for all circumstances. He brought cavalry, infantry, artillery batteries, and pontoon bridges. He brought with him an officer named George Armstrong Custer of Civil War fame, but in 1867 a lieutenant colonel attached to the Seventh Cavalry. Next, General Hancock hired Edmund Guerrier as an interpreter with the Indians at a salary of $120 per month. His first instruction to Guerrier was to ride out and bring in the leaders of the Cheyenne camp for a parley. Hancock particularly wanted to face the dissident leaders Tall Bull and White Horse.

Guerrier rode. He found Tall Bull and White Horse on the Republican River in Kansas and brought them to Hancock's camp, along with Roman Nose and Bull Bear. In an unusual night meeting, Hancock demanded of the Indian leaders that they bring in their entire Indian camp to his site, including their women and children. When they refused to obey his command, Hancock ordered his troops to move within a mile of the Indian camp to better watch them.

When Hancock again ordered the Cheyenne leaders to bring in their women and children, the leaders begged off, saying that their horses were too poor to make the journey. Hancock then gave the men army horses to make the journey.[13] What Hancock did not know was that Roman Nose was alert to Hancock's possible treachery against his tribe, and had planned his own revenge. He planned to shoot Hancock if his demands were not met.

But what Edmund did not know, for certain, was whether or not his beloved Julia was present in the Indian camp. As it happened, she was there, concerned about being chased and surrounded by government troops, dreading another slaughter. The trauma and flight following the Sand Creek Massacre had left an indelible mark on her. She was well represented in camp by Roman Nose, one of her handsome suitors before she decided to throw her lot with Edmund.[14]

Roman Nose, however, was boiling mad. In a meeting of the Cheyenne leaders at the camp, he told of his plan. "That man is the cause of all our troubles. Let me kill him, and then trust to luck. All of us may die, but we will have killed our worst enemy; if he should escape now, we might not be able to reach him again," he said.[15]

Guerrier knew nothing of this plot. As Hancock's interpreter, he stood beside the general during the conference that night. But, Bull Bear knew of Roman Nose's intention, and pulled Guerrier aside out of the line of fire, to protect his fellow Cheyenne. Then, Hancock reached over and drew Guerrier alongside him again. This pulling and tugging on Guerrier continued, although he made nothing of it at the time. Bull Bear at last motioned to Roman Nose to give up his scheme. Hancock was spared. Guerrier was later told by the Cheyenne of the reason for this tugging on him, and was surprised at his close encounter. "I never knew whether Hancock suspicioned trouble or whether he pulled me back to his side just to be contrary to Bull Bear, who had pulled me away," Edmund said.[16]

Guerrier was sent by Hancock to stay in the Indians' village, to tell the Indians that they were ordered not to leave the village, and to report back to Hancock every two hours. Hancock told Guerrier, "If those Indians run away, I shall hold you responsible." Guerrier, realizing immediately that these conditions were impossible to fulfill, did not want the actions of an entire camp of Cheyenne on his shoulders. He refused to accept under these circumstances. Hancock then backed off, asked Guerrier to go to the village and just to let him know if the Indians ran away.[17] Guerrier agreed and left Hancock's camp.

When he rode into the Cheyenne village, Guerrier found that the Sioux who had camped there with the Cheyenne already had disappeared. Then, he was taken into a tepee where the principal men had gathered.

"After a while Roman Nose came into the tepee where I was," Guerrier related, "after they had had a council and touching me on the shoulder said, 'My friend we are all going. So go and report that we are all going to leave the camp.' They gave back to me the two horses Hancock had given them and Bull Bear escorted me about half way back to Hancock, who was camped less than a mile away."[18]

Guerrier took his time on the path back to Hancock, in order to give his friends and relatives the time they needed to get away. Hancock reported that Guerrier did not return until 9:30, thirty minutes late on his duty. When he reported to Hancock that the Indians were leaving, the general ordered Custer to have his command surround the camp. Because he could hear Roman Nose singing in the Indian camp, Hancock did not suspect Guerrier of treachery.

When Custer's cavalry quietly surrounded the camp, Custer and Guerrier found it deserted except for one demented half-breed girl and two elderly Sioux who were too old to travel.

Custer was then sent with eight companies of the Seventh Cavalry to overtake the Indians, but not to attack. Guerrier was to convince them to return to Pawnee Fork where Hancock was headquartered. Of the scouts on this mission, including Guerrier, James "Wild Bill" Hickok, the courier Kincade and a party of Delaware, Guerrier was the only one familiar with the terrain, and was sent to scout ahead. Riding three miles in front of the troops, Guerrier spotted a Cheyenne and signaled to him to get away fast. Danger is coming. The Cheyenne used their escape technique of scattering in many directions and the trail grew faint. Darkness forced an encampment that night.

Spotting heavy smoke signals in the direction of the Smoky Hill, the command set out early the next morning in that direction. Custer took his troops up Walnut Creek but it became dry of water, forcing him to backtrack nine miles to obtain water for the horses. Although Custer did not blame Guerrier, Hancock assumed that Custer had been misled by one of his scouts. He wrote, "It was unfortunate that the information in the possession of General Custer concerning the country in which he was operating, and his distance from the Smoky Hill was not more accurate. As it was, he was misled by his guides, upon whom he was forced to depend, and induced to make a retrograde march of nine miles for water, losing many hours of valuable time thereby, when it was definitely ascertained that, by keeping directly on, he would have reached the Smoky Hill about fifteen miles from the point at which he turned back – probably as soon as the Indians he was following …"[19]

Guerrier was the only scout with Custer at that time who had knowledge of the country they traveled. He was born on the Smoky Hill and knew it intimately. Custer relied on Guerrier's words and scouting abilities totally. "The opinions of Guerrier, the half-breed, were eagerly sought for and generally deferred to,"[20] Custer wrote. Therefore, one can easily assume that Guerrier led the troops astray or feigned ignorance of the terrain in order to allow his fellow tribesmen to escape.

Guerrier, a quiet and unassuming man, did not advertise to his fellow tribesmen his role in helping them to escape Custer's forces. Possibly he should have, whether or not he would have been believed by them, as it was whispered about his children and grandchildren that their grandfather was a traitor to his tribe. His actions in this affair should put the lie to that accusation. He was Hawk. His vision was clear. And, he knew the Smoky Hill lands like his own hand.

Besides Guerrier's delaying tactics on this march, Custer himself played his own hand in being tardy in pursuit of the fleeing Cheyenne. Custer, ever in search of the amusement of hunting activities, took the time on his retrograde march to conduct a buffalo and elk hunt. He revealed to his wife Libbie in a letter an escapade on this buffalo hunt that could have proved disastrous. He became separated from his troops during the hunt, and accidentally shot and killed his horse and his dog, leaving him alone and afoot.[21] Custer was fortunate to escape with his person and his career intact at that point, as he not only endangered his troops by being unavailable in case of an Indian attack, but he disobeyed the direct order of General Hancock against hunting buffalo for fun. Hunting was permitted only by special details of personnel for the purpose of providing meat for the camp.[22]

Turning again up Walnut Creek after watering their horses, Custer and his troops, with Edmund Guerrier leading, crossed the Smoky Hill River only to discover that the stage station at Lookout, fifteen miles west of Fort Hays, had been attacked and burned. Three men had been scalped and nailed to the side of a barn, which was then burned. Custer believed this to be the work of the escaping Cheyenne, when actually they had circled around and headed south again. The Cheyenne blamed the Sioux for this attack. Guerrier told Custer that, in his opinion, the Sioux and Cheyenne would rejoin camps along Beaver Creek. Custer, however, decided to head back to Fort Hays to replenish food and forage, neither of which was available, causing further delays to his planned march after the Cheyenne.

Although Custer trusted the word of Guerrier as his chief scout, he decided to send for William "Medicine Bill" Comstock.[23] Comstock was familiar with the country thereabouts and knew all the tribes in the area. With Comstock now as chief scout, Guerrier was then forced to back off his misdirections, as Comstock would find him out and make a report to Custer."[24]

When Custer, Guerrier and the troops returned to Fort Hays following their fruitless pursuit of the Cheyenne, Custer was overjoyed to find that his heart's desire, his wife Libbie, had finally arrived to join him. Libbie quickly met Guerrier and Comstock. Theodore R. Davis was also present at Fort Hays. Davis, the correspondent from *Harper's Weekly* who followed the Custer campaign for his magazine, observed and spoke with Guerrier, then wrote about him. "His father was a well-known voyageur, who for a long time occupied the position of sutler at Fort Laramie. Guerrier wears the clothes of the whites, speaks pure English, and has no confidence in the Indians."[25] Davis, also an artist, sketched Edmund Guerrier and William Comstock for the *Harper's Weekly* issue on June 29, 1867.

Custer had been morose for several weeks, since the departure of General Hancock, and became difficult and punitive with his troops. He ordered the men on a fifty-mile overnight march and back with only an hour or two of sleep as punishment for falsely reporting Indian activity in the area. In another incident, he punished six men by having half their heads shaved and confining them to close quarters for leaving camp for the post without passes. As a result of his harsh treatment and the high incidence of scurvy from lack of proper food, the men began to desert in large numbers. Libbie Custer reported forty desertions in one night.[26] Theodore R. Davis wrote that the Seventh Cavalry had lost 800 men by desertion in less than one year.[27] In addition to the men themselves lost to the outfit, the men also took the best horses, saddles, equipment and food with them when they left.

Nevertheless, Custer, Guerrier, Comstock, and the remaining troops left Fort Hays toward the end of May 1867 looking for Indians. For six weeks, the regiment scoured Nebraska, western Kansas, and Colorado. As for the Indians, the Sioux and Cheyenne were raiding and attacking railroad workers, and the Kiowas under Santana in his major general's uniform given him by General Hancock, stole the Fort Dodge cavalry herd. Charles Bent and Roman Nose led a party of 200 to 300 Cheyenne Dog Soldiers on an attack at Pond Creek and Fort Wallace, where they had the fort under siege for two days. Colonel Albert Barnitz of the Seventh Cavalry rode to the fort's defense. Seven members of the cavalry were killed and seven wounded in the engagement. Custer's command also was attacked by large parties of Cheyenne, when he mistakenly divided his troops into three parts. Smaller units of troops were more likely to be attacked than a larger body, as the government was slow to learn.

Custer reunited his command for better safety and resumed the scout for Indians. Soon, however, a tragedy was discovered. On Beaver Creek in western Kansas, Edmund Guerrier was scouting two to three miles ahead of the main body when he spotted a cavalry boot on the ground, with part of the leg still encased in the boot. He found the remains of Lieutenant Lyman S. Kidder and his seven men riddled with arrows. Kidder had been sent from Fort Sedgwick in Colorado with new orders for Custer from General William T. Sherman.[28] After burial of the remains, the Custer cavalry continued on toward Fort Wallace. The men continued to desert in large numbers, noted by Edmund Guerrier in a 1916 interview:

> I was riding in a wagon, my horse having a sore back when I heard Custer inquiring for me. I knew what was up and did not wish to participate in any way in what was going to happen. The driver of the wagon said that he had not seen me, and I lay low. I heard Custer giving orders to Major Joel Elliott to overtake and shoot the deserters who could then be seen far out in the prairie moving away on foot. The men were out of sight when the shooting took place. The ambulance had been gone about an hour when it returned with the wounded.[29]

Custer reached Fort Wallace on July 13. Two days later on July 15, he rode with three officers and 72 men at breakneck speed across country to Fort Harker where he reported to General Smith, then dashed on to Fort Riley to see his wife Libbie. On this madcap journey, he lost 42 to 47 of his men through an Indian attack on his rear column, exhaustion, and desertion, but he was hell-bent on seeing his wife. For this unauthorized trip, the use of government property on private business, his failure to chase the Indians who attacked his party, and the inhumane and unlawful treatment of deserters, Custer was court-martialed in August 1867. He was sentenced to suspension from his command and forfeit of pay for one year.[30]

Major Joel Elliott replaced Custer in the Seventh Cavalry. But the scout Edmund Guerrier had had enough. He left his service with the Seventh Cavalry and rejoined the peaceful Indian camps, although not as a combatant. Guerrier found that the Dog Soldiers and other Cheyenne who had not signed the Treaty of the Little Arkansas were still incensed and resentful about the ceding of their lands on the Smoky Hill River in western Kansas as well as the growing influx of settlers, forts, trading posts and railroad workmen invading their territory. They had been absent when the treaty was signed and had no voice in the presentation of their objections to its conditions. William Bent and Edmund Guerrier continued to press for peace, as they realized the futility of continued conflict with government forces. Many Cheyenne finally relented and accepted the treaty.

Meanwhile, William Bent's son Charles continued his rampage. He had become a one-man army of fury and savagery. He made an infamous name for himself. After a price was placed on his head, William disowned him and was fortunate to be away from his stockade when an enraged Charles arrived with patricide in his mind.

Mary Bent was fond of her brother Charles, and always placed a lighted candle in her window at the fort as a signal that it was safe for him to come for a visit. On his last visit to the fort, however, he had something else in mind besides sisterly solace. His father, William, recounted the event:

> My daughter saw something that looked like an

Indian's head sticking up over the bank of the main irrigating ditch … went out … and discovered Charley. He said .. that he was after the old man, meaning me. I was off in New Mexico at the time and she … asked the durn'd scoundrel to come into the house. "No, I only wanted the ole man," and uncocking his rifle, he went off. That's the last we've seen of him.[31 32]

Charlie Bent, the youngest son of William Bent. The sketch by Theodore R. Davis appeared in the February, 1868 edition of *Harper's New Monthly* Magazine. *Courtesy (Scan #10042634), History Colorado, Denver, Colo.*

Sooner Death Than Captivity

12

The Cheyenne kept up their raids. Skirmishes with troops continued, as well as fights with enemy tribes, such as the Pawnees. Horses were important to the tribe, and many parties went after the horses and mules of the government or those of other tribes. George Bent was active in these raids. His father-in-law, Black Kettle, saw things differently, however. He still sought peace for his Cheyenne band. And, his father William Bent pursued this dream as well.

The government asked the warring tribes for another council, this time to be held in October 1867 on Medicine Lodge Creek, sixty miles south of Fort Larned, in Kansas, south of the Arkansas River. The site was a favorite camping ground for the Indians, where the Kiowa held their annual Medicine Lodge ceremony. The rolling land was graced with trees, water and grass for the ponies, along the wooded banks of Medicine Lodge.

George and Charles Bent interpreted letters of invitation to the peaceful Cheyenne, Arapaho, Kiowa, Comanche and Kiowa-Apache bands. But the hostile Cheyenne Dog Soldiers required a special messenger. Edmund Guerrier was led and protected by six young Cheyenne as he made his way to the camps of the hostile warriors with the invitation to the meeting grounds. Edmund returned successfully with his cousin's husband, Roman Nose, along with Grey Beard and eight other Cheyenne warriors.

When Edmund returned to the camp with Roman Nose, he found the site teeming with Indians, 2,500 of them at first, including Black Kettle's band of 150 Cheyenne. He quickly spied Julia among them, and crossed the ground to greet her with a warm Indian handshake. Julia, by then a lovely 20-year-old maiden, dropped her eyes after their first greeting, to hide the pounding in her chest and the blush on her cheeks.

Edmund promised to see her during the encampment, with her permission of course. But first he must hurry to check in and determine his duties, as he would be an interpreter at the treaty negotiations. She bade him goodbye as he turned to cross the camping grounds.

Indians were streaming in from all directions, eventually over 5,000 of them, including the rest of the 2,000 Cheyenne who had just completed their Medicine Arrows ceremony. It was a spectacular sight; over 800 lodges were arranged over a vast area, the tanned buffalo hides of the tepees gleaming creamy white, some of them decorated with painted legends. The tepees were aligned in circles.

The circle was a sacred symbol to the Indians. Thus, each of the ten bands of the Cheyennes camped in a circle, its position there assigned for generations, with the circle's opening facing the direction they traveled. In a settled camp, however, the tepees always faced the east. At the treaty grounds, each band joined in a larger circle of the whole tribe, enclosing a vast area of ground. In tribute to the Father Sun, the elders stepped out through the tepee flap each morning to greet the rising sun and offer their daily prayers. In the open space in the circle's center, the lodge of the sacred Medicine Arrows was set up.

Thousands of ponies dotted the hills and valleys, as whenever a tribe moved, its pony herd accompanied them, as well as their camp dogs and all their possessions.

When the main body of Cheyenne arrived, the newspaper reporters were awed by their personal majesty, colorful attire, and military precision. One reporter wrote:

> I shall never forget the morning … At a distance of about two miles from our camp was the crest of a low swell in the plains. The background was blue sky – a blue curtain that touched the brown plains. For a moment I was dumfounded at the sight of what was rising over that crest and flowing with vivid commotion toward us. It was a glittering, fluttering, gaily colored mass of barbarism, the flower

and perfection of the war strength of the Plains Indian tribes. The resplendent warriors, armed with all their equipment and adorned with all the regalia of battle, seemed to be rising out of the earth ... As they came into plainer view, the Indians spread their ranks wider and wider, to create as profound an impression as possible, and inspire us deeply with their power. Now they could be heard chanting and singing. Having arrived within a quarter of a mile of our camp, the Indians charged like a whirlwind, firing their guns and brandishing them over their heads. The charge was abruptly halted, and the Indians stood at rest, waiting for the negotiations to begin.[1]

A *New York Tribune* reporter was even more descriptive:

Five columns of a hundred men each, forty paces apart, dressed in all their gorgeous finery. Crimson blankets about their loins; tall, comb-like headdresses of eagle feathers, variegated shirts, brass chains, sleigh bells, white, red and blue bead-worked moccasins, gleaming tomahawks, made up the personnel of a scene never to be forgotten. Their chief, Mo-ko-va-ot-o, or Black Kettle, mounted on a wiry horse, sprang

> forward, dressed in a dingy shirt and dingier blanket, his long black hair floating behind him like a bashaw's tail, and waved his hands. In most admirable order they moved by the left flank by divisions; another wave and they marched obliquely across the Neo-contogwa – up to within 50 yards of commission camp, where they halted, but still continued their lively exhilarating chant until the Commission appeared in full dress within a few paces of the line.[2]

The reporters sent from the East and Midwest to report on the affair were impressed with the Cheyenne. *The Chicago Tribune* reporter described them as "singularly fine-looking men – splendidly framed, and with impressive, characteristic faces. They showed by every look and gesture their fitness for command. The more I saw of these Cheyenne the higher opinion I have of them. They are better looking than the others; they are cleaner and more of the Spartan fire burns in their veins. Sooner death than captivity is the motto of these warriors of the plains."[3]

Roman Nose, the prominent Dog Soldier warrior, was especially noted for his fine physical attributes. General Theophilus Rodenbough wrote his impression of Roman Nose:

> Roman Nose moved in a solemn and majestic manner to the center of the chamber. He was

> one of the finest specimens of the untamed savage. It would be difficult to exaggerate in describing his superb physique. A veritable man of war, the shock of battle and scenes of carnage and cruelty were as the breath in his nostrils; about thirty years of age, standing six feet three inches high, he towered, giant-like above his companions. A grand head, with strongly marked features, lighted by a pair of fierce black eyes; a large mouth with thin lips, through which gleamed rows of strong white teeth; a Roman nose, with delicate nostrils like those of a thoroughbred horse, first attracted attention, while a broad chest, with symmetrical limbs, on which the muscles under the bronze of his skin stood out like twisted wire, were some of the points of this splendid animal. Clad in buckskin leggings and moccasins, elaborately embroidered with beads and feathers, with a single eagle feather in his scalp-lock, and that rarest of robes, a WHITE buffalo, beautifully tanned and as soft as cashmere, thrown over his naked shoulders, he stood forth, the war-chief of the Cheyennes.[4]

George Bent later described the appearance of Roman Nose

when he was dressed for his war activities on the plains. His war bonnet sported a single buffalo horn on the forehead of the bonnet, which was adorned with forty eagle feathers painted in red and black. His painted face was formidable looking, with yellow on his forehead, a broad stripe of red across the nose, and black painted around the mouth and chin.[5] He rode a white horse.

Roman Nose was indeed a formidable figure, both in appearance and in influence with the Dog Soldier band. But General Rodenbough was wrong in his attribution of Roman Nose as a war chief. Roman Nose was never a chief. He was a warrior.

At the time of the Medicine Lodge Treaty, Black Kettle's sway over the Cheyenne as the leading peace chief was waning, and the Dog Soldier chief, Bull Bear, exerted the major influence over the tribe. General Harney believed that Bull Bear was the ablest man of the tribe. But Bull Bear procrastinated in signing the treaty. Finally, General Harney harangued Bull Bear, adding an irresistible hook. "The Great Father knows you are a chief, and your name must be seen upon its face, or he will not recognize it." That did it! Bull Bear signed the document with such force that his pen jabbed through the paper.[6]

The Cheyenne tribe consisted of ten bands, each band with four chiefs, plus four men who were principal chiefs. Although a warrior could be selected by the Council of Forty-Four to become a chief, thereafter he could not belong to a warrior society but then must become a man of peace. This was a fact of the Cheyenne tribal order that the white people never understood.

When a man was chosen by the Council to become a chief, he must learn the words of the Cheyenne's mythical hero, Sweet Medicine:

> Listen to me carefully, and truthfully follow up my instructions. You chiefs are peace-makers. Though your son might be killed in front of your tepee, you should take a peace pipe and smoke. Then you would be called an honest chief. You chiefs own the land and the people. If your men, your soldier societies, should be scared and retreat, you are not to step back but take a stand to protect your land and your people. Get out and talk to the people. If strangers come, you are the ones to give presents to them and invitations. When you meet someone, or he comes to your tepee asking for anything, give it to him. Never refuse. Go outside your tepee and sing your chief's song, so all the people will know you have done something good.[7]

A chief exerted moral authority over his people, not total authority. As a man of peace, he listened to his people, helped to settle differences, took care of the homeless and elderly, shared his belongings with a generous heart, and was brave in the face of danger. It was a heavy but honorable tribute to be selected as a chief of the tribe. The chiefs were selected every four years, were expected to serve for ten years and could choose their own successors. It was not a hereditary post.

At the time of the Treaty of Medicine Lodge, Black Kettle's moral authority ebbed, because of the war between the tribe and the government that caused so many young men to want to take up their guns and bows and fight. The force of the leaders of the warrior societies, therefore, gained the ascendancy.

And, when Bull Bear jabbed the document with his signature, the deed was done. The main signatories had aligned themselves with peace.

The Cheyenne signed this treaty on October 28, 1867, with Charles and George Bent acting as interpreters, sitting directly behind the Cheyenne leaders Black Kettle and Gray Head. George himself also signed the treaty. Edmund Guerrier was present also, listed by reporters as an interpreter but not officially recorded as such. Here was yet another treaty that the Indians were forced to concede through dint of the white's superior numbers, and it was the most important treaty the tribe was ever to sign, as it forced the tribe to give up their lands in Kansas and to settle on lands in Indian Territory bounded by the 37th Parallel and the Cimarron and Arkansas rivers. In addition to their promise to live in peace, the tribe also guaranteed the right of emigrant travel and the safety of the railroads.[8]

The newspaper reporters present were impressed by the education and self-expression possessed by Charles and George. Oddly, William Bent was not present during the treaty proceedings.

But his daughter, Julia, was found to be a great curiosity. She sat in the front row of the women's section. She was described by reporter Hall as "fat and ugly, having sunk to barbarism" after completing boarding school when she returned to the Indian camps. However, reporter Henry M. Stanley, of Stanley and Livingston fame, said she had a charming laugh, tiny feet, and added "a peep at her trim ankles might drive an anchorite insane."[9] Beauty, indeed, is in the eye of the beholder. Julia was dressed in her finest attire, a brain-tanned and fringed buckskin dress beaded in the Cheyenne style, her hair braided and tied with fluffy feathers, her hair pipe bone necklace falling gracefully down her breast. She lived in the Cheyenne camp and attended all the council meetings.

Julia was one of only a few women in the main assembly of Indians called into the inner circle of the council. She was accustomed to being a minority population for most of her life, as she had grown up at Bent's Fort where hordes of men lived and traded. Large groups of men did not faze her. As Julia had reportedly run away from school, it seems apparent that her father gave up his attempt to provide a formal education for her. She was not schooled further, and for the rest of her life spoke only Cheyenne, except for a few English words.

Edmund's education proved to be of invaluable assistance to the Cheyenne and to the government officials who treated with them, as did that of William Bent's sons, George and Charles. They had helped to forge the new treaty. Peace, however, would be harder to come by.

George Bent, however, was feeling a lot more than peaceful. He was exhilarated. His wife Magpie had given birth to his first child, a daughter, in the Cheyenne camp during the treaty proceedings at Medicine Lodge Creek. Feeling blessed and filled with largesse, George and his wife visited the tent of General Harney, where Magpie herself presented Harney with George's gift of a fine pony while cradling her newborn, Ada, in her arms.[10]

Edmund was glad to have a few brief moments with his sweetheart Julia during the days of the treaty, but nothing was settled between them. Julia hurried back to her father's home in Colorado when the tribes dispersed as the meetings ended, and Edmund moved south onto the new treaty grounds with the peaceful bands of Cheyenne. George Bent and Magpie also moved south of the Arkansas with the band of her father, Black Kettle.

Death of Kit Carson

13

Pleased that at last the Cheyenne and Arapaho had signed a treaty with the government that had a chance of succeeding, William Bent was even further gratified when he learned that his old friend of thirty-five years, Kit Carson, was mustering out of his six-year service with the army, and leaving his command at Fort Garland. Kit was then jobless, however, and needed an income for his pregnant wife and six children. William helped Kit apply for the position of superintendant of Indian affairs for Colorado, and recommended Kit to the government. William hoped Kit would be accepted, so that the two men would live near one another in order to renew their old friendship. A man on the prairie needs friends.

Happily, Kit's superintendency was awarded in January 1868, and Kit moved his large family to Boggsville,[1] a village on the confluence of the Arkansas and Purgatoire rivers near Bent's home. Kit, his wife Josefa Jaramillo Carson and their six children moved into three rooms of the six-room adobe house built by Thomas Boggs near the ranch's barn. On a visit to the Carson home, however, William Bent was shocked to find Carson weak and looking ill. Bent wondered how long he could last. Not long.

Early in 1868, George Bent rode alone to visit his family in Colorado. His brother Robert, his sister Julia, as well as his sister Mary and her husband, Judge J. M. Moore, all resided with William Bent at his stockade on the south side of the Arkansas River near the Purgatoire River, near Boggsville. William had been busy trading his wares to the Indians for their buffalo robes, which he then packed into bales to be hauled back to Missouri. His traders came and went from the Indian camps. His son George noticed that William seemed morose, and learned that their old friend Kit Carson was ailing and near death. George hopped back on his horse and rode toward Boggsville for a visit with Carson.

George already knew that Carson had lost his wife the previous day, apparently from complications from childbirth two weeks before. Kit was saddened over her death, and was obviously very ill. His diagnosis was a large aortic aneurism, which was restricting his breathing and eating severely.[2]

Kit told George Bent of his wife's death. He had just returned from a trip to Washington and Boston with a delegation of Ute to try to help the tribe in governmental negotiations, and was dog tired and ill when he stepped off the train. This was only a few days before his wife's delivery of their seventh child. Now, he was near death, had lost his wife and had seven children to care for. Although desperately ill, he felt well enough to conduct a piece of business with George. He had a very fine racehorse he wanted to sell. George had seen the horse and, impressed with the animal, bought it from Kit.[3]

So the deal was done. And just in time, as Kit had very little time left. He summoned Ignacia Jaramillo Bent, widow of Governor Charles Bent and sister of his wife, to care for the children temporarily.[4] But for the permanent care of his youngsters, one of them an infant, he turned to the Thomas Boggs family[5] who owned the house the Carsons rented. After all, Thomas Boggs had married Ignacia Bent's daughter Rumalda. Kit felt reassured that his children would benefit from being reared in the bosom of their extended family, and knew that Thomas Boggs could afford their care.

His loyal physician, Dr. H. R. Tilton, the post surgeon at nearby Fort Lyon, knowing that Carson's time was limited, moved him to the doctor's quarters at the fort as he feared that the spring rise in the Arkansas River under a dilapidated bridge might hinder rescuing Carson at a later date. Carson lingered for less than a month, and died on May 23, 1868. He was buried with military honors beside his wife Josefa at Boggsville.[6]

William Bent mourned the loss of his old friend, as knowledgeable about the ways of the West as William. A legend even during his own lifetime.

Efficient and Gallant Services

14

Following his visit with his family at his father's Colorado stockade and with Kit Carson at Boggsville, George Bent rode south again to rejoin Black Kettle's camp and the lodges of his two wives. By that time in 1868, George had married a second wife, Kiowa Woman,[1] unrelated to his first wife, and supported the two families. George found that Edmund Guerrier was then living with chief Little Rock's band nearby. Edmund and George discussed the turmoil in the Indian camps and the raids the young men were perpetrating, fearful that there was bound to be retribution from the government on the Indian camps.

After the Treaty of Medicine Lodge, many Cheyenne still were not ready to settle down south of the Arkansas River on a reservation under the white man's rule. Notably, there were the bands of the warrior Roman

Nose, and of the militant Dog Soldiers under Tall Bull. Even the peace-seeking chiefs, such as Black Kettle and Little Rock, were hard pressed to control all their young men and to keep them pinned down in camp. Eager young men would slip out of camp to meet others from different camps, and go to war on their own devices. These groups continued their raids on farms and small settlements, fought battles with their tribal enemies and engaged government troops. Black Kettle was honest in admitting that he could not control all his young men. Government troops, under the direction of General Philip Sheridan, kept busy chasing them.

By this time in 1868, the popular Union general, Ulysses S. Grant, had been elected president. William Tecumseh Sherman took Grant's post as commanding general of the army and Sheridan moved up to take the appointment of Sherman's old command of the Division of the Missouri. Sheridan meant business. His back was up. Sheridan did not scare the young Cheyenne warriors. They continued the raiding.

On September 8, a group of about twenty-five warriors bore down on Thomas Kimsey, returning to Boggsville where he was to be judge of elections for Bent County's first election. His companions were on horses and outran the Indians, but Kinsey's mule was too slow to avoid the encounter. He was killed and scalped.[2] The Cheyenne then rode to Boggsville where they killed several good oxen with arrows and stole some horses from local settlers, including one of their kinsmen, Robert Bent. [3]

Robert, miffed at the loss of his stock of cattle, signed on as a scout with Captain William H. Penrose's 7th Cavalry to track the war party responsible for it. He went further, by signing a depredations claim against the government for the loss of his stock.

Guerrier later reported on events that occurred during the month of August in this time of unrest when the eager young warriors left camp to fight on their own, against the directions of their peace chiefs. His statement revealed what happened:

> I was with Cheyenne Indians at the time of the massacre on the Solomon and Saline rivers in Kansas … and I was living at this time with Little Rock's band. The war party who started for the Solomon and Saline was Little Rock's, Black Kettle's, Medicine Arrows' and Bull Bear's bands; and as near as I can remember nearly all the different bands of Cheyenne had some of their young men in this war party which committed the outrages and murders on the Solomon and Saline. Red Nose, and The-man-who-breaks-the-marrow-bones, (Ho-eh-amo-ahoe) were the two leaders in this massacre; the former belonged to the Dog Soldiers, and the latter in Black Kettle's band. As soon as we heard the news by runners who came ahead to Black Kettle – saying that they had already commenced fighting, we moved from our camp on Buckner's fork of the Pawnee, near the head

> waters, down to the North Fork, where we met Big Jake's band, and then moved south, across the Arkansas River; and when we got to the Cimarron, George Bent and I left them and went to our homes on the Purgatoire.[4]

The young Cheyenne warriors, along with similar hotheads from other tribes, conducted these raids against the wishes of their chiefs who were for peace with the government. They rampaged along the Solomon and Saline rivers in Kansas and Colorado for two months in 1868, striking forty sites. They killed seventy-nine civilians and wounded nine, as well as killing six soldiers and wounding ten.[5]

The Dog Soldiers and George Bent were heavily involved in these attacks. An incident had happened at the Medicine Lodge Treaty campgrounds, however, that incensed the Dog Soldiers. A group of Kaw raiders were seen herding off many Cheyenne horses, humiliating to the great horsemen of the plains. After the treaty was signed, the Dog Soldiers chased after the Kaw, with Charles Bent on his white horse in the lead.

By accident, the Cheyenne raiding party met ten U. S. scouts with Major N. D. McGinley leading. The scouts and Dog Soldiers agreed to meet for a parlay, but when Charles Bent wheeled his horse to ride away, scout Coridoro and the rest of the scouts began firing at the Cheyenne. Charles was shot in the hip, but was able to ride away and return to his camp. His wound led to other problems. He developed a fever and died, according to his brother George, of malaria. Most likely his death was due to pneumonia. Charles, who had wished his father dead, died himself on November 20, 1868. Of all of William Bent's sons, Charles was the stuff of legends, due to his savage and brutal attacks on whites and their goods and settlements.[6] According to his older brother George, Charlie died at age nineteen, was married and sired one daughter. Charlie's widow later married the Cheyenne Oakerhater, known as David Pendleton.[7]

After scurrying south of the Arkansas River when the fighting broke out, as ordered by the Treaty of Medicine Lodge, the peaceful Cheyenne and Arapaho chiefs were alarmed about the actions and intentions of General Sheridan. As a result, four of the chiefs, including Black Kettle, went to visit General William M. Hazen, superintendent of Indian Affairs for the Indian Territory, at Fort Cobb.

Black Kettle greeted General Hazen with his repeated desire for peace with the government. He was concerned about his camp's position, fearful that General Sheridan might think that his people were unfriendly and send troops against them. He asked General Hazen to inform Sheridan that Black Kettle's camp was settled for winter on the Washita River, lands assigned to the tribe by the treaty. General Hazen was noncommittal and uncooperative. He told Black Kettle that he should take that message directly to Sheridan himself. Hazen could offer no help in the matter. Black Kettle and the other three chiefs returned to their camps with saddened and fearful hearts, as they had no assurance as to their safety from attack.

Sheridan planned a winter campaign, hoping to catch the

Indians in their winter camps during the time when their food supply was limited and their ponies were in their poorest condition. Toward that end, he sent George Custer, newly restored to his command of the Seventh Cavalry, south into Indian Territory searching for Indians to destroy in November 1868. A second army movement under Major Eugene A. Carr was to start from Fort Lyon in Colorado on December 1st. Custer struck first, before Carr left Fort Lyon.

Black Kettle was right. Sheridan was geared for an all-out war against all Indians, friendly or not. Six days after Black Kettle declared his peaceful intentions to General Hazen, Custer attacked his camp on the Washita on November 26. Black Kettle helped his wife Medicine Woman up onto the horse tied outside their lodge, and the two of them fled toward the river. All three were shot and killed. Black Kettle, his wife, and the horse. George Bent and his wife Magpie were not present at the massacre, as they had left earlier for a trip to visit his family at Bent's stockade. Black Kettle's twenty-one-year-old nephew, Blue Horse, refused to surrender and shot Major Frederick W. Benteen's horse from under him, but then was killed by Benteen. The Cheyenne lost eleven men, twelve women, and six children. The camp was destroyed, as well as their large pony herd shot, by order of Custer. Fifty-three women and children were taken captive.

Major Joel Elliott took a force of about fifteen troopers to pursue chief Little Rock, who was helping a group of women and children to escape. Little Rock was killed in the engagement, but the nearby Arapaho warriors came charging up, surrounded Major Elliott and his forces, and slew them.

Sheridan was delighted with Custer's slaughter of Black Kettle and his band, even though Black Kettle had moved his band to the south, well within the territory assigned during the Treaty of Medicine Lodge. Sheridan congratulated the command "for the efficient and gallant services rendered."[8] He was convinced that Black Kettle and his band were the "guiltiest of all."[9] Custer had "wiped out old Black Kettle and his murderers and rapers of helpless women."[10] [11] Black Kettle and the majority of his band were tarred with the brush of his few young men who slipped out of camp to fight and raid. Sheridan was one of the many in the government who did not understand the Cheyenne tribal system and the chief's duties and limitations.

Custer took the Cheyenne prisoners captured during the Washita River attack back to Fort Hays and confined them within a wooden stockade, the fifteen-foot-high walls topped by a sentinel walk around the perimeter. The band of mostly women prisoners were objects of curiosity for the group of overhead onlookers, including Libbie Custer who visited frequently with the women, one of whom was Making Out Road with her daughter Cheyenne Belle. The Cheyenne men who escaped the Custer attack pined for their women and children incarcerated at Fort Hays, and began a series of raids in western Kansas to demonstrate their displeasure over their separation from their families. They prowled along the Kansas frontier, attacking homesteaders, hunters and railroad workmen, derailing trains and raiding post stations. When the captives at Fort

Hays eventually were returned to Camp Supply to reunite with their families on June 12, the government seemed astonished that their raiding ceased almost immediately.

Meanwhile, the Dog Soldiers under Tall Bull and White Horse traveled north and joined the Sioux in raids into Colorado. After a chase, Major E. A. Carr with his 5th Cavalry unit and Pawnee scouts caught the raiders at Summit Springs, Colorado, and a battle ensued. Carr's forces killed 52 Indians, including Tall Bull killed by Major Frank North. The remaining band of Cheyenne fled north to join the Sioux.

While Carr and his forces chased and battled Indians during the summer of 1869, Custer, his brother 1st Lt. Tom Custer, and the other officers and men of the 7th Cavalry chased buffalo for sport at Fort Hays, entertaining a Russian Grand Duke, British nobles, P. T. Barnum, generals and the president of the Audubon Club with lavish buffalo hunts.[12]

Winter was coming. As cavalry horses generally were not used during the winter months, Custer and the 7th Cavalry headed for Fort Leavenworth to spend the next few months. Just as Custer rested his horses and men during cold months, so did the Indians, whose ponies found meager fare on winter grasses and were in too poor condition for any kind of exercise. The tribes of the plains had many years of experience in dealing with the seasons and knew that winter was the time to rest the ponies, find a safe and secure camping spot with plenty of water nearby, to conserve food supplies and physical energy. The men hunted when they could, prepared hunting paraphernalia in camp, and told winter stories to the children around the fire in their tepees in the evening. The women cooked, made clothing, and beaded and decorated the garments. It was a time of renewal for the tribe.

General Sheridan, however, gave little thought for the reasoning behind the Indian's rejection of making war on the plains during the winter. Sheridan saw the Indian's winter hiatus in activity as an opportunity to catch them when they were idle in a peaceful camp, and forced to rely on thin and undernourished ponies, if attacked. Sheridan thought only of his goal of exterminating the Indians, not of what may befall his own troops and stock during winter war on the plains.

Sheridan's winter campaign against the Indians was a disaster for the troops and animals and resulted in engaging no Indians except for the camp of Black Kettle attacked by Custer. Besides Custer and Carr, Sheridan sent General Penrose south from Fort Lyon with 313 cavalry and infantry to search for Indians, along with eighteen scouts. Among the scouts were Jesse Nelson, husband of Kit Carson's niece; Tom Boggs; Wild Bill Hickok; and Robert Bent.[13]

The Penrose Expedition met heavy snows and severe cold, and suffered from lack of food. Frostbite bothered the men. Upwards of one hundred horses and mules froze to death or perished from starvation. In an effort to find Penrose, Carr and his troops were dispatched from Fort Lyon as a relief and supporting unit. Carr's guides included W. F. "Buffalo Bill" Cody and Edmund

Guerrier. The pair stood guard together one night to spare the exhausted troopers. Carr's forces ran into the same heavy snowstorm that had struck Penrose. The heavy snow and wind blew over tents and wagons. Four pickets froze to death, and the cattle were lost in the storm. Horses and mules died. After much suffering, the Carr forces eventually located Penrose in a camp on the Palo Duro River.

Guerrier was then sent by General Carr to carry dispatches to Sheridan at Camp Supply that December. When he reached Camp Supply, however, Guerrier learned that Sheridan was then camped at Medicine Bluff Creek, farther south, with Custer's 7th Cavalry. Guerrier then traveled to Fort Sill to deliver the dispatches, accompanied by a group of Custer's scouts that included Jack Stillwell, Jack Corbin, Jimmy Morrison, and the Osage Hard Rope. When Sheridan told Guerrier of his plan to disarm the Indians and confiscate their pony herd, Guerrier advised him against it, saying that the Indians would fight to the death to retain their valuable possessions, thereby squelching Sheridan's ill-formed idea.[14]

Guerrier then left Fort Sill in the company of fellow scout John Hanley in order to locate General Carr in his Palo Duro camp. On the way, the pair met Company M of the 19th Kansas Volunteer Cavalry. The company clerk, A. L. Runyon, reported "The fourth day out, three scouts came into camp, on their way to Fort Lyon, with dispatches. One of them was Ed. Geary, the famous scout and interpreter … He thinks that the war with the Cheyennes is good for all next summer. He says that they number about three thousand effective warriors."[15]

Continuing their journey, Edmund had expected to find Carr in his camp on the Palo Duro River. After a hard trip in deep snow, however, Guerrier arrived at the Palo Duro to find that Carr had decamped with all his forces. Guerrier and Hanley were exhausted from their trip, and hungry, as were their mounts. Guerrier had every reason to expect to gather food for themselves and forage for their animals at the Palo Duro camp, but everything was gone. Distressed, he looked around the camp, but in his cold and hunger he missed an important sign. Carr had left food and forage in the log house, with an arrow on the chimney pointing down. "X" marks the spot. Guerrier, the Hawk, in an uncharacteristic lapse, missed it. He and Hanley rode away. Soon, Hanley's horse gave out. Then his boots collapsed, leaving his ankles raw and bleeding. Guerrier was in moccasins, his only footwear since rejoining his Cheyenne relatives years before. He had nothing to fear from overrun shoes and boots.

Guerrier, realizing their precarious situation, made a decision. He would give Hanley his mule to ride, and he himself would walk back to Fort Lyon. He knew he was in for a rough few days, but hoped to find wild game to sustain them on their journey.

Guerrier and Hanley traveled for eight miserable days in the snow, without food, in agony from hunger. Guerrier occasionally saw an antelope, but he was so weak that he could not aim properly and missed his kill. His trousers finally ripped at the seams, and as he had nothing to patch them with, he gathered a thick buffalo robe around his waist for warmth.[16]

John Hanley grew weaker, nearly incoherent. His mule

wandered off, causing Guerrier to waste hours tracking him into a ravine. Still able to make decisions in spite of his condition, he decided to walk behind the mule and drive him forward at a trot, the better to keep an eye on him. They traveled all night on the eighth day and reached Bent's New Fort at dawn.[17] Due to Guerrier's stamina, determination and knowledge of the country, the pair survived the near fatal ordeal.

Guerrier preferred traveling alone, at night, in hostile Indian country. "When there was more than one man, each depended more or less upon the other to watch for danger, while a man travelling alone was compelled to keep his eyes open all the time to save his scalp."[18] He chose a mule to ride rather than a horse, as a mule was tougher and more dependable. Besides his gun, he carried a bow and a quiver of arrows for concealed and quiet fighting. An arrow at 300 feet was sure death.

Though not superstitious, he paid attention to premonitions. One day he rode away from Fort Wallace in search of antelope. As he lay in the sun for a smoke, he spied a man on a hill nearby, then several more men appeared on the hill. Fearing hostile Indians, he removed the saddle from his horse, tied his shoulder-length hair into braids, and began making Indian signs with his blanket to the men to signal that he was friendly. He was amazed when the men changed into buffalo and raced away. After he made an Indian prayer, he decided that this strange event was a sign for him not to continue in the direction he was going, and rode back to the fort. A few days later, he learned that hostile Indians indeed were in the path he traveled. His premonition saved him.[19]

After his recuperation from the grueling ordeal, Edmund Guerrier continued to provide his services as a scout for the army. William Bent kept busy at his trading post, hauling supplies from Westport to the stockade and visiting Indian camps to trade his goods for pelts.

In 1869, William Bent set out on another trading venture into New Mexico and back over Raton Pass. As he neared his stockade, he was ill and feverish from the bad weather encountered during the trip. He reached his Purgatoire River ranch and went to bed with pneumonia. The Fort Lyon doctor was called, but was unable to save him. William died on May 19, 1869, a few days before his sixtieth birthday.

What a busy, rich and exciting life William Bent saw in his lifetime. The opening of the West, the settlement of Colorado, the Indian wars, and the peace treaties. And, William played a major role in all these events. The *Pueblo Chieftain* eulogized him, stating that his estimated fortune was between $150,000 and $200,000.[20] His will listed ownership of 652.6 acres of land, as well as two lots in Westport.[21] The truth, however, was far different. William had never owned the lands his forts and stockade occupied, and was deeply in debt. To daughters Mary and Julia went the household furnishings and family Bible. Robert received four mules, a wagon, and the remaining trading merchandise. To George went seventy-eight cattle, two mules and a wagon. Adalina was evicted from the Westport house, and received $2,214.[22]

Colonel William Bent, Fort Dodge, 1869. *Courtesy Western History Collections, University of Oklahoma Libraries.*

His family mourned the loss of their patriarch, the gentle capable man who steered their ship. An era was ending. The old traders were dying. William Bent and Kit Carson both dead, one year apart. But what of Bent's dream of peace for the Plains Tribes and the end of the Indian wars? He had spent many years of his life working toward that and his efforts had been rewarded with two treaties with the government: the Treaty of the Little Arkansas and the Treaty of Medicine Lodge. And yet, neither side was ready to give up its antipathetical position toward the other, and the antagonists were still slugging it out.

I Will Fight It Out With You

15

The summer of 1869 was a time of extreme unrest among the Indians, and many councils were held in the tents of the elders. At first, the Cheyenne balked at adhering to the reservation restriction set forth in the Treaty of Medicine Lodge Creek. They wanted to live free, as they always had, to go wherever weather, abundant food, and other circumstances dictated. But, Sheridan, in council with them, declared his intentions.

"If you refuse to settle peacefully around the agency selected for you," he roared, "I will tell you what I will do. I will fight it out with you."[1]

Many of the Cheyenne bands began to surrender at Fort Sill, and George Custer was sent to track down the rest. He found 260 lodges, mostly Dog Soldiers under Medicine Arrows, on the Sweetwater River. Medicine Arrows met Custer upon his arrival, and offered the hospitality of his tepee for a meeting.

Medicine Arrows placed Custer on his right hand in the tepee, in the place of honor. Then Medicine Arrows removed his pipe from its beaded buckskin case, filled it with tobacco, tamped it with his finger, and lit the pipe. He took four puffs on the pipe, swirling the smoke up toward the ceiling with lifts of his hands. Then he handed the pipe to Custer, who also took four puffs on the pipe. Medicine Arrows spoke to Custer as he always had.

"General, if you are acting treachery toward us," warned Medicine Arrows, "sometime you and your whole command will be killed."[2] Then Chief Medicine Arrows poured the ashes from the pipe's stem over the toes of Custer's boots to bring him bad luck.[3]

Custer right then and there disregarded the warning of Medicine Arrows. After leaving the chief's lodge, Custer called to his men to seize four of the Cheyenne chiefs, and had three of them sent to Fort Hays for imprisonment. At the Fort Hays stockade during the first week in May 1869, Lt. David G. Rousseau decided to move the three chiefs from the stockade into the nearby guardhouse for better protection, using force to compel their compliance. Lt. Rousseau neglected to use an interpreter to explain his actions, leading the Cheyenne chiefs to believe they were about to be killed when they saw the troopers approach with fixed bayonets. The chiefs drew hand-honed knives they had hidden in their clothing and rushed the guards, wounding the sergeant.[4] A guard then fired, killing two of the chiefs, and the third chief was wounded as he was knocked unconscious from a blow of the rifle butt.[5]

That summer, bands of Cheyenne began to drift in and settle around their designated agency at Camp Supply, notably those of Little Robe, Minimie, Buffalo Head, and even Medicine Arrows for a brief period. And the prisoners at Fort Hays were released to the care of Little Robe. Among the bands were the half-breeds Edmund Guerrier, George Bent, and Robert Bent, who made the trip to what is now western Oklahoma to take their places among the Cheyenne on the new reservation.

Julia Bent did not come south into the new Cheyenne-Arapaho lands in 1869 with her brothers.[6] The tribe was still too unsettled. The peaceful Cheyenne first had to explore their new territory and find areas to set up their camps around Fort Supply, and already there were rumblings about the area around fort Supply as being unsuitable for their camps. Many of the belligerent Cheyenne had not surrendered as yet. There was the possibility of more skirmishes.

Meanwhile, in Washington, D. C., President Ulysses S. Grant wrestled with a new problem. He wondered how to administer to these reluctantly-tamed, recently wild Indians who were filtering into their vast treaty lands. He decided to entrust the responsibilities as Indian agents in the Bureau of Indian Affairs to the Society of Friends, or the Quaker sect. The Quakers sent elderly Brinton Darlington as the new agent for the Upper Arkansas Agency, then

Indians in traditional dress. *Courtesy Western History Collections, University of Oklahoma Libraries.*

headquartered at Camp Supply. His new charges, the Cheyenne and Arapaho, very soon began to voice displeasure to Darlington about the site of Camp Supply as their headquarters, and about the reservation lands given them in the treaty. They preferred the environs of the North Canadian River where there was good soil, water and timber. President Grant then created a new reservation for these two allied tribes: The Cherokee Outlet on the northern boundary; the Cimarron River and 98th meridian on the eastern boundary; the Kiowa, Comanche and Kiowa-Apache reservation on the south; and the Texas state line on the west. This amounted to over four million acres, which Grant wanted split between the two tribes. Next, Darlington obliged the two tribes by moving the agency headquarters close to the North Canadian River in May 1870. The site chosen became known as Darlington, named for its first agent who became loved and respected by the Indians, located a few miles north of El Reno.

But agent Darlington had his own problem. He could not speak the language of his charges. He searched among the half-breeds for an interpreter, and decided to approach Guerrier. Darlington was impressed with Edmund's education, his fine mind and steady manner, as well as his knowledge of English and several Indian languages. He offered Edmund a position in the agency. Edmund then began his role as interpreter for Darlington in September 1871. He remained on the reservation, living in Darlington and then in Kingfisher, providing services for the government when needed.

Copy of Lt. Abert's drawings of Bent's Old Fort on the Arkansas River.
Courtesy Western History Collections, University of Oklahoma Libraries.

Indian agent Darlington received a letter dated October 15, 1870 from John W. Prowers at Fort Lyon. Prowers asked that Darlington request from Edmund Guerrier the surrender of his land patent from the 1865 Treaty of the Little Arkansas, the 640-acre grant he was awarded as compensation for the attack on Black Kettle's village at Sand Creek by Colonel Chivington. Edmund agreed. He and George Bent and others sold their patents to Prowers, a white man married to the Cheyenne Amache, daughter of Chief Och-kenee, One Eye. Prowers had been an employee of Bent's Fort, and later managed the stage station based at the remains of Bent's Old Fort after it was blown up by William Bent.[7] Julia Bent also sold her Colorado land patent to Prowers, who eventually owned a great swath of land on the north bank of the Arkansas River for the ranch. A town and a county were named Prowers in his honor.

In the spring of 1871, Edmund was hired by Colonel John W. Davidson, commandant at Fort Supply, to accompany cavalry detachments that were assigned to escort the Dog Soldier bands of Bull Bear and Stone Forehead, which were returned south to join their peaceful relatives. Upon arrival, however, the small bands were so impoverished that Davidson issued rations to them, as they obviously were no threat. But he also warned them that they would incur his punishment should they attempt to leave the reservation. Task accomplished, Edmund was discharged from those duties.

Guerrier was not idle for long. The next month, Darlington sent him with a delegation of Cheyenne and Arapaho to meet with President Grant and Indian Commissioner Ely S. Parker in

Washington. The Arapaho leader Little Raven was instrumental in pressing for the trip, as he wished to cement relationships with the federal government. Little Raven, Powder Face, and Bird Chief, Arapaho, as well as Stone Calf and Little Robe, Cheyenne, and Buffalo Goad of the Wichita made the trip, accompanied by Edmund Guerrier, John Smith, and Philip McCusker as interpreters. This was a grand trip covering a tour of the city, the naval yards, government buildings, and a meeting with Commissioner Parker, where Stone Calf told him, "We haven't an axe, we haven't an acre of corn growing today in our great country that the government has said they would reserve for us."[8]

In a trip to the White House, the chiefs were amazed at the rotunda and the various paintings, and refused to believe they were manmade. In a meeting with President Grant, they were asked about recent depredations in Texas, and responded that the Kiowa were responsible. They became alarmed and ran in all directions when shown an elevator in the Treasury building, an unimaginable contraption that frightened them.[9]

From Washington, the group traveled to New York where they toured Central Park, the zoo, the harbor, and were shown the ocean liner *Oceanic.* Next was a tour of Harvard University in Cambridge, where Little Robe mused that this school might serve to educate his son. After a stop in Philadelphia, they rode the train to Chicago and were feted with a large reception by the Indian Peace Commission. This extensive honor-laden trip was a peek at the vast eastern resources of the white man by these western chiefs, meant to awe and quiet them, but was also a source of many wondrous tales for their families in the Indian camps. Of course, it was a source of pleasure for Edmund Guerrier and the other interpreters.

As steady and reliable as Edmund was known to be, he nevertheless had his moments. He was paid $100 for his services while in Washington, and again was paid $100 in Lawrence, Kansas by Mr. Cyrus Beede at the office of Superintendent of Indian Affairs when the chief's contingent was scheduled to leave Lawrence by wagon on June 15 on its way to Indian Territory and home. But Mr. Beede had more to say about that. He wrote to Jonathan Richards, Kiowa Indian agent, on that date.

"For the most part they conducted themselves well while in this city [Lawrence]. This cannot be said as to all the interpreters. Ed Guerrier is left behind, and McCusker is I believe staying to take care of him or pretending to at least. It is really discouraging to undertake to civilize Indians with interpreters who cannot overcome their appetites for whiskey."[10]

Many a present-day vacationer in a big city with a pocketful of money can identify with Edmund's overindulgence. Edmund at last continued home and picked up his employment at the agency at the rate of $82.60 per month, an ample amount for his needs at that time.

Following his appointment as Indian agent by President Grant, Darlington immediately began to urge the precepts of former Indian agent General William Clark who, fifty years before, recommended that tribes be resettled on reservation lands, that the government provide common schools, and training in agricultural life, and annuities to help the tribes purchase cattle and horses. Darlington believed that education, instruction in farming and the provision of medical care were essential to civilizing the Indians. At first, only two families tried farming. Eight children enrolled in the newly-built Quaker-run school, all Arapaho at first, as the Cheyenne families still balked at sending their children to school. The Cheyenne eventually agreed to send their children to school, but wanted a separate school for their tribe, which was built nearby. It was reported that in 1875, Cheyenne Belle, daughter of Making Out Road and relative of Julia Bent, was the first Cheyenne girl to attend school when John H. Seger was the superintendent there, and where she was known as a beautiful and brilliant student.[11]

But in 1871 the population was growing. When Medicine Arrows arrived with the Dog Soldiers, Darlington counted 2,300 Cheyenne in his census, including 500 warriors. The Cheyenne were content for the most part, as Darlington allowed them to continue to hunt buffalo, still plentiful on the southern plains, and sent Robert Bent as the overseer in charge of the hunt. The Union Pacific railroad had divided the great herds, but meat was still abundant until the white buffalo hunters invaded their range and began the wholesale slaughter of the animals for their hides.

It is estimated that 7,500,000 buffalo were killed by the white hunters, a staggering number. They were at once so numerous that a herd required two days to pass by. But, they were too easily killed. If approached warily, they would stand in one herd without stampeding while being shot, one by one.

The Indians were incensed over the intrusion of the buffalo hunters, as they considered the buffalo as their sacred animal. "From the hide he made his tepees, winter robes, parfleche cases, saddle covers, winter moccasins, cradles and shields; from the horns, his spoons and dishes; from the long hair of the head, ropes and lariats; the sinew gave him his thread and bowstrings and back his bows; the shoulder blades and other heavy bones were used as instruments in dressing hides, and the brain, liver and fat in tanning; from the tail were made knife scabbards, handles for clubs, and wands used in medicine dances; the hoofs and horns were made into glue; in fact, so varied were the uses of the buffalo that its destruction was like taking away the Indians' life."[12] These buffalo hunters defiantly set up their camp at Adobe Walls, a small fort first established by William Bent as a trading center to obtain horses from the southern tribes. Adobe Walls was located in the Texas panhandle, on the south fork of the Canadian River near Bent's Creek.

In addition to the buffalo hunters, white horse thieves became a problem to the tribe. The ponies were held in large herds, difficult to adequately protect, and were considered fair game for the horse rustlers. And, the Indians fell under the sway of illegal alcohol, provided by unscrupulous traders. Some Cheyenne began swapping rounded-up horses to the traders for small amounts of whiskey. Edmund Guerrier was forced to send his pony herd to Camp Supply for safety. And George Bent lost his entire herd while they grazed near the Darlington agency to horse raiders or to whiskey traders.

Objections and pleas for intervention by the Indians went unheeded by the government. Little was done to protect the herds or to stop the practices of the whiskey traders on the reservation.

Sadly, their beloved Indian agent, Brinton Darlington, died in April 1872. John D. Miles was appointed to replace him. Agent Miles became a part owner of the Lee and Reynolds trading company, and hired Edmund Guerrier as a clerk in the store. Now, Edmund had three jobs: trading store clerk, interpreter, and rancher on his land. He was a busy man. He was also sent out to oversee a buffalo hunting party of the Cheyenne.

Although the bulk of the Cheyenne on the reservation were peaceful, agent Miles did not want to stir up their hostilities by broaching the subject that President Grant had exchanged their lands given in the Treaty of Medicine Lodge Creek for the lands Grant had chosen for them. Edmund Guerrier was of the same mind as agent Miles. Edmund refused to interpret this land swap to the Cheyenne, fearing the Cheyenne retaliation upon himself and dreading any disruption of the peaceful settlement process.[13] As it turned out, Congress never took action on the new treaty that would have divided the Cheyenne and Arapaho into two separate reservations. The two tribes remained together on their lands.

For the next two years, the Cheyenne were mostly quiet, although some of the young men, restless, periodically would join the Kiowa in raiding for horses or hunting their enemies, the Ute. But the inadequate food through the loss of their buffalo herds to white hunters, drunkenness because of unchecked whiskey traders, lack of

Fort Laramie Peace Commission, May 10, 1868. Left to right: Gen. Alfred H. Terry, Gen. William S. Harvey, Gen. William T. Sherman, Julia Bent (identified by author based on the fact that Bent's family was on temporary residence at Fort Laramie during this period. Those pictured also were with Bent at the Medicine Creek Treaty in 1867.) N.G. Taylor, Col. Samuel F. Tappan, and Gen. C.C. Augur. *Courtesy Bureau of American Indian Ethnology.*

protection for their horse herds, and lack of rations finally drove the Cheyenne once again toward war.

In June 1874, a group of Cheyenne and Comanche attacked a thirty-eight man force of white hunters at William Bent's old trading post at Adobe Walls, where they had been slaughtering the buffalo herd. The white hunters happened to have risen early that morning to make some repairs on the structure, so they were not taken unaware and were able to drive off the attacking Indians.

Following the raid on Adobe Walls, Kiowa and Comanche raiders in their wrath fell on two buffalo hunters and killed and mutilated both of them. Their bodies were found and buried by a survey party who then met deputy agent E. C. Lefebere and a Mr. Talley on their return trip from Adobe Walls to Camp Supply, and told their story. Lefebere's camp itself was attacked on June 11 and all their stock driven off, including both their horses. "We came back afoot" to Camp Supply, they said. Ed Guerrier arrived at Camp Supply about that time and relayed to the pair that they were needed at the agency. They sent word to the agency that "as soon as we can get horses, we will start. Probably we will come back with Ed."[14]

Other Indian raids resulted in the deaths of settlers and surveying parties. Once again, there was an Indian war on the plains. Agent Miles pleaded for government protection for his family and his agency, and received it in good measure.

Five armies were dispatched from all directions toward the Cheyenne trouble sites. Colonel Nelson Miles moved from Camp Supply and found a large village of hostile Indians on the Sweetwater

River. His forces attacked, and took no prisoners. Miles captured the pony herds, as well. The Indians fled to the Palo Duro Canyon, where they were attacked by Colonel Ranald Mackenzie. Mackenzie destroyed 400 lodges and captured 1,400 ponies. Then, Colonel George Buell found and destroyed 500 lodges and captured large herds. Pursued through the winter and attacked when found, 821 Cheyenne surrendered in March 1875. Most of the hostiles were subdued, except Medicine Arrows and White Antelope and their bands, which fled north to join the Northern Cheyenne.[15]

By 1875, most of the Cheyenne were back camping near the Darlington agency with the exception of the two hostile bands, but those at the reservation were still skittish. When in April, a blacksmith was knocked down by Black Horse as leg irons were being applied, shots were fired by the guard and Black Horse was killed. Some of the bullets rained into the main camp of Cheyenne, who returned fire and dashed toward a sand hill on the North Canadian River where they dug up a stash of guns and ammunition. They fled during the night, but stopped ninety miles northwest of Darlington. Three weeks later, they began to filter back to the agency, where thirty-one men and one woman were selected randomly by a drunken officer to be imprisoned at Fort Marion in St. Augustine, Florida. According to Cheyenne lore, the officer lined the men up in one row, and then chose every other man regardless of any complicity in the escapade.[16] One of those imprisoned was Oakerhater, who had married Charlie Bent's widow after his death following a battle wound.[17]

Others who had fled north were intercepted by Lieutenant Austin Henely and the Sixth Cavalry, who killed nineteen men and eight women and children. Most of the remainder of the "stampeders" returned to Darlington, with the exception of a few who stayed in the north.

Hoping to keep the Indians busy in their new lands, Indian agent Miles hurried to develop a master plan to encourage the Cheyenne and Arapaho toward becoming farmers, even though the agency had little money to buy farm equipment and supplies. Agent Miles divided the reservation into parcels for administrative purposes, hired a foreman and farmer helpers in each section to work with and instruct the Indians. One of the most successful of these was John H. Seger, whose Indians were more productive in farming. Seger established a school for the Indians, while founding the town of Colony.[18]

Edmund Guerrier and Indian Agent Miles were both in Mr. Seger's Colony office at one time when a particularly difficult and mean Indian named Hippy entered the office. Thinking he would not be understood, Hippy began to speak in the Comanche language that he had everyone scared, including Agent Miles. Edmund understood and spoke Comanche, however. He reported Hippy's threatening words to Miles, thus thwarting Hippy's mischief.[19]

There had been much turmoil in the Indian camps for four years. But by 1875, when the stampeders returned to the reservation and a group of troublemakers was incarcerated at Fort Marion in Florida, peace was beginning to reign again. And, this was the year of an event that would lead to the establishment of a town and the genesis of a family dynasty within the confines of the reservation.[20]

Robert Bent, right, and Navaho Tom Torlino at Carlisle Indian School in 1884. Torlino arrived at Carlisle in 1882 and was commonly referred to as Tom "Carlisle." *Courtesy Cumberland County Historical Society, Carlisle, PA.*

Old Man "Guerie"

16

When the Cheyenne wars were over, the tribe began the slow transition toward reservation life. Edmund continued his position as interpreter at Darlington and as clerk for Lee and Reynolds' trading post there. Robert Bent, who forged his home on a ranch, was given supervision of the Cheyenne hunters who were given permission to hunt in the vicinity of the reservation, as there were still buffalo on the range although their numbers were rapidly decreasing.

An amusing, if macabre, incident occurred on the reservation, of which Robert Bent was a part. Agent Captain Lee, who replaced agent Miles, sent an ailing agency "farmer helper" to Robert and suggested that Robert make any use of him around the ranch that he wished. The farmer very soon had an epileptic seizure and became rigid. Robert, supposing the farmer was dead or dying, sent a runner on horseback to tell Captain Lee at Darlington to hurry a casket to his ranch. Lee rushed to buy a coffin, hired a team to take it to Robert's ranch, and was greatly surprised to find the farmer, revived and alive, able to inspect his own casket when it arrived.[1]

Robert had his own sense of fun, but he did not like to brook nonsense from braggarts. He was in a saloon one afternoon when he overheard a few white cowboy loafers boasting of their prowess in fighting Indians during the recent wars. Robert, bemused, went outside to accoutré himself and his horse in Indian fashion, then came riding his horse through the swinging canteen doors into the saloon whooping and shooting his pistol in the air. The frightened cowboys took out the store's front windows on their way south toward Texas.[2]

Robert had married the Cheyenne Elk Woman by Indian custom, and the pair lived on Robert's allotment two miles west and four miles north of Watonga.

George and Robert kept busy with their affairs, but they also had more serious thoughts on their minds. Their father was dead, also their older sister Mary Bent Moore had died in Colorado. Now their sister Julia was the only living relative living in Colorado, having never come south to the new reservation. The two remaining brothers were instrumental in providing for her future by arranging a marriage between Julia and her long-time friend and sweetheart, Edmund Guerrier. Among the Indians, their role was customary. If a woman's father was dead, her brothers looked after her interests and arranged her marriage.

And so, it was done. They were married in 1875 at Fort Reno[3], according to their granddaughter Ann Guerrier Shadlow, probably by a priest as both were Catholic.[4] Julia was not the only traveler to Indian Territory on the journey, as she was provided with an ample dowry for her marriage. She was accompanied by cattle, many horses, sheep, fowl, household goods and cash.[5] Edmund was age thirty-five, Julia was twenty-eight. They settled in Kingfisher, a community just north of Darlington.

Although her marriage was an arranged one, Julia was pleased and content. Edmund was kind to her, and let her do as she pleased. He never made her cook, although she could make good biscuits. He hired a black cook, and sometimes even did the cooking himself. Julia had not learned to cook, as her Suhtai foster parents always cooked for her. "When a family has a foster child," said her granddaughter Ann Guerrier Shadlow, "they are afraid to make her work for fear that people will say 'They worked her.' That's part of the tradition. So, she was never made to do anything."[6]

In the summer of 1876, Edmund was again hired as an interpreter by the agency when small groups of Northern Cheyenne began to join their southern relatives at the Darlington agency. Although hostilities were feared and the troops at Fort Reno were alerted, these small bands came in peacefully and accepted the terms offered by agent Miles.

The Indian agent decided in 1877 to make a head count of

the Cheyenne currently residing within the reservations' limits. Only the men were listed by name, however, and the number of people in each household. Thus, we obtain some information but are left with a few mysteries as well. On July 1, 1877, the household of Edmund Guerrier held two men, three women, and five children, for a total of ten people. On December 10, 1877, his home included one man, two women, and one child. Then, in the 1880 Cheyenne census, Edmund's home contained two males, three women, and four children, for a total of nine people.[7]

Ed Guerrier. *Courtesy Archives & Manuscripts Division of the Oklahoma Historical Society.*

The mystery can be solved by remembering that Indian people, and Cheyenne in particular, are hospitable people who readily house their relatives and tribal members and friends when the need arises. When one person or family has abundance of something, that thing is shared with others. Needs are provided by those who have the means. Thus, we can safely assume that in the 1870s period of transition when the Cheyenne were gradually settling onto their lands in Indian Territory, Edmund was housing his or Julia's relatives and friends, and that

Arapaho Indian camp near the Canadian River, ca. 1870. Edmund Guerrier is center. *Courtesy Archives & Manuscripts Division of the Oklahoma Historical Society.*

those visitors living temporarily in his home eventually came and went when they obtained their own land and housing.

Edmund and his brother-in-law George Bent continued their friendly relations, as both worked at that time for the Lee and Reynolds trading company at Darlington and the two families visited one another frequently. Edmund and George teamed up together in business occasionally, as well. In 1877, the pair bought a fine horse from a Texas rancher named King, the horse with one lopped ear, branded it K W on the left hip, and used it often as a race horse during the tribe's competitive races, a favorite pastime with the Indians. The horse eventually wound up in the hands of the Cheyenne Red Lodge, from whom the horse was stolen.[8] The horse was well-known within the tribe and its loss was mourned, but Edmund had more pressing matters on his mind to think long about it, as he was very busy with his stock, providing for a continuous influx of relatives and visitors in his home. His next assignment for the government during the Northern Cheyenne breakout from the reservation was unsettling for Edmund and his Cheyenne family, however. It led to his distress over threats to his life.

1877 was the year of another large influx of Indians into the Cheyenne and Arapaho lands in Indian Territory. After the Northern Cheyenne bands of Little Wolf and Dull Knife were moved south into Indian Territory during the spring of 1877, those related Cheyenne joined their Southern Cheyenne brethren at the Darlington agency. Very quickly, however, they began to sicken and die of debilitating fevers and agues. They were accustomed to the high dry country of Montana, and could not adjust to the heat of Indian Territory. Of the approximately one thousand who arrived, forty-one died the first winter. In addition, they were the consumers of the buffalo and wild game abundant in the northern hunting grounds. In Indian Territory, the skinny beeves allotted to them in insufficient quantities further sickened them.

The following spring of 1878, Little Wolf went to agent John D. Miles at Darlington, saying that his people were sick and dying at the agency's locale. He requested the agent's permission to go back north, or the agent's leave to allow their representatives to plead their case in Washington. Miles refused. Miles noted that three of the Northern Cheyenne warriors had already left the agency, and demanded that Little Wolf turn over ten of his warriors as hostages until the three missing Indians were returned. This Little Wolf refused and returned to his camp. Shortly, Miles sent troops with a howitzer to the Indians' camp. He also sent Edmund Guerrier to continue his role as interpreter during this crisis. Guerrier delivered Miles' demand that Little Wolf come to the agency for another talk. When Little Wolf complied and went to see Miles at the agency, Edmund Guerrier reported Little Wolf's speech.

"My friends," said Little Wolf, "I am now going to my camp. I do not wish the ground about this agency to be made bloody, but now listen to what I say to you. I am going to leave here; I am going north to my own country. I do not want to see blood spilt about this agency. If you are going to send your soldiers after me, I wish that you would first let me get a little distance away from this agency. Then if you want to fight, I will fight you, and we can make the ground bloody at that place."[9]

Seeing that the Northern Cheyenne were firm in their resolve to leave and that their tempers were on edge, Edmund's relatives in the Cheyenne camp advised him to quit his interpreter's post, as they feared he might be killed. Edmund had advised them not to go. "If you do, you will have trouble."[10] More than that, he could not do. Wisely, he heeded the advice of his relatives. He stopped interpreting during these exchanges. But the Northern Cheyenne did not heed the advice Edmund gave to them. The bands under Little Wolfe and Dull Knife, true to their words, fled the agency's jurisdiction in 1878.

But when the Northern Cheyenne bolted for their homeland

George Bent and his Cheyenne wife Magpie, 1867. *Courtesy Western History Collections, University of Oklahoma Libraries.*

in the north, one woman, in particular, stayed behind. This was Standing Out Woman, a handsome and dignified but fun-loving Northern Cheyenne who took a shine to George Bent. The feeling was mutual. George made her his third wife. Magpie had borne him four children: Ada in 1867, Robert in 1870, Mary, and William and now she was pregnant again. Kiowa Woman bore George his daughter Julia in 1871 and George W. "Junior" in 1877, but she soon left Bent for the Cheyenne, Bird. George continued to provide support for his wives and extended families.[11] And, he kept up his visitations with his sister and brother-in-law, the Guerriers.

Edmund and Julia moved in 1880 from Kingfisher to Darlington, as reported in the agency newspaper, *Cheyenne Transporter.* On November 26, 1880, the paper reported "Ed Guerrier came in from Kingfisher last week and will make his home at the agency." West of Darlington, Guerrier built a small trading post, with a general store, boarding house, and restaurant combination. [12] Later, a post office was added bearing the name Geary. This location was on the trail from Fort Reno to Cantonment, a military station, and was a busy travel route for the army as well as for traders and travelers of various sorts. Julia, who knew no English, very likely steered clear of it, however, and stayed in their quarters. On the land around his trading post and restaurant, Guerrier was afforded space to graze his horses and cattle. He built for the family a two-story log house, described by Mrs. Mary Hudnall on a visit to the Guerrier household. Mrs. Hudnall was the daughter of John Prowers, who had purchased Edmund's Colorado land patent years before.[13] Yet Edmund and Julia preferred to live in the canvas tepee that he later erected in front of the new log house. They preferred to sleep on palettes on the ground within the canvas cone of their tepee, and there, they fit in with the habits of their Indian neighbors.[14]

Gradually, Edmund added other structures to the farm, including a chicken house, several one and two-room tenant houses, a hay barn, smokehouse and a large stock barn. Besides his horses for which he became well known, he stocked the farm with small pure-bred black cattle, draft horses for the wagon, hogs, chickens, turkeys, burros, and Shetland ponies. He traveled daily to his store and restaurant by horseback or buggy unless business called him out of the area, while Julia busied herself tidying the tepee and arranging visits with her relatives. Her brother George had settled in Colony, southwest of Darlington. She loved her weekly visits by wagon to the Lone Lodge family related to her foster parents who helped raise her, and who lived west of the Guerrier family near what is now Lake American Horse.

Edmund's love of blooded stock was well known to all on the reservation, and brought a certain amount of fame to him as well as personal pride in his breeding methods. He was known for fine horses. His friend George Smith, a long-time neighbor, wrote how Edmund sometimes was able to improve his stock. According to Smith, "One day a man from Kentucky, riding a thoroughbred stallion came to Ed's farm to trade for a good strong horse. His stallion was young and worn out from the long trip. He picked out one of Ed's best horses to trade for, but Ed did not want to trade. After much dickering, the trade was finally made and the man rode on his way to Texas. From that time on, Ed raised even better horses, sired by the Kentucky thoroughbred stallion."[15]

But in the midst of the busy days of the Guerriers, Julia found a quiet moment alone with Edmund to give him an important piece of news. She was pregnant. Edmund paused, and quietly sucked in his breath. He was to become a father. He had waited long years for this. He was over forty years old, and would at long last have a child. Although he was solicitous of Julia's welfare during her pregnancy, there was no need to fear, as Julia delivered a healthy baby boy in April 1881. His parents named him William, after both his grandfathers, William Bent and William Guerrier.

Edmund was proud to fulfill his new role as a father, but he was also concerned about his tribesmen, as the Cheyenne and Arapaho were experiencing difficult times as a result of their treatment by the government, which expected these Plains tribes to begin farming and to learn to support themselves, unrealistically. These men were hunters and warriors. They wanted to continue to live communally, not separated on individual farms apart from one another. Even with the expectation, the government refused to supply the Indian agent with the farm equipment needed to distribute to his charges. The few crops that were tried quickly burned in the hot dry western climate. The government then cut their beef rations to three pounds per person live weight, which yielded only one and a half pounds of beef weekly. Although the tribes had been

Robert Bent, mixed-blood Cheyenne. *Courtesy Archives & Manuscripts Division of the Oklahoma Historical Society.*

forced to switch from the traditionally-eaten buffalo fare to cattle beef, still the people were meat-eaters primarily, and could not safely exist on such meager rations. And yet, the government cut the ration again to yield only one pound per person weekly. Begin farming or starve. And starvation did occur. The new agent, John D. Miles, was criticized for playing favorites when he gave George Bent two heads of beef weekly plus twenty pounds of beef per day to feed his three families. Bent was also earning $100.00 per month as an employee of Lee and Reynolds trading company, and agent Miles was a part-owner of that company, clearly a conflict of interest from his standpoint as the tribe's agent. Guerrier may have been receiving the same favored treatment from the agent, reason enough for their fellow tribesmen to grumble about the pair.

But Guerrier, the Bent brothers and other half-breeds had another thought that they presented to agent Miles as a way to help the tribe gain needed income. As the Indians were not farming the land currently, then allow others to lease the land from them, and pay the Indians rent money. Agent Miles finally was successful in persuading the government to allow the Indians to lease their lands, but this proved to be a mixed blessing. Many problems arose, including an influx of white men to the territory. The Indian leaders rebelled, and demanded that the leasing be stopped. The chiefs also wanted Edmund Guerrier, Robert Bent, and George Bent banned from the reservation as they were supporters of the cattlemen leasing the land.[16] The men stayed, but leasing was halted in 1885 by President Grover Cleveland, who ordered the cattle off the reservation within forty days. The greedy cattlemen were incensed, but had to obey.[17]

During this period, Guerrier's entrepreneurial enterprise was prospering. While he traveled to Las Vegas, New Mexico in April 1882 to buy a herd of sheep for his ranch, he designated an employee to run the operation in his absence. The *Cheyenne Transporter* newspaper reported on April 25, 1882 that "Charley Scott has charge of Ed Guerrier's mess house and is feeding the bachelors of the place, and transients who come this way, in first class shape. He is having a good run of trade, and gives general satisfaction to his guests.'[18]

In September, Ed traveled with his brother-in-law Robert Bent to Las Animas, Colorado on business. November saw him in Winfield, Kansas where he interpreted for the Cheyenne in a court case. The *Cheyenne Transporter* reported his return. "Ed Guerrier, who has been attending court at Winfield a couple of weeks, acting

Cheyenne Chiefs and their children visiting Gettysburg Battlefield in 1884 en route to enroll the children at Carlisle Indian School in Pennsylvania. The group was escorted by Edmund Guerrier as interpreter. Guerrier is in the light suit second from right in second row. *Courtesy Archives & Manuscripts Division of the Oklahoma Historical Society.*

as interpreter for the Indians who were testifying against one Van Meter, charged with stealing ponies of the Indians, returned last week, bringing with him one of the handsome barouches[19] we have seen in the west. That's pretty enough for a queen, Ed. Couldn't the Transporter spread agony if only we possessed a like carriage? We believe it was made by the Winfield Carriage Works."[20] Guerrier was not finished indulging his bent toward fine clothing, blooded cattle and horses and handsome adornments around him.

The government was insistent that these two tribes send their children to schools at Darlington for the Arapaho and at Caddo Springs for the Cheyenne children. But the Cheyenne families, in particular, were reluctant to send their children to school. Some children of the more important chiefs were selected to attend Carlisle School in Pennsylvania, thought to be a little more prestigious for the chief's children. Edmund Guerrier accompanied a group of these students along with their parents and tribal dignitaries, acting as interpreter, when the students traveled to Carlisle for schooling in November 1884. The group stopped to visit the Gettysburg Battlefield, where a group picture was made.[21] The old chiefs surely must have sensed the melancholy of the Gettysburg battlefield, warriors as they were, as they had suffered their own losses in battles and massacres at the hands of enemies.

The following year, 1885, the Guerrier household was again blessed with an addition to its ranks. A daughter was born, one whom Edmund named Anna, known thereafter as Annie.[22] Two more children were born at an unknown date, a son, and a daughter they named Rosa, after Edmund's sister. Edmund later sent Rosa to France for tutoring. After four years in France, tragedy struck as she sailed back to the United States. She became ill on the ship and died, either on the ship or when she returned to her parents' home.[23] Her parents mourned, but quietly got themselves back into their household and career routines as, after all, they had two living children to rear and many mouths to feed.

Besides his ranching and interpreting jobs, and his trading post/boardinghouse/restaurant, Edmund often had other matters to attend to. In 1887, he and his brother-in-law George Bent were called upon to testify in court. The old lop-eared race horse had been found, as it was well-recognized by the tribe for its fleetness of foot. When the horse was stolen from Red Lodge, it had come into the hands of the owner of a livery stable in Atoka, Indian Territory by the name of Downing, who sold the horse to someone else. Edmund and George swore they had bought the horse from the Texan named King, identified the horse, and their word was taken as they were known to be "intelligent half-blood Indians."[24]

But Edmund was distressed, as were the other tribal members, at what the government next planned for the Cheyenne. The final blow to the communal sovereignty of the Cheyenne and Arapaho tribes came in 1887, when the United States Congress passed the Dawes Act, a General Allotment Act that awarded one hundred and sixty acres to each tribal member for farming, an amount which doubled to three hundred twenty acres if the land was suitable only for grazing. The land was to be held inalienable for twenty-five years, not nearly long enough to protect the Indian land holder and his heirs from the greed of land-seeking white people. Citizenship for the Indian was promised for the future, but meanwhile all allottees were to be subject to the laws of the state or territory. And, disastrously for the Cheyenne and Arapaho reservation, all the excess land not allotted to tribal members was to become available for sale to whites in one-quarter sections of one hundred sixty acres each, the proceeds of the sale of this land to be held in trust by the United States Treasury for the tribes' benefit. This act, when implemented, destroyed the tribe's land base, its traditional communal living style, its long-established tribal order, and the effective functioning of the tribe as an entity. For the Indians, the concept of "Each man for himself" was an alien one. They only knew their long-accustomed pattern of communal land ownership for the entire tribe. The white man's individual use of the land was foreign to their thinking. They looked forward to the implementation of the Allotment Act with confusion and apprehension.

In the spring of 1889 when it was learned that the Choctaw Oklahoma and Gulf railroad was to be built one and a half miles southeast of the post office named Geary, the area's residents decided to move the post office nearer to the railroad, and did so. Edmund received the first mail from that post office. Soon a sizeable town of seven hundred gathered around the settlement, also named Geary. A blacksmith shop, newspaper, bank, barber shop, two drug stores and various saloons, restaurants and merchandise stores followed its founding. The name Geary grew out of the difficulty

Cheyenne Indian Camp at Darlington, O.T., ca. 1889. *Courtesy Archives & Manuscripts Division of the Oklahoma Historical Society.*

most people on the frontier had in pronouncing the French name of Guerrier. Rather than trying to pronounce it, strangers arrived looking for "Ole Man Guerie," or Geary. Thus, he was known that way, and the town as well.

Now in 1890, he was a fifty-year-old patriarch. He sold his trading post/restaurant on the Fort Reno-Cantonment road to L. M. Hartley for $400.00. He calmly pursued his business as a farmer and rancher, wondering what the turn of the century would have in store for him.

In the midst of the distress that the entire Cheyenne tribe was feeling over the government's breakup of its communal land into individual allotments, an even more personal blow hit the Guerrier family. Robert Bent died and was buried on his ranch.[25] Robert, the oldest of the Bent children, was known as a steady hand, a responsible and successful rancher, respected by the government during the role of interpreter he filled in Washington, and beloved by his younger siblings. Now, only Julia Bent Guerrier and George Bent remained of the five Bent children. But Julia had her own family now, her husband and protector and their two living children.

During this period when allotments were being chosen and assigned to tribal members, the tribe became restive and unhappy. The old chiefs were losing their power. Many whites gathered at the reservation's borders awaiting the opening of the excess land. The people were in poverty. There were few jobs available, even to the young people who had received education at the reservation schools or at Carlisle. The people turned to a new religion for solace, that of the Paiute religious leader named Wovoka, who promised all who danced the ghost dance that their prayers would make the white people disappear and the buffalo herds return to the plains. How they wished that would happen. Thus, in 1890, all work stopped and the children were withdrawn from school while their parents prepared for the dances by making Ghost Dance shirts, embellished with special symbols.

Edmund Guerrier was not surprised at seeing his wife's activity in the tepee when he returned from his Darlington store one day. She was making a buckskin shirt to wear in the next day's Ghost Dance nearby, and was just painting the special symbols on the skins.

George Bent, 1905. *Courtesy Archives & Manuscripts Division of the Oklahoma Historical Society.*

Edmund did not believe in Wovoka's prophecy, but pacified Julia by allowing her to take the wagon and participate in the dance.

For two to three years, the people gathered in camps to sing and dance the Ghost Dance, hoping to bring about Wovoka's vision. Julia Guerrier was one of these. In 1892, Edmund himself, in the company of Washee and Sitting Bull, made a pilgrimage to visit Wovoka to check out this holy man. He was not impressed. His message to the Cheyenne when he returned from this visit was definite. Stop Ghost Dancing.[26] The Darlington Indian agent lived with this distraction amiably, but on the Pine Ridge Sioux reservation in South Dakota, mayhem resulted when a Sioux Ghost Dance gathering was gunned down at Wounded Knee, with the loss of many lives.

Finally, the dreaded day came. The Dawes Act allotments were made, with only 3,329 allotments going to the Cheyenne and Arapaho tribes. Of the 4,294,415 reservation acres that were guaranteed to the two tribes in their Treaty of Medicine Creek, only 529,692 acres remained to them. The rest of the land, all three and a half million acres, was then available to the whites waiting on the reservation borders.

Edmund selected his allotment as the land he had been occupying for his ranch. This was good land that ran along a creek that emptied into the North Canadian River, where he had not only water available, but fine grass for his stock. The Guerrier family was awarded four adjoining allotments, those of Edmund, Julia, William and Annie, six hundred forty acres in total.[27]

In 1892, when the excess lands were opened by the land run on April 19, twenty-five to thirty thousand white men swarmed into the territory, watched over by the soldiers at Fort Reno. Then, the rape of the Cheyenne and Arapaho Indians began in earnest.

Whites stole the Indians' timber, farm tools, saddles, horses, cattle and anything else that was not nailed down. Indians were accused of crimes unjustly and had no means to defend themselves. When an allotment was leased, whites often refused to honor the contracts. George Bent leased two sections for $110 cash but had difficulty obtaining the lease money and evicting the lessee. A poll tax was instituted to discourage Indian voting. Then, the western counties voted in the right of the open range, which allowed their cattle to overrun the Indians' farms.

The new counties began to assess the Indians' property in order to impose local taxes, in violation of the United States government's assurances that the property bought with annuity, leasing or interest money exempted the Indians from local taxes. In an attempt to forestall the county's tax burden on the Indian, Indian agent A.E. Woodson decided to make his own inventory of Indian property. He listed the personal property of Edmund Guerrier as valued at $935, consisting of 80 head of cattle, 35 horses, farm implements, a wagon, and furniture worth $5.00.[28] And sadly, Edmund was a wealthy man compared with most of his tribe.

William Guerrier began his first school days in the basement of a house in Geary. As he grew, he helped his father at the Darlington store, waiting on customers and interpreting for the elders who spoke no English. These were still wild and lawless times in that part of the country prior to statehood. The Indians experienced thievery and chicanery and knew they could expect little or no help from the law or the government. The Guerrier ranch seemed to be fair game for the cattle and horse rustlers. William and his friends became adept at tracking down the rustlers, retrieving their stock, and sometimes killing the thieves and hiding their bodies after a shootout.[29]

One day, in a derisive mood, William began mocking an elderly medicine man he met in a pasture. The medicine man, John Sorehead, whose Indian name was Bob-Tail-Horse, then told William, "Before you leave this pasture, you will need my help." William confidently walked away, but before he reached the fence, began to choke, desperate to regain his breath. John Sorehead walked over, reached into William's throat, and pulled out a large chuck of chicken fat and skin, saving him from asphyxiation.[30] William was thereby convinced of the powers of the medicine man, and began to interpret for him when needed.

There were many other social pressures weighing on the Cheyenne at the same time as the Dawes Allotment Act was breaking up their tribal lands. When Major A. E. Woodson succeeded as Indian agent, he began to attack their cultural/social values as well. He denied the tribe permission to hold their annual Sun Dance. He launched an attack on their use of peyote in religious ceremonies. And he became obsessed with antipathy toward their ancient marriage customs. He agitated the legislature and proposed a change in Oklahoma Territory statutes: recognizing divorce and the right of remarriage for a spurned plural wife; outlawing plural marriages; and awarding custody of her children to the rejected plural wife. This statute passed the territorial legislature on March 12, 1897. All prior marriages and divorces in the Indian style were grandfathered as approved, but henceforth all Indian plural marriages were to be punished, as well as marriages by Indian custom.[31]

And sure enough, the punishments began. On January 20, 1898, for example, the Blaine County Cheyenne couple Snake and Small Back were arrested and jailed in Watonga by Probate Judge W. H. Boudre for the crime of marrying on June 15, 1897 by Indian custom. Snake and Small Back pled guilty and were sentenced to six months in jail, "to be kept separate and apart."[32]

I Never Mistrusted a Truer Friend

17

Guerrier was in the community of El Reno one afternoon in about 1900. El Reno was a town that had developed a few miles east of Fort Reno and south of the Cheyenne agency at Darlington. It was a growing and busy town on a north-south Rock Island railroad line, with a spur into Oklahoma City to the east.

In the main district of town, Edmund was hailed on the street by his old friend from scouting days, Ben Clark. Ben had received pass tickets from Buffalo Bill for his Wild West Show that was coming soon to Oklahoma City, and he wondered if Edmund had received pass tickets also and planned to attend. Edmund begged off as he was not feeling well enough to make the thirty mile trip right then. But, he asked Clark to remind Buffalo Bill of the night he and Edmund stood guard on the Pawnee

Fork of the Arkansas River during the winter 1868-1869 Carr Campaign from Fort Lyon. If he remembered the incident, ask him if it was not a fact that he was afraid of Edmund that night because he was half-Indian, and was on guard all night against Edmund possibly sticking a knife in his back.

When Ben Clark posed the question to Buffalo Bill, William Cody's eyes filled with tears as he recalled the incident clearly.

"Yes, I was afraid of him that night," said Cody. "I didn't know him before then but I never mistrusted a truer friend in my life, for no truer heart ever lived than Ed Guerrier. Tell him that."[1]

Ben Clark relayed back to Guerrier the information that Bill Cody had, indeed, been afraid of him that night of standing guard, but later regretted his mistrust and eventually came to depend upon the friendship and reliability of Edmund Guerrier. Edmund, a sensitive and thoughtful man, quickly knew that Cody was afraid of him that night, so was not surprised that Cody verified his own fears.

Edmund was sixty years old now, feeling the first pangs of aging. But his life on his ranch continued unabated, watching his children William and Annie mature. William was a young man now, age nineteen. He took up the trades of carpentry and demolition, as well as tree work. Coming into town one day after a lengthy spell of lumberjack work, he decided he wanted a drink from the saloon. Entering, the saloon keeper took one look at his long flowing dark hair and buckskin clothes, now dirty, and announced, "Get out. We don't serve Indians here." William, unfazed, walked across the street for a shave and hair cut, bought new clothes, then reentered the

Southern Cheyenne Agency, Oklahoma, 1927. Left to right, Mrs. Big Heart, Gen. H. L. Scott, Mrs. Ed Guerrier, and Mrs. George Bent.

saloon unrecognized and was immediately served his drink.[2]

When Charles E. Shell was named superintendent of Cheyenne-Arapaho tribes, he began a close scrutiny of the habits of his charge, quickly discovering that the use of liquor by the Indians was voluminous. As it was a federal crime to sell or barter liquor to reservation Indians or those whose lands were held in trust, Shell secured the services of a federal officer and several detectives to sniff out violators, whom Shell then threatened to prosecute. He was especially concerned about liquor traffic to Indians in the smaller towns such as Geary and Kingfisher. The tavern owner who refused William his drink was just obeying the law. Still, Indians found ways to buy liquor, especially when they received funds from employment, interest payments, and lease money.[3]

Shell also began to enforce the 1904 Burke Act, which charged that an allotment alone did not provide the basis for citizenship and the Indian allotment holder's right to sell his land. Too many Indians were being fleeced by unscrupulous land-seekers, the Indians by then less than thirty years away from their old tribal, free-roaming days when individual ownership of lands was unknown. From 1904, only those Indians deemed competent, thrifty in occupation and industry, would be approved by the superintendent to hold title to their allotments in fee simple, rather than trusteeship under the Bureau of Indian Affairs. Many Indian families, although eligible, refused to consider the change, as it would mean that their lands would be subject to property taxes. The family of Michael and Cheyenne Belle Balenti were an exception. Cheyenne Belle's son George returned from schooling at Carlisle demanding that the family be allowed to manage their own property. Shell relented in the case of the older Balenti children, but remained firm that the minor Balenti children's' leases be managed by the agency office.[4]

Another large problem noted by agent Shell was rampant prejudice against the Indians, both in classrooms in schools and in the territorial courts. White judges, law officers and juries were loath to credit an Indian's word against a white man. One western Indian Territory town tried assimilating white and Indian children in its school for one year, but declined to further experiment the following year as the Indian children were shunned and ridiculed by their white fellow students.

Certainly, the Cheyenne and Arapaho tribes were destitute. In 1904-1905, the per capita income was $139.16 from all sources. Two years later in 1906-07, their per capita income had dropped to $78.03.[5] Very little had been accomplished in the way of farming skills, there were few opportunities for employment, and many families had sold their land just to have money for food and basic essentials.

Meanwhile, the Constitutional Convention was meeting in Guthrie, Oklahoma Territory, drawing plans for the new state of Oklahoma, becoming official in 1907.

During this time leading up to statehood, William Guerrier had begun to travel, to spread his wings away from his parents and his home. In his travels he saw many women, some of them attractive in his eyes. He wanted to be married, but had not found the right woman for him until he found one in a most unlikely place.

William Guerrier had first seen Nellie Adams at the St. Louis World's Fair in 1904, this beautiful Sioux woman. Nellie was a trick rider in a Wild West Show he witnessed in the area. He wanted this woman for his wife. William was then age twenty-three. He knew it was time to settle down and begin building a family. But until his visit to St. Louis, he had not found the woman who kindled his heart.

But with Nellie, there was a problem. A large one. She had been married twice and had two little girls. One husband, a High Eagle, was Sioux. The other, a Provost, also a Sioux. At the Fair, William promised himself to keep abreast of her whereabouts.

As fate would have it, Nellie's husband was desperately ill with tuberculosis and died shortly after she returned home to South Dakota from her Wild West Show tour. William learned of this through the Indian grapevine, traveled to South Dakota to look for her, and brought her back to his family in Geary, Oklahoma as his bride. At first, Nellie left the two girls with her parents in South Dakota, but later at Edmund's insistence, William traveled north again with Nellie and brought her daughters to Oklahoma. Pearl was unhappy there and eventually went back to live with her grandparents. But, her sister Dorothy stayed in Oklahoma with William and Nellie. These girls became half-sisters to their own children, soon to come.[6] Edmund was pleased that his son William had chosen a wife, and liked having a step-granddaughter in his lodge. He had a fondness for children.

Edmund Guerrier was well known in the early years of the state of Oklahoma. He had many visitors on his farm, some sent to him by word of mouth for his knowledge and assistance. Besides the traveler from Kentucky who provided Edmund with a thoroughbred stallion, another visitor arrived who, through his reporting and writing skills, would further the name and fame of the scout and interpreter Edmund Guerrier.

This was Fred S. Barde, the former writer and reporter from the *Kansas City Star* newspaper who had retired to live in Guthrie, the first capital of the new state. In 1910, Barde interviewed Guerrier under the brush arbor on his farm north of Geary. Barde found him to be still strong and well preserved at his age of seventy years, with deeply-lined features and thin grey shoulder-length hair. His eyes were strong, his memory intact.[7]

And soon, in his tepee, Edmund was told that his daughter-in-law Nellie was pregnant. Finally, his family would become complete with the birth of his first grandchild.[8]

Edmund Guerrier with George Bent's daughter, Julia Bent, right, and Cheyenne student Laura Standing Elk at Carlisle Indian School. *Courtesy Cumberland County Historical Society, Carlisle, PA.*

The Birth of Piavinnia

18

Julia Bent Guerrier quickly leaned to cradle the baby down to the waiting pad of clean cloths, then bent to cut the cord with her knife. In a glance, her eyes flew over the countenance of the new baby, her first grandchild.

It was a girl, very pretty, with strong and healthy lungs, Julia noticed as she listened to the wails of the newborn. Julia was pleased. She selected a Cheyenne birth name for her. Piavinnia. Pretty Wing.

In the soft light of the center fire, the tepee walls glowed, spreading a golden radiance over Julia's features and those of her daughter-in-law, Nellie Guerrier. The baby cried and whimpered as Julia cleaned her with soft toweling. Julia sent her daughter Annie to tell her brother William that he now had a baby girl. Annie glided silently from the open flap of the large tepee. William was waiting on the porch.

William Guerrier softly grunted his pleasure at this news. He was pleased to have a daughter, his first child. Wanting to see this noisy child for himself, he walked toward the tepee and entered. Piavinnia was still announcing herself to her family, promising to be a sturdy youngster. William called his father, Edmund Guerrier to leave his place on the porch steps and come see his first grandchild.

Edmund entered, the firelight catching the golden glints in his dark but slightly graying shoulder-length wavy hair, worn to the shoulders in the French style, unbraided. Edmund was short, barely five feet six inches. Half Cheyenne, he was fair of skin and good looking. He was proud at that moment. Proud to be married to his sweetheart, Julia Bent, daughter of William and Owl Woman. Proud to carry on the French line of Guerrier that he had inherited from his father, William Guerrier, and Cheyenne from his mother, Tah-tah-tois-neh.

William asked his father to honor his first child by naming her. Edmund did not have to think long about it. His choice was Anna, a treasured family name, the name of Edmund's daughter, William's sister.

Edmund looked around the tepee and saw the wooden ladder-like rack with hanging rawhide parfleches filled with their personal items moving gently in the soft breeze. His eyes traveled toward a few small buckskin bags, beaded by his wife, draped on the tepee poles. He noticed the bedding of his wife on the north curve of the tepee, and his own on the west side facing the opening flap on the east. Their thick sleeping pads were covered with hand-woven Navajo and Ute blankets. Seeing the Ute blankets made him remember his many trips to Ute country to visit with his friends, and their generosity with many beautiful gifts.[1] There was plenty of room in the tepee. The baby Anna's bedding was laid on the south tepee curve, by the fire.

It was a cool evening on that June 6, 1911, and a fire had been lit to boil water and to warm Nellie and the baby. The fire also provided light for the birthing. Nellie, her long black hair stretched out behind her, was resting. Her beautiful features lay in repose, a quiet time. She listened to the squeals of the baby nestled in her arms, who very quickly came to be called by a diminutive name, Ann.

Edmund chose to take his accustomed place in the family circle, sat down and folded his legs to lean against his brightly-dyed porcupine quillwork-decorated back rest and quietly watched the scene before him. Before long, the dancing firelight glancing off the faint curl of smoke drifting upward toward the smoke hole, the muffled sounds of the women arranging Piavinnia's layette, and the soothing sense of his heart's joy in welcoming his grandchild lulled him into a semi-dream state. As he looked at Ann, he thought of how this all happened, to the very beginning of his life's road toward this moment, so long ago.

But after Ann was born, the family had only a short while to become accustomed to the newborn, as Nellie became pregnant again. Charles Freeman Guerrier was born January 14, 1913.[2] Charles was an honored family name, that of his grandmother's uncle who was killed in Taos by an angry mob while he was the first governor of territorial New Mexico, and that of his grandmother's brother who proved his bravery and daring as a Cheyenne Dog Soldier in the Indian wars with the government.[3]

The first six years of Ann's life on her grandparents' farm were memorable for the freedom she and her younger brother Charles enjoyed. She played in the yards, in the fields, and in the house of her parents William and Nellie, but her true place was with her grandmother Julia in the tepee. In the Indian world, that was traditional. Grandparents reared their grandchildren. Julia disciplined Ann very gently, in the Indian way. The children were never spanked. She lived in the tepee with her grandparents, her half-sister Dorothy and her brother Charles.

There was another reason for living in tepees, as did three-fourths of Cheyenne-Arapaho families. Not only were they accustomed to the conical dwelling and the center fires, but they realized that their very lives may depend on it. Tuberculosis was rampant. It hit the Indian tribes particularly hard. Word flew from tepee to tepee that all should live in the open air and not shut themselves up in houses, as that was when people began to die. Edmund and his family followed this admonition.

Edmund and Julia had amassed many beautiful Indian goods. Besides the colorful Ute blankets given to Edmund as gifts when he traveled extensively among the Utes, there were trunks filled with pictures of the family as well as Indian and non-Indian notables, beaded cradles and traditional Cheyenne clothing.

Ann made her first trip to South Dakota with her mother, to Nellie's home on the Sioux reservation. Nellie took Ann there specifically to be christened at the Holy Rosary Mission. She was only two years old at the time, but remembers acting up while they waited in a train station. She was being uncontrollable, running up and down the benches, and Nellie was unable to catch her. But a station attendant dressed all in black looked directly at Ann and made his hat go up and down on his forehead, which terrified Ann so much that she ran to her mother's side and stayed there.

While in South Dakota, Nellie petitioned to have Ann enrolled on the Sioux tribal rolls. Therefore, Ann was officially Sioux, rather than Cheyenne. Her tribal allotment was in Sioux territory on the Pine Ridge reservation. It was poor land, and she sold it later in her life.

In Oklahoma, however, the family owned large tracts of land. Annie, Edmund, Julia, and William were awarded Cheyenne allotments contiguous to each other, three miles north and one-fourth mile east of the present town of Geary. In addition, the government awarded Edmund a six-hundred-acre spread in payment for his services as scout and interpreter prior to his marriage to Julia. That land was located in the sand hills north of El Reno, after crossing the bridge, first turn to the left.

Edmund's El Reno land was the site of many Indian burials. His and Julia's child, Rosa, who died following her return from France, was buried there.

Edmund had many friends among the Ute tribe, one of whom

was a small man named Yellow Nose, who had been captured by the Cheyenne and had continued to live with the tribe after its move to the reservation in Oklahoma. He lived a long life, and was buried in the Geary cemetery upon his death, near the granite monument to Edmund Guerrier. According to George Bent, Yellow Nose, "a little man not very tall," was the man who captured Custer's flag at the Battle of the Little Big Horn in 1876.[4]

On Edmund's farm, the children had burros and Shetland ponies for their use, along with saddles to ride them. The ornery ponies bit Ann's legs and gave the children trouble. At the age of three, Ann was knocked to the ground unconscious when the pony she was riding raced to the barn and drove her head into the upper half of the closed barn door.

Ann had other playmates besides her brother and half-sister. The yard and the road leading to the house were always filled with people camping. They came to camp when Edmund killed a beef, and some families stayed permanently. Ann and Charles often enjoyed visiting and sharing a meal with these campers and playing with their youngsters. Edmund put up a tent and banked it all around for the Sheridan family, a family without a man, who stayed for a long time. His kindness and generosity to those in need were well known in the tribe.

Annie Guerrier lived with her parents on Edmund's farm well into her spinsterhood. But she finally married Emory Hicks Ballou, following his gifts to the Guerrier family, and the pair built a house on Annie's land one-half mile south of Edmund's farm. "Hicks" and

Annie preferred being close to the family, however, and moved into the two-story log house on Edmund's property behind the tepee. Annie had a still-born baby, and died of uremic poisoning after the birth, December 12, 1914.[5]

Her niece Ann recalled that Annie Guerrier Ballou was a beautiful woman, with chestnut-colored hair that shone golden glints. Ann attended her burial, south of the quarter mile by a ravine. She was buried fully dressed, with all her possessions: Mexican dishes with lids, blankets and quilts, pots and pans, and wearing her jewelry. This was a traditional burial in every way.

Although Hicks moved from the Guerrier house, he came to visit often and took Ann and Charles for walks. Julia was stoical about the loss of her only living daughter. She grieved, but quietly within herself. She had a living son and two grandchildren with her, and she rejoiced in having them in her sight and in her prayers.

During these early years on his Geary farm, Edmund devised his own method of educating his grandchildren. His granddaughter Ann was outgoing, talkative, inquisitive, and quick of mind. He doted on her. He began teaching her to read with the many books and magazines he had, resulting in her knowledge of and interest in current events. She read to him, with comprehension, and learned spelling. She learned her multiplication tables, as well as short and long division. He taught her English as well as the Cheyenne language the family used at home, and how to count and make change so she could interpret and help the older Cheyenne who traded in Edmund's store. She loved to sing, her stentorian voice

A gathering at the Oklahoma State Fair in 1917. Julia Bent, with "x" underneath, is the daughter of Col. George Bent. The Chief behind Julia is Cheyenne.
Courtesy Archives & Manuscripts Division of the Oklahoma Historical Society.

having carried over from infancy.

Her name for Edmund was Nam Shim, or grandpa. But her name for Julia was Bi Naeko, or My Mother. Ann felt that to be true.

Julia made her melt-in-the-mouth biscuits, like cotton, and Edmund cooked, too. Their primary diet was boiled food mainly of rice, meat and potatoes, with very few vegetables as neither cared for them, supplemented with occasional venison when a deer ventured into the yard. Besides doing a little cooking, although the family had hired a black woman as a chef, her husband a foreman on the farm, Julia took care to school Ann in traditional Cheyenne ceremonies, a task she relished.

In 1917, the Cheyennes held a two-day dance near Watonga to celebrate the animals. Julia attended, and took Ann to the last dance of its kind ever held by the tribe. The Animal Dance attracted many tribesmen, who camped along the river, and was observed with prescribed ritualized behavior. Upon arrival, each person remained inside his tent awaiting the arrival of the holy man, a very old man with a staff in each hand, who was covered with animal skins and displayed animal horns on his head. He was flanked by two warriors. Each person in the tent gave the holy man a gift, then was allowed by him to stay outside the tent. Ann, an inquisitive six year old, asked Julia for permission to participate and was given a square of material to present to the holy man.

The next day, the people dressed in the skins of various animals, many with horns attached. The men, clad in buckskin leggings and shirts, were covered with skins, their caps adorned with the horns of buffalo, deer and antelope. The women in long dresses, were also covered with pelts, as were the children, some with horns attached. Then, the dance began.

As the people ran back and forth alongside the river, the holy man pointed his staff at an animal person, who staggered and bled from the mouth. Other animal people ran to support the wounded, until a second holy man came to him and performed a ceremony to stop the bleeding.

"In those days, there were men who could stop bleeding, as well as fix broken bones and other magical things. Now they are all gone," Ann said.[6]

Besides enjoying the many Cheyenne ceremonies, Julia loved to visit with her brother George and his family at Colony. Soon, however, she was to be hit with an unexpected blow, the death of her beloved brother. George Bent contracted influenza during the pandemic siege of 1917-1918, and died on May 19, 1918, at the age of seventy-five. When a friend came to tell Julia of his death and escort her to his home in Colony, Julia's grief came pouring out in sobs. She had not known he was ill, and was shocked with the news. Julia took Ann with her on the trip, as Ann was then age six.

George, because of his active participation in the Cheyenne-U. S. wars, fluency in Cheyenne and English, garrulous nature and longevity, was the Cheyenne most recruited by historians to tell his stories. Diligent with his replies to correspondence and to active interviews, he was heavily involved with author George Hyde, who eventually produced the book *Life of George Bent*, as well

William Bent. *Courtesy Archives & Manuscripts Division of the Oklahoma Historical Society.*

as with other writers. George died in debt, unfortunately, with no funds to pay for his funeral or to pay off the two mortgages on his homestead in Colony, very likely due to the expenses of his large family and his alcohol dependency.

George was Julia's oldest brother, and the only living Bent sibling she had. He was her anchor when she moved to the reservation to marry Edmund, and lived in a nearby town, and was available for frequent visits with his youngest sister. His death presented her with a great loss, and left her as the only remaining child of William Bent and Owl woman. She concentrated on her grandchildren for solace, and in time was able to adjust to life without George, with the help of her ceremonies.

Julia was heavily involved in Cheyenne rituals. She took her granddaughter to an Arapaho Sun Dance near Greenfield, Oklahoma. During that time of the tribe's activities, the young men were given the assignment of riding horseback to gather brush with which to cover the Sun Dance arbor. Each rider could select a young woman to ride behind him on the horse while he gathered the brush to tie into a pony drag, then return to the Sun Dance arena. Ann recalled the scene of one young man arriving, the horse dragging brush, the young woman behind him with a shawl draped across her head. She was struck by the beauty of the scene.

"Knock Co (grandmother), I can't wait to be big, too. I want to ride behind someone during the ceremony."

The onlookers laughed, amused by Ann's remark.[7]

But, Ann's peaceful young years on the Guerrier farm with her grandmother Julia were coming to an end soon. A major change was around the corner that would lead to a drastic alteration in her climate and would introduce her to her maternal relatives in the north.[8]

Guerrier Rancher at Pine Ridge

19

When Ann was seven years old, Edmund decided to move his family to South Dakota. She considers that move the worse mistake he ever made. He moved into the land of his daughter-in-law's relatives and tribe, a harsh land more bleak and bitter than the lush farm lands he owned on the Canadian River. In the family, only Nellie was Sioux. But, Nellie wanted to go home, and Edmund obliged her by keeping the entire family together.

Everything moved with them. Julia went first, taking the children by train. Edmund arrived shortly by train, bringing his cattle, horses, sheep and chickens with him. Nellie's Sioux relatives then joined hands to build the Guerriers a large two-story log house on Nellie's Sioux land allotment.

The house was built along the bank at the mouth of a canyon, beside a large ell-shaped hill with a road alongside. Downstairs were the dining room and kitchen, with a large room upstairs where the family slept. A trap door in the downstairs floor was used as a food saver and storage place, where one hundred pound sacks of flour and sugar were kept, as well as syrup and other things.

There was a root cellar out the back door where they stored potatoes and onions. William butchered, and built a smokehouse to cure the bacon and ham. A fenced garden grew cabbage, fruit and vegetables. To store these, they dug holes in the garden, lined them with straw and put the vegetables in there. William was always crazy about Oklahoma's sweet potatoes, and disappointed that they would not grow in South Dakota.

On trading days, the family loaded the wagon with excess potatoes, cabbage and vegetables, along with the meat William had butchered, and drove to the Holy Rosary Mission to trade their goods for other necessities. William rode his horse alongside Nellie driving the wagon. Families came to the Mission from the surrounding territory not only to trade, but to have their babies baptized, as Ann had been on an earlier trip.

When the annual cattle sale was held each year, the entire family accompanied Edmund and stayed several days until his business was completed.

Living on the Pine Ridge Sioux reservation could be a lonely life as it was isolated from centers of population, although the Guerrier family had only its own relatives living nearby for socialization and companionship. Realizing this, Edmund made an effort to take the family to Gordon, Nebraska, the nearest town of any size, to shop for a week and mix with others besides the family. He took a large tent in the wagon, and set it up outside the town while they stayed to enjoy some fun. But at home, Edmund knew that the children must learn responsibility.

Edmund called the children together one day and bade them sit quietly to listen to his message to them. Everyone in the family had to have a job, he admonished. He gave each of the children five horses, and the job of herding and tending to the cattle. If they are going to be little cowboy and cowgirl, he said, they must learn how to do the job and how to get up on their animals when no one is around to help them.

Quickly, they learned how it must be done: Tie the horse short up to the post on the other side of the fence, throw the blanket over him from your side of the fence, then the saddle that you cinch from your side by reaching through the fence, then climb the fence and get on the horse. This procedure afforded the children safety from being kicked. Their ponies were skittish and cantankerous, but they liked to run and so did Ann. She named her horse Blue Bell.

Edmund was proud of his black cattle, and kept his land fenced to contain them. He sold some, but always kept the blooded stock. The cattle man on the next ranch sometimes found that his cattle had broken through the fence onto Edmund's land. As it was the responsibility of Ann and Charles to herd the cattle, they also had to drive out the neighbor's herd.

Once a large mean bull from the neighbor's land invaded the Guerrier pasture. Ann got down off her horse and chased him, whipping him on the nose to make him move. When she whipped him on the nose, he snorted at her and bellowed. Every time he took a step, she whacked his nose and he backed up. Nellie screamed as she stepped out the back door and saw Ann whipping the bull. She looked so small and fragile against the enormity of the bull. William shouted too, alerting Edmund who rushed to the scene on horseback and whisked Ann onto his saddle to take her to safety. Don't punish Ann, he advised Nellie. She was only doing her job, the very job that he himself had given her.

Most of Nellie's large family lived nearby on their own allotments. Her father had four wives, who all lived together with him in a large long house. Her sister Susie had married a half-breed who owned an ice place where the family obtained its ice. Sister Lucie and her husband lived away from the rest of the family. Stella had married a Mexican man, and they built a home north of the hill the Guerrier family lived under. Nellie's four brothers were Sioux warriors and, by custom, had not married as they did not want to move away from their families to live with their wives' people.

The warriors were delighted with Ann and Charles upon meeting these two Oklahoma youngsters, as both children wore moccasins and boots in the Indian style and adopted Indian ways. Ann wore traditional clothing. She owned buckskin dresses as well as cloth dresses sewn with dentalium shells, and one cloth dress adorned with elk's teeth. The warriors placed the children on horses and adorned them with Indian eagle feather war bonnets.

One day, the four Sioux warrior brothers honored Ann with a special ceremony, just for her. Placing her on the ground, each warrior dressed in full regalia rode by her single file, touching her on the left shoulder with his lance from astride his horse. Ann was frightened by the display of their majesty and the size of each powerful horse as it rode by, but managed to stand her ground with certain aplomb.[1]

Their life in South Dakota was carefree and fun for the children. Although during the week they had to herd cattle, check the chickens and pigs and help in the smokehouse, on the weekends they were let loose and left to their own devices. That meant they were on their horses all day, running up and down arroyos and into swamps, as there were three allotments to roam: Nellie's and those of her two older children, Pearl and Dorothy. Sometimes they picked berries and put them into pouches they carried. In the winter, they were pulled in a sleigh over the snow.

Ann's memories of her life in South Dakota did not include her mother, as Julia and Edmund fed her, taught her, and cared for her in the traditional role for grandparents. Edmund's studies of pharmacy at St. Louis University led him to be concerned about his grandchildren's health and nutrition. From a certain kind of wood, he pulverized the charcoal and occasionally had the children have a bite of it with their meal. When he butchered, he lined up all the children around the opened cow, removed the gall bladder, then dipped a piece of the liver or entrails into the gall and made each child eat a piece. Bitter, but that was his was of providing vitamins for his grandchildren.

This idyllic slice of childhood for an Indian girl growing up on a South Dakota ranch, running free with her own ponies, would end soon, as Ann's life and that of her family would change drastically very shortly.

The Deaths of Edmund and Julia

20

Edmund's health had been failing during the span of World War I years. His heart was wearing out. He became unable to perform his usual ranching duties or to tend to his special breed of cattle. When the war ended in 1918, he wanted to go back to Oklahoma, fearing that he did not have much longer to live. Although half French, his Indian nature led him back to his homeland, his area of Oklahoma that he had called home since 1869. Indian people, to this day, make frequent trips to their ancestral and tribal homes, even though they may live great distances from them. He broached the subject to Julia.

Julia heard him say that he did not feel well enough to do the work on the ranch in South Dakota, and that he wanted to return to his own Cheyenne people in Oklahoma. She reminded him that Nellie was pregnant. It might not be safe for her health to begin packing their belongs and making the long trip at that time. Nellie might lose her baby. So, they decided to wait until after the birth of William and Nellie's third child, a daughter born in 1919 whom they named Rose.

On the journey back to Oklahoma, they did not bring the stock. Nellie reluctantly sold the horses, and swore she could hear them crying for days.[1] It was painful for Edmund and Julia to recognize that they were in straitened circumstances.

Back again in Oklahoma, Ann noticed that Edmund's land had been sold, and the soil plowed up. Edmund also sold his six hundred acres north of El Reno. But they still had grandmother Julia's land, as well as the allotment lands of her father William. The economy was poor, the cattle market depressed. Times were hard for the Guerrier family as Edmund approached eighty.[2]

After their return from South Dakota, Edmund and Julia lived with William and Nellie in a new house that William had built for his wife, a frame home on his property north of Geary. But it was not a happy time. Edmund was ill, and William and Nellie began to experience marital problems. William began to drink frequently, which caused Nellie much sadness and tears. Sometimes William lived alone away from the family, in another small house. Their children noticed the discord, which dampened their childhood spirits.[3]

Whatever the problem between William and Nellie, another even larger trauma loomed with the family. Edmund had been correct

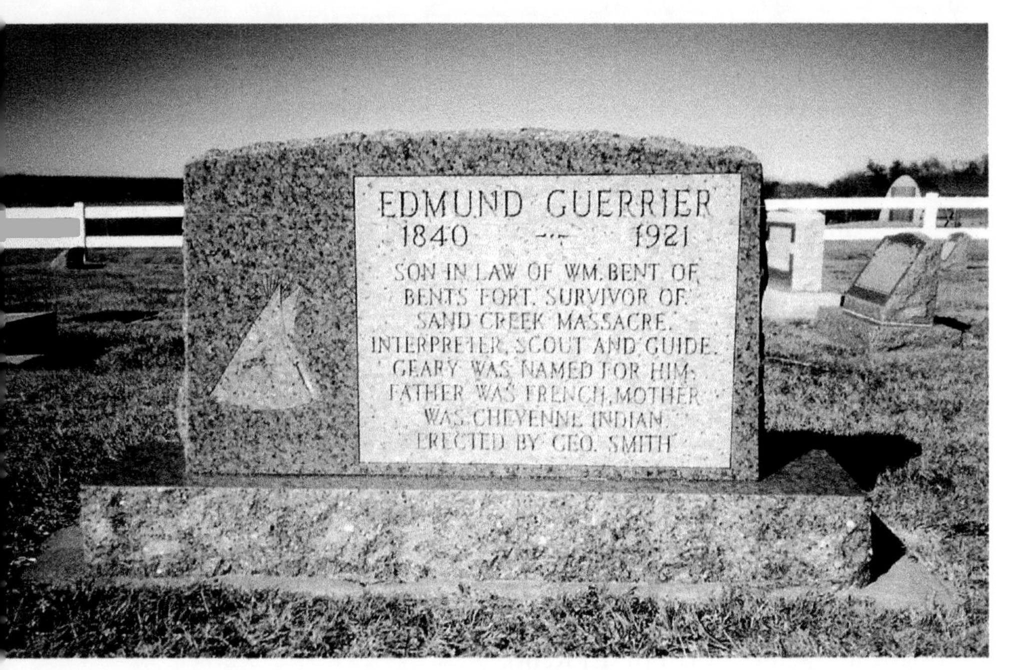

Gravestone of Edmund Guerrier in Geary, Oklahoma.
Erected by George Smith. *Courtesy Author's Collection.*

in his self-diagnosis. His life ended. Edmund Gasseau Chouteau Guerrier dropped dead one day in the doorway of the bedroom and could not be revived. His heart gave out on February 22, 1921. He died at the age of eighty-one, a long life for those times. He was buried in the cemetery at Geary, the town named for him. This vigorous, educated half-breed had forged a life of respect and dignity for himself as scout, interpreter, farmer/rancher, and trading post operator.

His gravesite in Geary was honored by a red granite market erected by George Smith of Geary, a friend of both Edmund and Henry Guerrier, a farmer who leased Henry Guerrier's wife's land. The marker, a tribute as well to the friend who paid the expense himself, reads:[4]

> Edmund Guerrier, 1840-1921. Son-in-law of Wm.
> Bent of Bent's Fort. Survivor of Sand Creek Massacre.
> Interpreter, scout and guide. Geary was named for
> him. Father was French, Mother was Cheyenne Indian.
> Erected by Geo. Smith

Julia was distraught over Edmund's death. She also fussed because her grandchildren were in school away from home. She wanted them to be with her. The family patriarch was gone, its loving mainstay. Immediately following his death, William and Nellie decided to place Ann and Charles at Concho School, a government boarding facility north of El Reno.

By that time, in 1921, the Darlington Cheyenne Agency and the Concho Arapaho Agency had been combined, with headquarters at Concho. The Darlington Agency, where Edmund Guerrier had operated a trading store in Oklahoma, had been closed. Ann was ten years old, had never been to school and had never been separated from her family. The separation was difficult for her, although she bore it with her innate determination and strength. Many Indian children sent to boarding schools, either forcefully or willingly through dint of circumstances, were removed great distances from their homes and native tribal lands. These children suffered the loss not only of their own tribal cultures and values, due to being absent sometimes for years. This hurt the grandparents and parents, and the children as well, because the children were separated from the ones who traditionally raised them. Ann, however, was more fortunate in that respect as her boarding school was within her own tribal and cultural area, and her extended family was only a few miles distant.

At Concho School, she was first placed in kindergarten. Not only had she not received formal schooling prior to that time, but she was sent to school alone with no adult to enroll her or tell the school of her accomplishments. The school staff groaned their displeasure at having to teach a ten-year-old who had never been in school, but not for long. They quickly discovered that she was endowed with a fine mind and had received tutoring in many areas. She was advanced to the sixth grade, quite a feat at her age, and a tribute to Edmund's pains in schooling her at home.[5]

In her military voice, Ann could shout "Left! Right!" when the students marched, and knew herself as a mouthy showoff.[6]

Ann stayed at Concho School for the next six years, with the goal of becoming a nurse. She made the highest score on the test required for nurse's training, but then the school rejected her application as she wasn't old enough and therefore had to wait another year to begin the initial course. She asked why, then, they let her take the test. No answer to that one.

When her daughter Ann was sent to school at Concho, Nellie Guerrier applied for a position as matron there, and was accepted. She was thereby able to keep an eye on her daughter and wield a heavy hand during Ann's teenage years. She occasionally locked her daughter in her dormitory room and away from potential boyfriends. She also hid Ann's mail, but Ann was alert to that and used her own tactic to circumvent it. She "stole" her mail, read it, and then replaced it back into Nellie's stash.

Although Ann's beloved grandfather Edmund Guerrier had died in 1921, there was another Guerrier almost identical to Edmund, although they had different mothers. That man was his half-brother Henry Guerrier, the half-Sioux brother who was adopted by the Cheyenne and later awarded a Cheyenne allotment. Surely the fine hand of Edmund can be seen in the care of Henry, his adoption into the tribe and his allotment located just north of Edmund's own land.

Henry had first married No-ah, but she died prior to allotments. He then by Indian custom married Bear Woman, the daughter of Stands in Timber and his wife Many Roads. During 25 years of marriage, Henry and Bear Woman produced a family of seven children.[7]

Edmund and Henry had the same size and facial features, but their natures were very different. While Edmund was smooth-tempered and easy going, Henry's temper was hot and quick to explode. One likely reason for this anger in his was that Henry's Sioux stepfather abused him unmercifully. He broke both of Henry's arms so badly that thereafter Henry was not able to raise his arms above his waist.

Toward the end of his life when Henry entered the Concho hospital, Ann was pursuing her nursing career at that hospital. Ann was with the widower Henry Guerrier when he died there on May 1, 1927 at the age of 73, "still with coal black hair," said Ann.[8]

At the same time, Ann's mother Nellie herself was ill as well. She had not been well for some time, and was suffering from cancer. When Nellie died at Concho hospital, her son William collapsed with grief and sobbed uncontrollably. Ann was shaken by seeing her father so distraught. "It killed me dead," she recalled, reliving the moment. After Nellie died, Ann took her brother Charles and young sister Rosa back with her to Concho, where they all boarded. The Concho staff allowed Ann, Charles and Rosa to gather every evening on the porch of the dormitory. Ann, during the day, went to school halftime and worked in the employee's dining room halftime.

Meanwhile, Julia Bent Guerrier was aging, and needed care. Nellie's sister Ellen and her husband Bill Bent were available to provide it. Ellen had married William Bent, son of George Bent. In other words, the cousins William Guerrier and William Bent had married sisters, Nellie and Ellen. Bill and Ellen had lived in South Dakota among her relatives, but decided to move to Oklahoma to be with Nellie before her death. While Nellie worked at Concho school, Ellen and Bill had provided care for grandma Julia.

Before Nellie died, she set into motion a plan she had devised for Ann's future by arranging a marriage for her, in the traditional Indian way. But Nellie didn't tell Ann any of this.

While Ann worked part-time in the employee's dining room, she had noticed a quiet Arapaho man who took his meals there. This was Oscar Pratt,[9] a Concho graduate who was at first its Athletic Director, going on later to repair and maintenance work on the grounds. Oscar was six years older than Ann, then age sixteen. She paid no attention to him, having no idea that he would very soon play a large role in her life.

One day after the noon meal, he approached her. He

Ghost Dance, Darlington, O.T., 1890. *Courtesy Archives & Manuscripts Division of the Oklahoma Historical Society.*

announced that she was to come with him, as they were to be married. Aghast, Ann recoiled and demanded to know why he would say such a thing to her. She knew nothing about marrying him. She hardly knew him, after all. Oscar explained that their marriage had been arranged by her mother, Nellie, and that he already had the marriage license. There was no question about it. She was to go with him and would marry him.

Realizing that she had no choice in the matter, Ann left with Oscar, and they were married in Watonga. She was sixteen, liked

school, and wanted to stay there to complete her studies in nursing. She knew nothing about being married. Although deeply romantic in her fancies, she was an innocent in the sexual ways of a man and a woman. After the wedding, she wept and could not stop crying. Oscar, taken aback, asked if she wanted to go back to Concho, because she was so unhappy about their marriage. Yes, she did. She asked him to take her back to school, and he obliged her request.

Three months later, Ann still worked in the cafeteria. The marriage had not been consummated. But that situation was to end one day at noon when the superintendent entered the room and made an announcement. He quieted the room and asked all to listen to him. Their student Ann Guerrier and Oscar Pratt were married, for over three months. Again, Ann was dumbstruck. She had told no one about the marriage, but now everyone would know. Now, they had to act. [10]

Right away, they moved into an apartment on the Concho grounds. Ann had married a stranger. Try as she might, she never became comfortable with him as her husband.[11]

In 1929 when Ann was eighteen, her grandmother Julia suffered a stroke, which left her mind confused and her speech rambling. Julia, the Cheyenne-speaking daughter of William Bent, the former ghost dancer of that group promulgated by Wovoka who believed that the dance would make the white people disappear and the buffalo reappear on the plains, was being battered by physical infirmities.

The following year, Ann and Oscar's first child was born, a daughter they named Dorothy. Still in their small apartment at Concho, Ann took care of her infant, and soon became pregnant again. She brought her grandmother Julia to their apartment to live with them for awhile, but the Concho superintendent soon came to her a visit. He admonished her, saying that she had no business trying to lift her grandmother. "That's what the hospital was for. There is a place in there for older people, and she needs that kind of care, so just put her in the hospital,"[12] he said.

Ann did so, and since their apartment was near the hospital, she visited Julia daily with baby Dorothy. But Julia's health continued to deteriorate, and she died on March 8, 1931 at the age of eighty-five. She was buried in the Geary cemetery near her husband Edmund.[13]

The two half-breed Cheyenne, Edmund Guerrier and Julia Bent, had merged a union of two of the early families who were instrumental in the settlement of Colorado during the 19th century, and in the taming of the flat lands of western Oklahoma into farming and ranching activities.

Edmund and Julia lived long lives for that period of American history, Edmund at age eighty-one and Julia to age eighty-five. Edmund founded a town that was named for him, Geary, Oklahoma. Together they established a family that was to make a contribution to their state as well as to their tribe.

Piavinnia On Her Own

21

When Ann Guerrier's grandmother Julia died in 1932, she grieved for her beloved Bi Naeko, her mother in every way except birth. But her life had to go on. She had her own problems now. At age twenty, she was in a marriage that was arranged for her without her knowledge and consent. She had a husband whom she felt she barely knew. And, she had a young daughter to rear. Within a few more years, she delivered two more daughters, Mickey and Marlene.

All was not well within the marriage. Oscar began to drink and leave their home after supper for an evening out on the town. Ann was the mother of three young toddlers, very young herself, and was bereft of emotional support, attention, and affection of her husband. This arranged marriage was not working out well, unlike that of her grandparents, Edmund and Julia.

Ann, by that time, was a handsome woman with a good figure on her five-foot tall tiny frame. She had high cheekbones on her light complexion, and a mane of brown hair glistening with the golden highlights inherited from her French grandfather. Her flashing brown eyes were slanted, another family trait.

Ann decided to separate from Oscar. His problems of drinking and disappearing were unbearable to her. She began to work at a local laundry, taking her youngest daughter to work with her daily. One day a car drove up to the laundry, chauffeured by a black man. Buffalo Robe opened the back car door and entered the laundry. Buffalo Robe was a medicine man who had married George Bent's widow after George's death in 1918. Buffalo Robe spoke to Ann, his "daughter," that he and his wife wanted to talk with Ann and would wait in the car for her lunch break. Over lunch, he chided Ann for working and leaving her children here and there. She was invited to live with Buffalo Robe and his family.

Relieved, Ann gratefully agreed, happy with the support offered from this branch of her family. With her three young daughters, she went to live with Buffalo Robe and Grandma Bent in Kingfisher that summer. Oscar soon found her, however, and enticed her back to El Reno with him, and she quickly became pregnant again. She had decided to reconcile with him, as she was tired of living in someone else's home and being a burden and responsibility to family and friends. But the reconciliation did not last, and she took the children and went to live with her half-sister, Pearl High Eagle, who lived in the country. She and Pearl raised chickens, and harvested beans and tomatoes, which they canned for the winter supply. Ann, lonely, had a borderline romance. As a Catholic, however, her interest was in preserving her family life with Oscar and rearing her children properly. Again, she went back to Oscar.

Although Oscar was becoming successful in his new position as an interior decorator with an El Reno firm, his bouts with alcohol recurred as usual and the old patterns of behavior began to repeat themselves. Ann developed a plan in her mind, then carried it out one evening when Oscar staggered through the front door drunk. She invited him to go into the bedroom and lie down to rest. When he quickly fell sound asleep, she tied his arms and legs to the four bedposts that that he could not move when he awakened. Then she telephoned Oscar's employer and reported his recent behavior with alcohol. The employer thought this over, then offered to send Oscar out of town to the firm's office in Enid, Oklahoma. Possibly the change of scenery from his usual drinking haunts might help Oscar change his habits. Ann immediately began washing and drying his clothes, while throwing a steak and potatoes on the stove to feed him.

Soon, Oscar awakened, demanding to know who had tied him to the bed. She announced that he was going to Enid. When he refused to go, she said he could just stay tied to the bed, then. He eventually agreed. What else could he do? The family stayed in Enid for two years, but the drinking pattern recurred, forcing Ann to bring herself and the children back to El Reno, where their son Charles was born.[1] Oscar followed her, impregnated her again, and then deserted the family. Ann was left without rent money. She was penniless.

What could she do to provide for her family, she wondered? Ann was ever resourceful, brave when she needed to be. She determined to take care of herself and her children. She had a plan.

In 1938, Oklahoma was in the midst of the same economic depression that affected the entire country. Jobs were scarce, especially for a pregnant woman with four small children.

Without money for rent, she decided to make her own home. She would fabricate and erect a tepee. Making a tepee is no small project. Ann, dauntless, was unafraid of tackling the unknown. After all, she was born and spent her early years in a tepee.

After obtaining some money for supplies at the Indian agency, she bought enough canvas to fulfill the required yardage, bought poles to cap the tepee top from the lumber yard, then had hooks installed in the poles to hook the canvas over the tepee top. The next purchase was twine. All the things she needed to make a tepee. She had all of the gear unloaded in the country, spread the canvas on the ground to measure it, and for the next two days made a large tepee with eight strips of canvas. A friend, George Hawkins, helped her erect a brush arbor, and his mother donated a tent to Ann's make-shift household. Then, she was ready to have her furniture and goods delivered to her new home. And she had plenty of it: sewing machine, three bedroom suites, Hoosier cabinet, stove, kitchen goods, dining room pieces, washer, and dryer.

Oscar was missing, but Ann determined against divorce. Her church disapproved and, after all, he was the father of her children. Eventually, Ann's Aunt Laura found her and was shocked at Ann's primitive living conditions. Aunt Laura bought a house in El Reno for herself and Ann's family, and invited Ann's father William Guerrier to join them. William divided the large garage in half and made himself a room there. The conditions were cramped, but at least it was a home with four walls and a roof for the family.

When Ann's baby Rick[2] was born, Oscar showed up at the hospital to see the new baby and said, "That's not my baby!"[3] Because Rick's skin tone was darker than that of the other children, Oscar refused to believe that Rick was his child. Ann sucked in her breath, emotionally devastated that Oscar would reject his own son. Of course he was! Reuniting briefly, Oscar stayed long enough to again impregnate Ann, this time with Harvey, and left.

Harvey Phillip Pratt was born April 13, 1941 and was named for the doctor who delivered him. When Ann saw that Harvey was born with a "veil" over his face, she knew immediately that he would develop special powers of "seeing" and sensitivity.

This see-saw marriage went on for a while, and saw Ann through one more pregnancy, with her youngest son Tony.[4] By then, Ann had had enough and refused to let Oscar back into the house and into her life. She now had seven children and knew she had to take care of them. She went to work in a flour mill, hard physical work for a small woman, but she was glad to have a job.

Taking the big step, Ann filed for divorce, but was only awarded separate maintenance for six months, which Oscar never paid. Needing an income desperately, she took a chance and went to Wichita, Kansas, hoping to find a good-paying job in the World War II aircraft industry there. She felt fortunate to be hired by Beechcraft to work in its Wichita plant. When that job ended, she worked in a Chinese restaurant. Oscar visited, in the mistaken belief that Ann would reunite with him again. This time the answer was "No!".

"It was really rough," Ann recalled. "The children and I slept in one rented room, when I did sleep at all. I had no clothes, no shoes, and needed glasses."[5]

Wichita was refuge and home for the next eight years. The three girls attended boarding school at Haskell Indian School in Lawrence in northeastern Kansas. The four boys stayed with Ann.

"We were very poor," Ann's son Charles later reminisced. "We lived in rooms over a penny arcade. I still remember the sounds of the penny arcade machines, clanking and beeping, especially at night as the arcade was open all night. Momma worked in a Chinese restaurant, where the customers assumed she was Chinese because of her Mongolian features and slant eyes. My brother Rick and I sold papers downtown at night—lots of papers. We played a trick on the older man who had a spot selling papers. Rick would come up close to the man's spot, and when he left his spot to chase Rick away, I would take his place selling lots of papers until he returned. Then, we would do it all over again. Momma said I made as much as a man, selling papers.

"One time my brother and I found an old tire somewhere. This was during wartime and tires were scarce, but we didn't know it. We were just Indian boys, with a plaything. We would roll the tire up and down the alley. One day, a man came along and said, 'Boys, this is a good tire. I'll give you five dollars for it.' So we sold it, and made some money."[6]

An ugly incident occurred during the World War II years while Ann was on a train filled with soldiers as she travelled between Wichita and El Reno. Her oriental features caught the eye of a drunken uniformed soldier, a fellow passenger on the train.

"Oh," he yelled, "Here's one of those traitors! A Jap spy!"

Ann hit him between the eyes with her wooden-handled carpetbag.[7] She was rightfully incensed. As a group, Indians are highly patriotic people. Their costumes are covered with ornately beaded American flags. Their young men go to war in great numbers, and are honored by their friends and relatives with special dances. Veteran societies are well supplied with devoted members. The United States government in 2001 gave tribute in special ceremonies to the "code talkers" of World War II, that group of soldiers encompassing among other tribes the Cheyenne, Navajo, and Choctaw, who were able to converse with one another and pass information along in their native tongues – "codes" the enemy were never able to crack.

While Ann was able to keep her eyes on her sons who lived with her in Wichita, she was saddened that all was not well with her daughters who attended Haskell Indian School. Dorothy was fourteen, and out of control. As time went on, Dorothy's behavioral problems were to worsen.

Another problem was brewing within the family, however, this time a medical one. Both Oscar Pratt and their daughter Mickey were diagnosed with tuberculosis and were hospitalized at the sanatorium in Shawnee, Oklahoma. Ann moved to Shawnee and worked in a laundry there in order to be near them. The entire family was forced to have chest x-rays every three months because of their exposure to the bacillus. But the treatment was too late for Oscar, who died there. Mickey fortunately recovered.

While in Shawnee to be near her sick family, however, Ann's life took a happier tone for a while. She found the love of her life while she worked at the laundry, another employee named Eddie Parker. They talked, flirted, and had lunch together. Eddie was a charming man. Very affectionate, a good lover, and highly attentive to Ann, who married him three months after Mr. Pratt died. "He was a brave man to marry a woman with seven children," said Ann.

Soon, however, Eddie destroyed the marriage when he had an affair. He begged to come back, but Ann refused. There were some things beyond toleration, and infidelity was one.

Eddie continued to call Ann for a year in an effort at reconciliation, but she would have none of it. Finally, she filed for divorce, a difficult decision for a Catholic woman. Although she had divorced Oscar Pratt, he had since died so in the eyes of the church she was free to remarry.

Once when Eddie called, his speech was slurred and she

thought he possibly had been drinking, but Eddie had had a stroke. Before he died, his relatives called and asked Ann and Charles to visit him, as Eddie was asking to see them. Ann refused, but Charles went to see him. Ann loved Eddie, but she was unable to forgive him for his egregious breach of faith.

A beneficial change was developing in Ann's life, however; one that would lead to the best years of her adulthood.

Someone is Protecting You

22

Ann moved to Oklahoma City, where she participated frequently in Indian dances and meetings. A man named Martin Shadlow came to her house one day and proposed marriage. She didn't know him well, this tall ugly Otoe-Missouria Indian from northern Oklahoma, but she had seen him at powwows. He was much older than Ann. In order to pave the way for his question to Ann, he took her sons for a meal in Anadarko and gave each one money, in the Indian way, before asking their permission to propose to their mother. Her answer?

"I'll have to think about it."[1]

They courted. He brought her gifts, and groceries for the family hoping to be accepted as a member of the household. Finally, they were married by a Methodist minister in Arkansas while on a trip. Martin worked in an Oklahoma City lumber yard, while Ann worked at a cleaners making alterations. She was a master dressmaker and seamstress. She and Martin dined out, attended baseball games and boxing matches, and had a good life together. They attended Indian dances near and far, where Ann competed both in the buckskin and shawl categories, winning frequently, while Martin rested on the sidelines.

Martin had been married previously, but had no children. This was to change suddenly when Laketa Pratt, the Kickapoo/Pottawatomi wife of Ann's son Charles, died unexpectedly, leaving two small children. Charles was devastated with her loss. He could not take care of the children and work at the same time. He went to his mother for advice.

Ann, in the traditional role as grandmother, immediately offered to take the children and rear them. She discussed her plan with her husband Martin, and he agreed that he would become the grandfather figure in their lives. He became a good role model.

Ann and Martin reared the children to adulthood. They were Laketa Pratt, named for her mother, and Gayther Pratt, known as Chapa (beaver, in the Cheyenne language). Ann felt fortunate that she had a good steady man who helped provide for the family, who gave her gifts and allowed her the freedom to act as she wished. Ann made costumes for Laketa and Chapa and reared them in the ways of the powwow, instilling traditional and family values.

When Laketa was four or five years old, her great-grandfather William Guerrier came to live with them during his final illness. The two of them shared a bedroom with two twin beds. In his bed or in a lounge chair, William would pound out a peyote rhythm on the

Chapa Pratt and wife Marlene in El Reno, Oklahoma.
Courtesy Author's Collection.

wooden floor with his cane as he sang the ritual songs of the Native American religion, emphasizing the deeply traditional training he experienced in his parental home, primarily from his mother Julia. William's condition worsened, and he was placed in a nursing home in Oklahoma City prior to his death at the age of 86, with burial in the Geary cemetery near his parents, Edmund and Julia.[2]

Laketa Pratt at graduation from high school in 1980.
Courtesy Laketa Pratt Collection.

As Ann rallied from the loss of her father, she and Martin continued for many years on the path of their quiet guidance of her grandchildren. Martin, however, weakened and began having heart problems. A pacemaker was installed, but his health continued to deteriorate.

Ann's grandchildren Laketa and Chapa continued their participation in tribal and pan-Indian activities. Laketa received the honor of being chosen as Arapaho Princess in 1978 at age seventeen. In that capacity, she was attending an Indian Hobbyist powwow in Terre Haute, Indiana when the police came to inform her that her grandfather Martin Shadlow had died, and that her father Charles, having an art show in Chicago at the same time, would drive to Terre Haute to pick her up for the drive to Oklahoma for Martin's funeral at the Otoe-Missouria cemetery in Red Rock.

Following Martin's funeral, Laketa was Arapaho Princess for the annual American Indian Exposition in Anadarko that year, as well as Powwow Princess for the Labor Day powwow at Colony, Oklahoma, the home of her great-great-uncle George Bent.[3]

Laketa Pratt, Arapaho Tribal Princess, 1978.
Courtesy Laketa Pratt Collection.

Indians have very strong beliefs in the life of the inner spirit and its importance in daily living. One story told by Ann Shadlow brilliantly illustrates these feelings:

"Following my year of mourning after Mr. Shadlow's death, I was Head Dancer at Native American Center. My whole family was there. Charles, Harvey, Laketa, Chapa, Mickey, Marlene, and other grandchildren and great-grandchildren. We took up one whole side of the hall. When I made my give-away, I had a very pretty white shawl, which I placed on the drum of the singers, and the singers had a raffle among the people for that shawl. It brought $84. We had seen there a big, tall and lanky man in a black slouch hat pulled down over his eyes. He stood watching everything going on. When the raffle was over, he bought the shawl from the person who won it, and came over to me and said, "Stand up, grandmother. This is too beautiful a shawl, and it belongs to you, and I want you to have it back. I am giving it to you."

"I didn't know what to say. The next day, he showed up at the house and said he wanted to spend the night with us. I made him welcome in the Indian way, and said he could spend the night. We made him a bed in the back bedroom. The next day, he took Chapa away from the house for a talk. 'I want your sister,' he said. 'I want her to come and cook for me.' 'I don't know,' Chapa replied. 'I'll have to ask my sister and my grandmother.'"

"At that time, Laketa was eighteen and Chapa was seventeen. When Chapa told me what this man had said, I talked with him and Laketa. 'Don't panic,' I said. 'Just tell this man that Laketa is a young girl, and she does not want this at this time. Just be calm.'

"He came back again later that day, and said he wanted to spend the night with us again. So, he stayed the night. The next morning, he spoke to me. 'I want your granddaughter to make breakfast for me. No anyone else. Just her.' So I went in and woke Laketa and told her, 'Get up and go make breakfast. Just be quiet and calm.'

"Laketa made bacon and eggs for the whole family. Afterwards, he asked Laketa and Chapa to go with him, as there was something he wanted to show us. Laketa said, 'Not by myself, I won't go.' So she and Chapa went with him to his hotel room. Laketa was terrified. He asked them to help him to carry out to the car three large boxes, which they then brought to the house. We had heard that there was a feather man in town, and this was the man. He was Cherokee. He went up into Canada and trapped eagles and brought them back into the country, and he sold and traded eagle feathers. He had 120 whole eagles. In other of the boxes, he had the feathers, which he made right then into an eagle feather fan for Laketa, which she still carries. He made an eagle feather bustle for Chapa by inserting the feathers into other feathers and wrapping them, which I had never seen. Chapa is still wearing it, too, with the deer antlers in his bustle.

"The last night he spent the night, he was in the bedroom with the door closed, and we heard the awfullest racket you ever heard. Yelling and whooping, scuffling, and the sound of blows in the middle of the night. We listened, but no one went to see about

Laketa Pratt, Ann Shadlow, and Choppa Pratt. *Courtesy Laketa Pratt Collection.*

him or find out what was happening. The next morning, he spoke to me.

"You have someone in this house who is protecting you," said the black-hatted stranger.

"Yes. Mr. Shadlow is gone, but he is very protective of his family. The feather man's knuckles were scraped, raw and bleeding, where he had been in a fight with Mr. Shadlow. Sometimes we see that man at various powwows, but he has never come around again."

As Ann mourned for her husband, so did Martin Shadlow protect her and her family. With this peace of mind, Piavinnia began to stretch her wings. Her grandmother named her "Pretty Wing" at birth, not for naught, as Ann in her older years determined to live out the name her grandmother Julia gave her. She had a destiny to fulfill.

The Best Indian I Can Be

23

Ann reached a turning point. She began the most important period of her life at the age of sixty-five, when she retired from her position in the alterations department in 1976. She had a goal in mind, and it had nothing to do with her age. Never mind sixty-five. She was healthy and active, filled with energy and determination. She made a conscious and deliberate decision. She would not allow her retirement years to merely drift along without direction. She wanted to make a difference, to become the best Indian she could possibly be within her environment. Even though she had a small amount of white heritage in her background, she felt that she was 100% Indian. She set out to prove it.

Her illustrious career in the Indian world began to blossom, and the awards and honors that followed proved what a unique person she was. She did not have to worry about her sons, as they prospered in their fields, and her children supported her efforts. Her son Tony was a detective with the Midwest City Police Department. Rick was a house painter. Harvey filled various positions with the Oklahoma State Bureau of Investigation, eventually becoming Assistant Director, and was beginning a second career as an Indian artist in the traditional style. Charles, a welder in his early years, had begun to experiment with crafting Indian art objects in metal, and at this time had become very successful as an Indian artist. In 1975, he received the Grand Award for his "Blue Corn People" at the 30th Annual American Indian Artists Exhibition presented by the Philbrook Museum of Art in Tulsa.

In her hometown of Oklahoma City, she began to provide services for various community organizations, and was soon active as an organizer of the Intertribal Senior Citizens group. There she coordinated powwows, food sales and craft programs on a twice-weekly basis and for special holiday events. This program prospered and was eventually taken over by the local Salvation Army. And that was just a beginning for her career in the Indian world.

With her children in careers of their own and only her high school age grandchildren to look after, Ann was free in her retirement years to do as she wanted, at long last. She determined that she would emphasize her Indian heritage and introduce her grandchildren to the world of their Indian culture even more intensely. The genes of her Guerrier and Bent ancestors kicked in, urging her to participate more fully in the important affairs of her surroundings, as they had done. She began her pilgrimage toward

Ann Shadlow being kissed by George Tahbone at a dance in Grand Prairie, Texas. *Courtesy Laketa Pratt Collection.*

fulfilling her Indian role in society by a decision to participate in the most Indian of all festivals in Oklahoma at that time, that of the Indian Exposition held annually in Anadarko. In order to become better known, she walked in the downtown parade and entered the evening dance contests, fully outfitted in her summer dance costumes of satin in bright colors. She camped on the grounds of the fair with her grandchildren, joining the crowded circles of tents and tepees for the week of the exposition. She became a familiar figure at this yearly event.

In the 1970s, the Oklahoma City Native American Center began a series of outreach craft programs for its Indian population, and tapped Ann to teach a class in shawl-tying. This was a traditional and ongoing Indian woman's activity, needed to make the many beautiful shawls worn in dances and presented as give-away gifts.[1]

The author enrolled in that shawl-tying class and, impressed Ann's poise, bearing, and knowledge of Indian lore and arts and crafts, approached her to fill a position with the Indian Education program in the Oklahoma City Public Schools. Ann accepted, and became the Indian Cultural Heritage Instructor in the Title IV program for the 1976-77 school year. She dressed daily in her traditional attire, and visited each school in the program, telling stories about her costume, relating various Indian myths, and teaching the round dance and buffalo dance in full school assemblies.[2]

Still a strikingly handsome woman, she presented a vivid picture in her buckskin fringed and beaded dress, wide dance belt, and belt trailer adorned with German silver conchos, beaded

Ann Shadlow, left, and Jo Ann Kessel in buckskin dress in Wilburton, Oklahoma, 1977. *Courtesy Author's Collection*

Ann Shadlow in beaded buckskin with feather fan, shawl, and beaded bag. *Courtesy Laketa Pratt Collection.*

Cheyenne moccasins, and the Sioux beaded leggings made by her grandmother. She had a rapprochement with children, who responded to her warmth. When that program ended, she continued to be called by the public schools to present her program, and taught a class in beadwork for students and their parents.

Again, the Oklahoma City Native American Center welcomed her with a special position, that of Cultural Coordinator for preschool to high school age children. The many activities she led kept her fully occupied, as she taught arts and crafts, sewed the costumes for the preschoolers, and directed a weekly disco program.[3] She made her programs interesting and educational, with an eye toward cultivating their inner strengths and inculcating pride in heritage, and the children responded warmly. She became known as "Grandma" to the Indian children of Oklahoma City, who greeted her with hugs when seeing her at powwows in the area, as she never gave up her dancing, a weekly event. Her vitality allowed her to attend a dance in Albuquerque, drive home for a day of rest, then leave again for another dance in Texas. At that stage of her life, she seemed indefatigable.

Her son Charles Pratt was honored in 1978 with a one-man show of his metal sculptures at the Southern Plains Indian Museum in Anadarko. Ann was naturally proud of him, but he was equally proud of his mother for her own state-wide honor received the same year as his.

Ann's name became known in the area because of her various activities as a cultural coordinator, community planner, dancer,

A Charles Pratt sculpture of a wolf. *Courtesy Author's Collection.*

Charles Pratt. *Courtesy Laketa Pratt Collection.*

and provider of programs for children. She was a natural for the next step in her post-retirement career, that of being selected in 1978 by the State of Oklahoma as Outstanding Senior Citizen. She proudly accepted her award on the stage of Oklahoma City's Myriad Convention Center from the hands of Oklahoma's then governor, David L. Boren.

For the next few years when traveling to other cities for powwows, she often entered the dance contests sponsored by the event, and frequently won. She won in all categories of dress, that of buckskin, shell dress, and cloth dress.[4] The 1986 Guthrie Indian Days Powwow saw her riding on the parade float, acting as Head Lady Dancer, and winning first place in her shell dress at the dance contest. She was very serious in pursuing her efforts at becoming well known in the Indian world, and took every opportunity to make herself known in a positive role.

But, that was only a beginning. Her highest honor arrived like a streak of lightning, and took her breath away. She was selected as "Indian of the Year," a national intertribal award made once annually by the American Indian Heritage Association, based in Washington, D. C. She flew to Washington in November 1986 to receive the award for the year 1987, and to attend the banquet and festivities in her honor. This national pan-Indian award was a special tribute, and brought many accolades and honors from other organizations and individuals. Wearing her special white fringed shawl with the words "Indian of the Year" embroidered in red, she attended a Catholic mass at the Santuario, an 18th century church in Chimayo,

New Mexico. The Spanish-speaking priest introduced her to the congregation, where she was greeted with many congratulations.

Another prestigious honor was being chosen by the Oklahoma Hospitality Club for its 21st annual "Ladies in the News" Charity Fashion Show given at the Marriott Hotel on March 13, 1987 in Oklahoma City. At the luncheon and style show, Ann appeared in three different styles of Indian dress: her aunt's seventy-five year old buckskin dress beaded in the Cheyenne style; a navy blue trade cloth dress adorned with elk's teeth; and a red wool dress covered with cowry shells. Her sense of style was as unique and dramatic as she was herself. In ordinary dress, she mixed black or red with white to complement her hair and skin tones, and often donned a red torero straw hat, the flat brim dancing with red ball fringe. This eye for fashion and love of a bon vivant appearance may have descended from her grandfather Edmund, himself a natty dresser in his time.

In what was becoming an outstanding year for her, the Oklahoma Indian Women's Federation saluted her with the statewide title of "Indian Woman of the Year."

Ann gained additional fame as a storyteller, as did her distant relatives, the artist Charles Marion Russell and his mother. Her vivacious personality and extroverted manner were put to good use when she told Indian tales, that of the trickster Iktomi and various animal stories. During the Red Earth Festival that was held annually in downtown Oklahoma City, a canvas tepee was erected for her, where she entertained adults and children who entered. True to her heritage, she ably used not only her colorful costume, but voice

Ann Guerrier Shadlow, with Tim Ramsey, was named Indian Woman of the Year by the Oklahoma Federation of Indian Women in May, 1987 at Lincoln Plaza Forum, in Oklahoma City. *Courtesy Laketa Pratt Collection.*

inflection and physical gestures to emphasize her stories. Indians reared in the traditional society of her youth learned Indian sign language, and Ann was no exception. This quiet communication filled the need to be understood among the many tribes that spoke different languages. Expressing herself with gestures, therefore was inherent in Ann's communication with others, only adding to the overall drama of her presentation.

She was called to present her stories during the annual Story Teller Festival in Oklahoma City, then again at a similar festival in Arlington, Texas.

By this time, Ann's son Charles had moved his home and

Ann Shadlow, 1987 Indian Woman of the Year, visiting the office of Sen. Don Nickles in Washington, D.C. *Courtesy Laketa Pratt Collection.*

studio to Santa Fe, where he bought an adobe home on three acres on the Upper Old Santa Fe Trail. In doing so, Charles went back to his family's roots, those Bent and Guerrier roots so active on the Santa Fe Trail one hundred seventy years ago. Charles had become known for his exquisite life-size ears of corn, each kernel individually crafted in turquoise, coral and other stones to emulate varicolored Indian corn.

Charles' demeanor was the opposite of his mother. Quiet and reticent, he displayed the stereotypical stoicism that had long been the cultural white view of the American Indian. During his many travels to Indian art shows across the country, he often stopped in

Oklahoma City to visit his mother. His habit was to walk into the living room, find a chair, and sit silently. Ann found this foreign to her garrulous habits. Once, she spoke to him in remonstrance.

"Son, when you come in, you just sit there and say nothing. Why don't you talk to me?" said Ann.

With eyes twinkling, Charles said, "I don't have to. You do all the talking!"

One day, Charles told his mother of a dream he had, which involved her and expressed his concern for her welfare.

"Mama, I had a dream," Charles told Ann. "In my dream I was told that I would dance the Sun Dance eight times. So, this year I will begin. I will dedicate the Sun Dance to you, praying for your good health."

Dreams are an important part of the inner lives of Indians and are seen as omens or as directions for one's life. They are always recognized and heeded, as in earlier years the Vision Quest fulfilled that role. Thus, Charles set out on his journey of atonement and prayer by dancing in his first Sun Dance with the Northern Cheyenne in Montana. He would dance seven more times. Berthrong wrote that the Sun Dance offered a time for "supplication for supernatural aid … and favors from powerful spirits."[5] It also represented a rebirth of life and a season of growth.

Ann and her family accompanied Charles for his Sun Dance in Montana, but upon her return soon found that she was sought again. Her determination to fully express her place in the Indian world continued to reap benefits.

Being the remarkable woman that she was, she was chosen in 1987 to represent "The Voice of North America." By her own accounts she knew she was a mouthy Indian, rather rare in the Indian world, yet to be chosen as the voice to represent all of North America was a special tribute. She spoke during the World Day of Prayer at Oklahoma City University in March. The same month, she was special guest of honor at the Denver Powwow, where she also participated in the dancing.

A good storyteller has a way of drawing listeners to him like a magnet, and Ann's stories had that quality. They were so dramatic that the Indian Center of the Kirkpatrick Museum in Oklahoma City presented a children's play based on one of her Indian history tales. She was teaching the good values of pride in self and heritage. Society needs people who live for spiritual values and are willing to share those beliefs, and Ann gave willingly of her time, money and enthusiasm toward that goal. She had lived her life graciously until the age of sixty-five, when her life's experiences and beliefs all merged into her drive to pass on her values to others.

She was honored with Appreciation Awards by the Oklahoma City Powwow Club as a lifetime member and founder, and by the Native American Center. She dressed in Indian costume and appeared on television for the Indian Education program of the Oklahoma City Public Schools. This program aired on Channel 43 on February 16, 1987, a Public Broadcast System for the state, in Oklahoma City.

She was recognized as Indian Mother of the Year on the stage of the Myriad Convention Center during an event sponsored by the Bahai faith, for the brotherhood of man.

In 1993, she spent a weekend camped in her tent on the grounds of the Cheyenne-Arapaho Agency in Concho, north of El Reno, where she was honored with selection of "Indian of the Year" by the Oklahoma Indian Nation Powwow Club. Here she was, being feted at the site of her school days, and the recipient of an award from her tribe, all of it occurring in the environs of her grandfather Edmund Guerrier's successful trading post at the agency one hundred years before. The progression of her Guerrier and Bent ancestry was not lost on Ann, who was fulfilling her grandfather's teaching role by passing on her life's pride and values to the next generation.

"He was the kindest man I ever knew," said Ann of her grandfather Edmund Guerrier. "He was always gentle and even-tempered with everyone."

For this quality and his quiet and willing service as scout and interpreter, his education and his intelligence, Edmund was known by all. When young man Edmund Guerrier became "Old Man Guerie" on his allotment north of Geary, his compassionate ear and thoughtful services continued to be sought. In her own way and time, his granddaughter carried the torch of service to her people.

She and her grandchildren were found camping with their tents and cooking equipment again, and for the next two years, at the northeast Oklahoma City grounds of the Oklahoma City Powwow Club. Ann was a lifetime and charter member of this organization, and graciously accepted her selection as special Honoree for the annual weekend dance.

"Being honored costs money," Ann said. "One must have a give-away, and it takes a lot of effort to gather material and fringe for shawls, and to make them. Then, there are other gifts given, such as money and Pendleton blankets. It can become expensive."

Yet, she did it willingly.

A special invitation arrived by telephone, a call to Ann from the Bent's Fort United States Park Ranger Craig Moore asking her to participate in a Bent Reunion weekend at the fort. She quickly accepted and was escorted to the fort by Moore. Ann was provided a tepee just outside the fort's main gate and asked to present her program in costume, and to talk with the fort's visitors. There she was, granddaughter of Julia Bent (on whose awarded land the fort was built), great-granddaughter of William Bent and Owl Woman, at the site of the historic original fort, dressed in buckskin and beadwork, in a tepee resembling the 1840s lodge of her ancestors. Certainly a memorable time for her.

The current fort is an exact replica of the original, with every room and amenity carefully reproduced: trade room filled with goods; buffalo robe press in the courtyard; executive dining room for owners and guests with blue and white Canton ware dressing the long table; carpentry room with tools of the period; well room for drinking water; Susan Magoffin's furnished bedroom; the large corral. The task of reconstruction was simplified due to the many descriptions and drawings made by Lt. Abert and other visitors to the fort.

Nor had the countryside around the fort changed. It is flat, except for the height of the cottonwood trees bordering the Arkansas River south of the fort. Across the river south are plains to the horizon, slightly humped with rolling hills between hidden gulches and stone outcroppings. Nutritious short grass grows on rock shale soil, providing beneficial pasturage for cattle, the main industry in this sparsely settled part of southeastern Colorado. Antelope are seen on this desert of the high plains.

Because Ann grew up within an Indian family of some means, surrounded by her relatives who practiced traditional Indian values in childrearing, she did not experience racial discrimination.[6] She did not attend school until she was ten years old, and thereby avoided incidents she might have encountered at school. When she finally attended school, it was in an Indian school with her family nearby for support and protection. She was therefore able to fulfill her role as Indian mother, wife and grandmother within her own culture, thereby deriving strength from her traditions. She passed these traditions on to her children and grandchildren with great care.

Her son Harvey Pratt, named for the physician who deliver him, meanwhile had retired from the Oklahoma State Bureau of Investigation as Assistant Director. But not for long. The OSBI soon brought Harvey back to work for them in order to take advantage of his artistic skills. Harvey became the forensic artist who sketched wanted perpetrators from the descriptions of the victims, as well as drawing and sculpting in clay possible likenesses of deceased persons

An ink on paper drawing of Anna Guerrier by Harvey Pratt. *Courtesy Laketa Pratt Collection.*

Painting by Harvey Pratt. *Courtesy Author's Collection.*

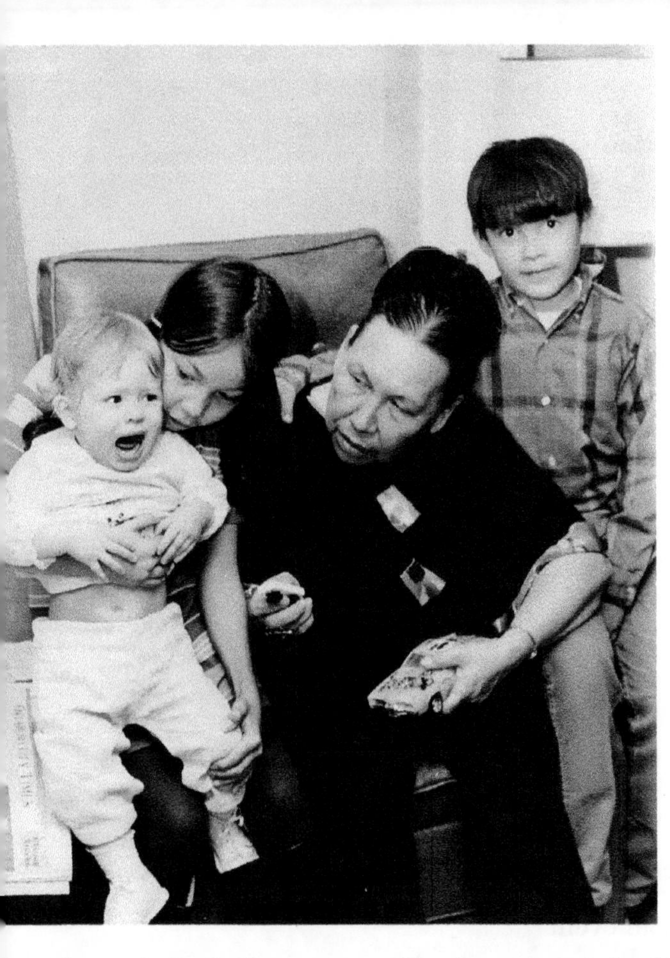

From left, Laketa Pratt holding Harvey Pratt's daughter Tracy, Ann Guerrier Pratt Shadlow, and Chapa Pratt, ca. 1972. *Courtesy Laketa Pratt Collection.*

from their skull contours. He also painted the history of the agency of a main wall. Ann followed Harvey's career with interest, even as she continued to reap honors herself.

The local evening news featured Ann in a program entitled "The Wisdom Keepers."[7] She told the story of rearing her young brother and sister when their mother died, and of her arranged marriage. Her desire, she said, was to pass on the teachings of her Indian heritage, most importantly to love our children and to put them first in our lives, rearing them with patience. And that, of course, was exactly how she was reared by her grandparents.

She next was sought to participate in a commercial cassette

recording of lullabies from various cultures, entitle "Lullabies of the World."[8] Her song represented the only American Indian voice, and it thrilled her that she could pass on the Suhtai lullaby that her grandmother Julia Bent Guerrier sang to her when she was a child living with her beloved grandparents in their tepee.

Ann Shadlow in a ceremonial buckskin robe painted and beaded by her son Charles Pratt. *Courtesy Laketa Pratt Collection.*

Her family, proud of their mother, sponsored a powwow for her at the south Pennsylvania Armory in April 1996, an event where all her friends could come and honor her.

In 1989, the town of Geary honored Ann by naming her as Parade Marshall in its centennial celebration of the founding of the town. For Ann it dredged up sweet and sad remembrances of her grandparents and of her happy childhood on their ranch.

Ann's youngest son, Tony Pratt, retired from the Midwest City Police Department. But Tony was not ready to give up his career so soon. He then accepted a position as Chief of Security for the Cheyenne-Arapaho tribes at its headquarters at Concho, near El Reno.

While Tony was on assignment in El Paso, something

Ann Shadlow and Jo Ann Kessel at Rancho De Chimayo, New Mexico. August, 1989. *Courtesy Author's Collection.*

Ann Shadlow in a beaded buckskin dress. *Courtesy Author's Collection.*

Ann Shadlow and great granddaughter Tashina Pratt.
Courtesy Author's Collection.

happened at home in Oklahoma that was to bring great joy and honor to the family. When he returned, he learned that his brother, Harvey Pratt, was chosen by the Cheyenne to become a chief of the tribe.

"Tony was just sick. He turned green," said Ann.

In spite of feeling a touch of jealousy, Tony joined the rest of the family in a great sense of pride at this prestigious honor bestowed on his brother. But, Tony was ill, and met his death from cancer on May 11, 1997. He was buried with full police attendance from his Midwest City force, Concho representatives, and police from adjacent areas. Following the funeral, the family provided a large meal and give-away.

Ann for the first time was experiencing the loss of one of her children. She was deeply wounded.

"Waah. Waah. My boy. I miss him so much."

"No," she replied when asked to be Head Dancer at a powwow. "I cannot. I am in mourning for my son for the next year.

Ann Shadlow, right, holding Tashina Pratt's hand at the Oklahoma City Pow Wow at the Indian Hills Dance Grounds. *Courtesy Laketa Pratt Collection.*

Laketa Pratt with Grand Award beaded doll at Red Earth Celebration Art Show, Oklahoma City, 2013. *Courtesy Laketa Pratt Collection.*

Even then, I cannot and will not dance until I have been smoked and blessed by a holy man."

An Indian reared in the traditional ways of the tribe will know its values, its dances and their meanings, its customary beliefs of the world it inhabits and its spiritual connection to the environment and to a higher consciousness. That person honors an Indian shaman and may have occasion to consult a holy person for health, psychological or family problems. Ann Guerrier was no exception. One of the Indian healers she knew was Marcellus Williams, or Bear Heart, a Muskogee (Creek) from Okmulgee, Oklahoma. Marcellus preached from the pulpit, was a Road Man of the Native American Church, and in his early years was trained by two Muscogee shamans to learn their ways of healing. A grounded, sensitive person, he also studied psychology at Bacone Indian School in Muskogee, and eventually became an adjunct consultant at the Psychiatric Memorial Hospital in Albuquerque, New Mexico.[9]

Thus, Ann was following the mores of her tribe regarding the appropriate time of mourning and soul cleansing before continuing with her social functions.

The author drove Ann Shadlow one summer afternoon to the site of a Cheyenne Sun Dance in the country near Hammond, Oklahoma, a three-day period of fasting and dancing under a brush arbor, the top of its main pole festooned with cloth and other offerings. The participating dancers that year included shaman Marcellus Williams. The dancers fast for three days, and are allowed only water distributed by the ceremonial water man, as they dance

Ann Shadlow dressed in a beaded buckskin dress, purse, moccasins, and fringed shawl. *Courtesy Laketa Pratt Collection.*

Ann Shadlow in a red cloth dress with Cowrie shells and beadwork. *Courtesy Laketa Pratt Collection.*

in one place to the drum and blow their high-pitched bone whistles emulating the eagle's cry. Quiet reigns all round the brush arbor, and visitors sitting outside the arbor are allowed no food or drink. It is a time of quiet meditation, filled with thoughts of one's life and goals, as well as prayers for the health and welfare of the person to whom the dancer dedicates his dance. The shaman later told the author "I knew you were there. I could feel it."

Before leaving the area, Ann and the author visited the tented pavilion, which the Pratt family had set up to provide coffee and drinks to visitors. Ann advised, "Don't spill the coffee, as that will bring rain," unwanted for that outdoor event. Of course, uncharacteristically, the author spilled a cup of coffee on the vinyl-covered table. And within ten minutes, as the pair set out for Oklahoma City on Highway I-40 under a clear blue sky, a vigorous shower pelted the car.

Ann's many activities reached a slowing point, however, as she approached the age of ninety. Her health began to fail. But her staunch spirit sustained her through the health problems and even continued to support her when she had to enter a nursing home for care.

Ann Guerrier Shadlow represented the continuing strength of the union of the two families of Guerrier and Bent. As the beloved descendant of Edmund and Julia, Ann could rest at age ninety with the knowledge that she had taken her rightful place in the annals of early Oklahoma and the twentieth century Indian world. She had proved she was the best Indian she could be.

Her family began preparing for Ann's eventual death at the time she entered a nursing home. Her son Charles purchased the materials for her burial outfit well in advance, and his daughter Laketa Pratt began the sewing of her attire. When Ann died on November 15, 2002 at the age of ninety-one, all was ready. Laketa had crafted a red trade cloth dress that was embroidered in a floral design, and matching cloth leggings. She made for Ann a leather dance belt with German silver conchos and a long drop, hung with matching beaded leather possible bag, knife sheath, and needle case. Laketa made moccasins beaded in a yellow, orange, and red on white design, with a matching medallion necklace, choker, and earrings. At Ann's wake in El Reno on November 17, Laketa dressed Ann in this outfit, braided her hair with feather hair ties, and added bright red lipstick and nail polish. A handsome woman in her life, Ann again exemplified her spirit even in death.

Ann Shadlow and granddaughter Laketa Pratt in dance dress. *Courtesy Laketa Pratt Collection.*

The miles-long procession of cars wound its way from Sacred Heart Church in El Reno to the Geary cemetery on November 18.

Harvey Pratt, windswept tie, at his mother's gravesite in
El Reno, Oklahoma. *Courtesy Author's Collection.*

Ann Guerrier Shadlow's burial site is near that of her parents William and Nellie, and her grandparents Edmund and Julia. Her headstone also lists her Indian name, Piavinnia.

Following the graveside service, Ann's coffin was lowered, and her sons and grandsons used shovels to fill in the grave with soil, piling the dirt three feet high. "That's the least I can do for my mother," said Harvey Pratt.

Three hundred people, along with her six living children, fifty-nine grandchildren, sixty-two great grandchildren, and twenty-three great-great grandchildren, gathered at the community center in Geary to give thanks for the life of Ann Guerrier Shadlow and to honor her.

Laketa Pratt winning the Grand Award with her Plains Indian Doll at the 2013 Red Earth Festival Art Show with *Piavinnia* author Jo Ann Kessel. *Courtesy Author's Collection.*

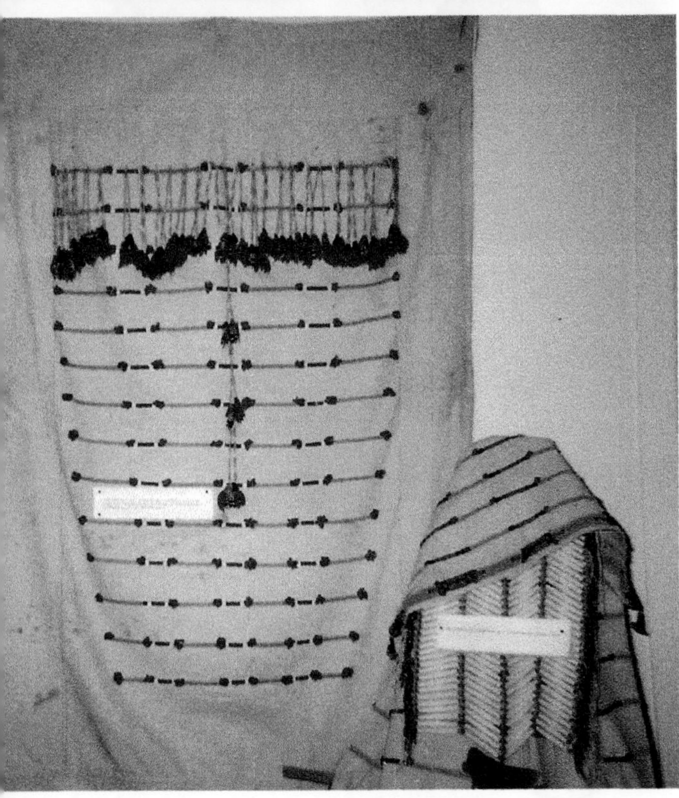

Tepee canvas door covers embellished with dew claws and feathers by Charlie Pratt. *Courtesy Laketa Pratt Collection.*

Charlie Pratt with his brass buffalo head sculpture. *Courtesy Laketa Pratt Collection.*

Charlie Pratt with one of his sculptures. *Courtesy Charlie Pratt Collection.*

Ann's family continued to prosper, most notably her two sons in the field of art. Charles Pratt moved his home and studio from Santa Fe to Gallup, New Mexico and continued winning awards in sculpture at art shows. His daughter Laketa is employed by the Cheyenne-Arapaho Tribal Headquarters at Concho, north of El Reno, and is enjoying success with art projects such as beaded moccasins and dance belts, beaded buckskin wall hangings and handmade fully-outfitted Indian doll figures.

Ann's son Harvey Pratt collaborated with an investigator with Bigfoot phenomena in the American northwest by co-authoring two books on their studies, Harvey supplying drawings based on witness descriptions.[10] [11] Still active at Indian art shows, Harvey was featured in a large show sponsored by the Science Museum Oklahoma in December 2012, displaying watercolor paintings, drawings of Bigfoot, and his trove of photographs, dresses, and other items of family memorabilia.

An Oklahoma state honor was bestowed on Harvey Pratt on January 12, 2013 when he was inducted into Oklahoma Law Enforcement Museum and Hall of Fame at the Oklahoma History Center. Currently the police forensic artist for the Oklahoma State Bureau of Investigation, Pratt also has been recognized as Outstanding Southern Cheyenne by his tribe.

The Bent-Guerrier legacy continues through Ann Guerrier Pratt Shadlow and flows through her progeny, enhancing the history of the West and especially the state of Oklahoma.

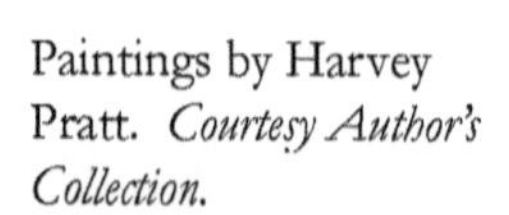

Paintings by Harvey Pratt. *Courtesy Author's Collection.*

A candelabra of white pine, seed beads, and brass on wooden stands by Laketa Pratt. *Courtesy Laketa Pratt Collection.*

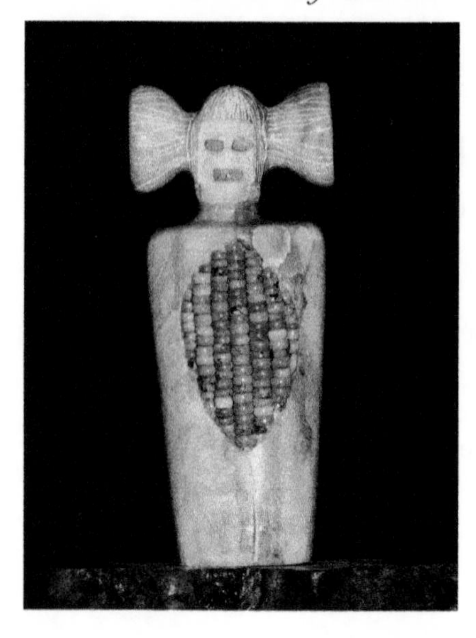

Hopi Corn Maiden from Alabaster and accented with turquoise beads by Laketa Pratt. *Courtesy Laketa Pratt Collection.*

Bibliography

George Bird Grinnell. *Bent's Old Fort and Its Builders.* Kansas State Historical Society.
Harvey Pratt. Interview with author, June 14, 2002, Oklahoma City, Oklahoma.
Fred S. Barde. "Edmund Gasseau Chouteau Guerrier." Article, *The Chronicles of Oklahoma*, Oklahoma Historical Society: Oklahoma City, Winter 1969-70, Vol. XLVII, #4
Stella M. Dramm, Ed. *Journal of a Fur Trading Expedition on the Upper Missouri 1812-1813.* St. Louis Historical Society: St. Louis, 1920.
Bent, George, and George E. Hyde. *Life of George Bent written from his letters,* Norman: University of Oklahoma Press, 1968.
Hoig, Stan. *The Sand Creek Massacre.* Norman: University of Oklahoma Press, 1961.
Stan Hoig. *The Peace Chiefs of the Cheyenne.* Norman: University of Oklahoma Press, 1980.
Mitchell Marks. *In a Barren Land.* New York: William Morrow and Company, 1988.
Maria Sandoz. *Cheyenne Autumn.* New York: McGraw-Hill Book Company, Inc., 1953.
George Bent Testimony, Estate of Slow Smoking. Washita County, Oklahoma, March 27, 1914
Ann Guerrier Shadlow. Interview, April 24, 1989. Oklahoma City, Oklahoma.
William Clark Kennerly. *Persimmon Hill: A Narrative of Old St. Louis and the Far West.* Norman, Oklahoma: University of Oklahoma Press, 1948, page 218.

Notes

Chapter 1
1 George Bird Grinnell. Bent's Old Fort and Its Builders. Kansas State Historical Society, page 31. Smith later became one of Colorado's first urban entrepreneurs when he opened one of the first stores in Denver in 1858.
2 Harvey Pratt. Interview with author, June 14, 2002, Oklahoma City, Oklahoma. Pratt is the great-grandson of Julia Bent and Edmund Guerrier, and is a chief of the Cheyenne tribe. Pratt states that although most reference works cite the name of Grey Thunder, he is officially known among present-day Cheyenne chiefs as White Thunder.
3 Fred S. Barde. "Edmund Gasseau Chouteau Guerrier." Article, "The Chronicles of Oklahoma," Oklahoma Historical Society: Oklahoma City, Winter 1969-70, Vol. XLVII, #4, page 366.
4 Stella M. Dramm, Ed. Journal of a Fur Trading Expedition on the Upper Missouri 1812-1813. St. Louis Historical Society: St. Louis, 1920, page 70. Of Algonquian stock, the matrilinear Cheyenne were first noted in 1680 as living on the Missouri River in Minnesota. Called Shahiyena by their enemies, the Sioux, the tribe was forced to move first to North Dakota, where they continued to live in earthen lodges and farmed, and from there they were found by Lewis and Clark in 1804. Relatively peaceful with the whites until 1865, the tribe by that time had divided, one part (Northern Cheyenne) living in Montana while the other bands stayed in the Kansas-Colorado area. Known as the Southern Cheyenne, they were induced to stay in the south to trade with Bent's Fort on the Arkansas River in southern Colorado, and because William Bent had married the daughter of the Holy Man and Keeper of the Sacred Medicine Arrows, White Thunder.
5 Bent, George, and George E. Hyde. Life of George Bent written from his letters, Norman: University of Oklahoma Press, 1968, pages 135-136.
6 Ibid.
7 Barde, Fred S., page 362.
8 Harvey Pratt. Interview with author, June 13, 2002. Oklahoma City, Oklahoma. Pratt, former Assistant Director of the Oklahoma State Bureau of Investigation, was recalled from retirement to become the forensic artist and sculptor at the OSBI. He is the great-great-nephew of Robert Bent, and is a chief of the Cheyenne tribe.
9 Hoig, Stan. The Sand Creek Massacre. Norman: University of Oklahoma Press, 1961. page 137.
10 Ibid., page 53.
11 Stan Hoig. The Peace Chiefs of the Cheyenne. Norman: University of Oklahoma Press, 1980, pages 106-107.
12 The Peace Chiefs of the Cheyenne, pages 104-105.
13 Life of George Bent, pages 322-333.
14 Life of George Bent. Pages 322-333.
15 The Peace Chiefs of the Cheyenne. page 110.

Chapter 2
1 "Edmund Gasseau Chouteau Guerrier." Page 368.
2 Ibid.

3 Paula Mitchell Marks. In a Barren Land. New York: William Morrow and Company, 1988, pages 183-184.
4 George Bird Grinnell. Bent's Old Fort and Its Builders. Kansas Historical Society, n.d., page 39.
5 David Fridtjof Hallas and Andrew E. Masich. Half Breed. Da Capo Press: Cambridge, Massachusetts, 2004., pages 141-146
6 Maria Sandoz. Cheyenne Autumn. New York: McGraw-Hill Book Company, Inc., 1953.
7 George Bent Testimony, Estate of Slow Smoking. Washita County, Oklahoma, March 27, 1914.
8 Half Breed, pages 149-151.
9 Craig Moore, United States Park Service, Interview. Sand Creek Massacre site, September 23, 2009.
10 Life of George Bent, page 157.
11 Ann Guerrier Shadlow. Interview, April 24, 1989. Oklahoma City, Oklahoma. Granddaughter of Edmund Guerrier and Julia Bent. Ann followed this tradition when her husband Martin Shadlow died, by cutting a chunk from her hair and slashing her arm, as witnessed by author.
12 Harvey Pratt, Interview. Pratt states it is known that Edmund Guerrier was shot in the arm and thereafter bore a scar.

Chapter 3
1 David Lavender. Bent's Fort, Lincoln, Nebraska: University of Nebraska Press, 1954, pages 16-17.
2 Frank McNitt. The Indian Traders. Norman, Oklahoma: University of Oklahoma Press, 1962, page 27.
3 Bent's Fort, page 25.
4 Ibid., page 224. Lilburn Boggs became governor of Missouri in 1836, built the state capitol and organized the state university. But his legacy was stained by his antagonism toward the Mormon sect. While Anti-Mormon riots raged, Lilburn Boggs sent six thousand state militia to rid the state of them. They were driven out. One enraged Mormon shot Governor Boggs through the head and neck as he sat by the window of his home one night. Boggs lived, and later won a seat in the Missouri Senate. Lilburn eventually moved to California with three of his sons, where he died on a farm in Napa on March 16, 1860.
5 Ibid., pages 224-225.
6 Helen Clark. "The Genius who Was Charles Marion Russell." Article. True West. Iola, Wisconsin: Western Publications, Vol. 30, #8, August 1983.
7 George Schriever. "Remington and Russell." Article. Southwest Art. May 1977, pages 42-43.
8 William Clark Kennerly. Persimmon Hill: A Narrative of Old St. Louis and the Far West. Norman, Oklahoma: University of Oklahoma Press, 1948, page 218.
9 Wikipedia, "Silas Bent (naval officer)," http://en.wikipedia.org/wiki/Silas_Bent_%28naval_officer%29 (accessed September 2, 2011). For twenty-five years until 1861, Bent cross the Atlantic five times, the Pacific twice, rounded Cape Horn four times and the Cape of Good Hope once. But he was a southern sympathizer and resigned his commission at the beginning of the Civil War, thereafter managing his wife Ann Elizabeth Taylor's estate in Louisville, Kentucky. Honoring Bent, the US Navy inaugurated in 1966 the Silas Bent class ships commissioned solely for oceanographic survey work. In 2009, the nuclear submarine Silas Bent was commissioned.
10 Louis Houck. A History of Missouri from the Earliest Explorations and Settlements Until the Admission of the State into the Union. Vol. I, II, and III. New York: Arno Press and New York Times, 1971, pages 14-15. The son of Walter Carr of Albermarle County, Virginia who was a personal friend of Thomas Jefferson, William Chiles studied law and was admitted to the bar, immigrated to Louisiana Territory and settled first in Ste. Genevieve where he married Dr. Aaron Elliot's daughter, Anna Marie. He later moved to St. Louis and, after the death of his wife, married Dorcas Bent in 1829. He died March 31, 1851 at 68 years.
11 John Francis McDermott, Ed. "Myths and Realities Concerning the Founding of St. Louis," article. The French in the Mississippi Valley. Urbana, Illinois: University of Illinois Press, 1965, page 9. The grant to Laclede and Maxent was made by Jean D'Abbadie, the last French commandant in New Orleans.
12 Clarence W. Alvord, Ed. Illinois Historical Collection. Vol. 5, Kaskaskia Records, 1778-1790. Springfield, Illinois: Illinois State Historical Library, 1909, page 421.
13 Persimmon Hill: A Narrative
14 Storrs, James E. and Gale, Kira. The Death of Meriwether Lewis: A Historic Crime Scene Investigation. Omaha, Nebraska: River Junction Press, 2009.
15 Persimmon Hill, page 41.
16 Stephen Ambrose. Undaunted Courage. New York: Simon and Schuster, 1996, page 403.
17 Persimmon Hill, page 62.

Chapter 4
1 Bent's Fort, page 26.
2 Gene and Mary Martin. Trail Dust. Boulder, Colorado: Johnson Publishing Company, 1972, page 4.
3 Bent's Fort, page 91.
4 Bent's Fort, page 105.
5 Bent's Fort, page 129.
6 Bent's Fort, page 132-133.
7 AllanW. Eckert. Twilight of Empire. Boston, Massachusetts: Little Brown and Co., 1988, pages 105, 106, 622. The St. Vrain family had been noted in the high governmental offices of France for many years. But the elder, Felix de Hault et de Luziere in Hainault, in the north of France, was forced into exile during the Reign of Terror following the French Revolution. He then settled in the Spanish-owned territory later to be known as the Louisiana Territory. His eldest son was appointed Governor de Lassus of Upper Louisiana. Another son was Jacques St. Vrain, an officer in the French Navy, and the father of Ceran and Felix St. Vrain. Felix became quartermaster of the Second Regiment of the Illinois Militia while living in Kaskaskia, next a Randolph County commissioner and public administrator. In October of 1830, Indian Agent William Clark appointed Felix as the new Indian Agent for the Sac and Fox Indians. Felix was stationed at Fort Armstrong on Rock Island. The brother Ceran became a respected trader on the Missouri River, once formed a partnership with William Guerrier, then became a partner in the Bent, St. Vrain and Company that built Bent's Fort, Adobe Walls, Fort St. Vrain and traded extensively in Santa Fe and Taos. Ceran's brother, Marcellin, also worked for the company at Fort St. Vrain and in Taos.

8 Ann Guerrier Shadlow, interview. Ann stated that Yellow Wolf never wore the regalia of battle finery when going to war or on a raid. He only wore his breech cloth.
9 Bent's Fort, page 139.
10 Bent's Fort, page 1page 145-148.
11 Lewis H. Garrard. Wah-to-Yah and the Taos Trail. Norman, Oklahoma: University of Oklahoma Press, 1972, page 42.
12 Ibid.
13 Trail Dust, page 4.
14 Richard Dunlop. Great Trails of the West. Nashville, Tennessee: Abingdon Press, 1971, page 38.
15 George Bent to George Hyde. Letter. March 19, 1906. Oklahoma Historical Society, Oklahoma City, Oklahoma.

Chapter 5
1 The Indian Traders, page 36.
2 George Bent. Testimony in the estate of Slow Smoking. Washita County, State of Oklahoma, March 1914. Bent testified that the children of White Thunder and Tail woman were Owl Woman, Island and Slow Smoking, daughters, and Pushing Bear, son.
3 Bent's Fort, page 255.
4 David Fridtjof Halaas and Andrew E. Masich. Halfbreed: The Remarkable Story of George Bent. Cambridge, Massachusetts: Da Capo Press, 1970, pages 43-44.
5 Bent's Fort, pages 43,44.
6 James W. Abert (edited by John Galvin). Through the Country of the Comanche Indians in the Fall of the Year 1845: The Journal of a U. S. Army Expedition Led by Lieutenant James W. Abert. San Francisco, California: John Howell Books, 1970, page 3.
7 Halfbreed, pages 31-38.
8 Bent's Fort, pages 79-82.
9 Stan Hoig. The Western Odyssey of John Simpson Smith. Glendale, California: Arthur H. Clarke, 1974, pages 18, 25-26, 39, 43-44.
10 The Rath Trail.

Chapter 6
1 St. Louis Genealogical Society. Research material dated 2-23-2011 in letter to author.
2 Ibid.
3 SLGS Research: Florence (11-27-1784 to 11-3-1832) married Joseph Philibert from Trois Rivieres, Canada; Marie Louise 92-1-1786 to --) married three times to Joseph Laprise, Pierre Marasse and August Durocher; Felicité (9-20-1787 to 10-30-1832) married Charles le Guerrier, Sr.
4 SLGS Research. The deed from Florence and Joseph Philibert to Felicité and her children was recorded November 18, 1811, the lot fronting Main Street forty feet wide and 150 feet long, next to the Philibert lot and that of Pierre Chouteau.
5 Marie Claire (1807 -) married Gabriel Philibert; Charles, Jr. (1808-2-17-1863) married Constance Giguere; Victoire Eulalie (9-29-1811 -); Guillaume "William" (1-4-1812 to 2-16-1858) married Tah-tah-tois-neh; Isabelle "Elizabeth" ((7-23-1814 to July 7, 1895) married Leon Longuemare 1-2-1834; Felicité (5-20-1817 to before 1896) married Charles Longuemare 4-18-1836; Marie Julia (8-25-8120 to 5-29-1892) married Benjamin Philibert 5-19-1842. The sisters Isabelle and Felicité married brothers Leon and Charles Longuemare from Paris, France. Marie Julia and Marie Claire married related Philiberts.
6 Missouri Legislative Census, Fall of 1817. Washington D. C. 1819. In the fall of 1817, St. Louis held 4,725 males, the women and children not counted at that time, out of only 19,218 males in the entire Missouri Territory.
7 Ceran St. Vrain to B. Pratte. Letter. April 27, 1824. St. Louis, Missouri: Missouri Historical Society.
8 Sandoz, Mari. The Beaver Men. Lincoln, Nebraska: University of Nebraska Press, 1964, Page 272. In 1816, Congress outlawed alien fur dealers on United States territory. However, a trader who married an Indian woman was considered a member of the tribe and therefore belonged to the United States.
9 Barde, Fred S. "Edmund Gasseau Chouteau Guerrier." Article. The Chronicles of Oklahoma. Oklahoma City, Oklahoma: Oklahoma Historical Society, Winter 1969-70, Vol. XLVII, #4, page 362.
10 Fly, Shelby. The Saga of the Chouteaus of Oklahoma. Apache News: Norman, Oklahoma, 1988.
11 Broadhead, Edward. "William Guerrier () – 1858 and Edmund Guerrier 1840-1921." Article. Pueblo, Colorado: Pueble County Historical Society, November 1984, pages 3-8. Broadhead reported William Guerrier's second wife as a Brule Sioux who gave birth to Henry.
12 Cheyenne Tribe Rolls. Henry Guerrier is listed as enrollee #910 at tribal headquarters in Concho, Oklahoma, born in 1854, a widower in the 1926 census, and died March 1927 at the Concho hospital.
13 Ann Guerrier Shadlow. Interview, April 29, 1989, Oklahoma City, Oklahoma. Ann was present at Henry's death, she stated it was Henry's Sioux stepfather who severely physically abused Henry.
14 S.L.G.S. Research. William Guerrier's will dated April 6, 1858 in Sandy Point, Territory of Nebraska lists his heirs as Edmund Guigot, Julia, Rosanna, Florence and Henry, all to receive equal shares of his estate upon his death. William signed with his mark.

Chapter 7
1 Patricia K. A. Fletcher, Dr. Jack Earl Fletcher, Lee Whiteley. Cherokee Trail Diaries. Caldwell, Idaho: Fletcher Family Foundation, Caxton Printers, Ltd., n.d., page 67.
2 Life of George Bent, page 435. One son was name Elfego. His father, George Bent, sent Elfego to the United States for schooling in 1847. Elfego and his wife, Guadalupe Long, later lived in El Rancho, Colorado. Their son Albert Silas Bent (born October 20, 1864) was baptized on December 7, 1864 by Joseph M. Coudert at the Catholic church in Taos. Elfego met his death in Taos on December 9, 1865.
3 1910-1960: A Church of the Plains, page 24.
4 George Bent to George Hyde. Letter, March 19, 1906. Oklahoma City, Oklahoma: Oklahoma Historical Society.
5 Bent's Fort, page 254.
6 Mari Sandoz. Beaver Men; Spearheads of Empire, New York: Hastings House, 1964, pages 109, 138.
7 Edward Broadhead. "William Guerrier ( )-1858 and Edmund Guerrier 1840-1921." Article, Pueblo Lore. Pueblo, Colorado: Pueblo County Historical Society, November 1984, pages 3-8.
8 Ibid.
9 History Central: Union Generals. General Francis

Preston Blair, Jr., USA. AOL ONLINE. Francis Preston Blair, Jr. (born February 19, 1821 in Lexington County, Kentucky) studied at College of New Jersey (now Princeton) and received his law degree from Transylvania College in Kentucky. As a Brigadier General in 1862, he commanded the Union line at Vicksburg when General Pemberton surrendered that city to General Grant. After his troops battled their way to Atlanta, he led his XVII Corps across the south with Sherman's march, and was in Goldsborough, North Carolina when General Lee surrendered at Appomattox. He was highly praised by Grant and Sherman. In 1868, he became the Democratic nominee for Vice President. He was appointed to fill a seat in the Senate in1871. He died in St. Louis July 9, 1875 at the age of fifty-four.

The Presidential Guest House at 1651 Pennsylvania Avenue N.W., Blair House, was purchased by Blair, Sr. in 1836, and has kept the Blair family name.

10 Bent's Fort, pages 230-231.
11 Ibid.
12 "The Story of Gov. Bent's Massacre as Told by his Daughter Teresina Bent Scheurich Who Was a Witness." Article. Undated and unpublished manuscript. Recalled from her age of five years at the time of the massacre. Taos, New Mexico: Bent Museum, September 14, 2003.
13 Ibid.
14 Ibid.
15 Ibid.
16 The Indian Traders, page 42.
17 Bent's Fort, page 326.

Chapter 8

1 This splinter group from the Missouri River originally lived in earth lodges in the north, and were known as the Suhtai or SuTaio. Suhtai were gradually absorbed into the larger group of Cheyenne, and their language was lost.
2 Bent's Fort, pages 333-335.
3 Life of George Bent, page 83. "There were four children, all born at the old fort, from the marriage of my father and mother about 1835," wrote George Bent, William's son. "Mary was born January 22, 1838, Robert about 1840. I was born July 7, 1843, and Julia was born in 1847. Our mother died at Julia's birth, and sometime later our father married her youngest sister, Yellow Woman. By this second marriage there was only one child, my half-brother, Charles."
4 Life of George Bent, page 97.
5 Bent's Fort, page 337.
6 Halfbreed, page 52-53.
7 Gregory M. Franzwa. The Santa Fe Trail Revisited. St. Louis, Missouri: The Patrice Press, 1989, pages 241-242.
8 Bent's Fort, pages 338-339.
9 C. W. Hurd. Boggsville, Cradle of the Colorado Cattle Industry. Boggsville, Colorado: Boggsville Committee, 1950s, page 57. Bent's destruction of his fort was not complete. Ranchers and bankers in nearby settlements verified the presence of the fort many years later.
10 Halfbreed, pages 54-55.
11 George Bent. Affidavit in the Estate of Slow Smoking, Washita County, Oklahoma, March 24, 1914. Scout Woman died in 1884 at age twenty in Indian Territory.
12 Edmond Gasseau Chouteau Guerrier, page 362.
13 Cherokee Trail Diaries, page 61.
14 Cherokee Trail Diaries, page 271. Guerrier and Ward were licensed in July 1848 by Indian agent Thomas Fitzpatrick to trade in the Upper Platte and Arkansas agency.
15 J. Tutt to Major Dougherty. Letter; April 14, 1853, St. Louis, Missouri: Missouri Historical Society.
16 Ed., Leroy R. Hafen. The Mountain Men and the Fur Trade of the Far West. Glendale, California: The Arthur H. Clark Company, 1968, Vol. VI, pages 365-366.
17 The Mountain Men and the Fur Trade of the Far West, page 367.
18 David Dixon. Hawk: The Life and Times of Edmund Guerrier. Thesis. Slippery Rock College, Slippery Rock, Pennsylvania, page 20.
19 Ibid, page 21.
20 Cherokee Trail Diaries, page 261. The Evans-Cherokee packer train on its way to the California goldfields in 1849 recorded that Bent's U-shaped stockade at the Big Timbers burned in 1849. Possibly Bent rebuilt the stockade in whole or in part and used it until he made a decision to build another Fort, the stone Bent's New Fort.
21 Ann Guerrier Shadlow. Interview. Julia described her recollections of Bent's New Fort to her granddaughter Ann Guerrier on many occasions during Ann's childhood.
22 Bent's Fort, page 355.
23 Albert Boone, grandson of Daniel Boone, was the brother of Panthea Boone Boggs, who married the husband of Juliannah Bent, Lilburn Boggs, following Juliannah's death.
24 Angus Boggs was the son of William Bent's sister, Juliannah Bent Boggs, and Lilburn Boggs.
25 Halfbreed, pages 80-81.

Chapter 9

1 Ann Guerrier Shadlow. Interview. Shadlow recalled that her grandfather Edmund Guerrier often spoke of his football days and classes in pharmacy at St. Louis University.
2 The Mountain Men and the Fur Trade of the Far West, page 369.
3 The Mountain Men and the Fur Trade of the West, pages 368-371.
4 Ibid, page 371.
5 Conflicting stories are documented concerning the date and place of William Guerrier's death. The date and place given in this narrative are from: Dan L. Thrapp. Encyclopedia of Frontier Biography. Spokane, Washington, The Arthur H. Clark Company, 1990. Vol. II, page 597.
6 Ibid, page 362.
7 Ibid, pages 596-597.
8 Harvey Pratt, Interview. Pratt related family history, and the observations of his mother Ann Guerrier Shadlow, granddaughter of Edmund Guerrier.

Chapter 10

1 Gregory M. Franzwa in Santa Fe Trail Revisited reported that Bent bought the home on April 6, 1858 from William Matney Jr. After Bent's death, Seth Ward's widow, Mary Ward, bought the home from Bent's widow, Adalina Bent, in 1870.

Another version is in an article by Mrs. Sam Ray in the Kansas City Times of July 30, 1965 entitled "Sunset Hill House Link to Fur Trade

Days." Ray stated that William Bent built this house on his 400-acre farm, which covered Sunset Hill and Loose Park areas of Kansas City. Seth Ward bought the house and the 400-acre farm in 1871 and built a fifteen-room house in front of the Bent house, connecting the two structures. The William Bent-Seth Ward home was listed for sale in November 2011 for $3,000,000, a 5-bedroom, 4½ bathroom home on 1.1 acres with a seven space garage, 6,688 feet with seven fireplaces, a prestigious property near the country club. This information was provided courtesy of author Shirley Christian of Overland Park, Kansas and Rena Carter of Oklahoma City, Oklahoma.
2 Early Far West Notebook. August, September, October, #111. 1907. Mrs. Shaw's Notebook, page 32. Denver Public Library, Denver, Colorado, taken from papers at the Pioneer Museum in Colorado Springs.
3 Introduction: A Place Named Taos. n.d., n.p. Listed are Catholic Church of Taos records. July 6, 1858.These same church records also contained an entry of baptism for Juana Carson, their young teenage adopted Navaho daughter, on December 22, 1860. The same church baptized Albert Silas Bent, son of Elfego Bent on December 7, 1864. And, Rumalda Bent married Juan Rite there in November 1865.
4 Halfbreed, page 72.
5 In a Barren Land, page 145.
6 Bent's Fort, pages 358-361.
7 Ibid, page 365.
8 Ibid, pages 365-366.
9 Ibid, pages 367-368.
10 Ray in "Sunset Hill House ..." gives the name as Robert M. Moore. The Carson-Bent-Boggs Genealogy lista R.M. as Robinson M. Moore, born 8-26-1833 in New Haven, Huron County, Ohio, died autumn of 1894. Descendant of Sir John Moore of Glasgow, Scotland. Moore became Probate Judge of Bent County, Colorado.
11 George Hyde to Jos. Thoburn. Letter. Oklahoma Historical Society. Oklahoma City, Oklahoma.
12 Halfbreed, pages 84-91.
13 Bent's Fort, pages 372-374.
14 Ibid, page 105.
15 Life of George Bent, page 173.
16 Bent's Fort, page 370.
17 Boggsville: Cradle of ..., pages 58-63. In 1866, heavy rains overflowed the banks of the Arkansas River and ruined the buildings. In 1867, the army moved Fort Lyon to its present location, seven miles from Las Animas. The army abandoned Fort Lyon August 31, 1889, but reopened it in 1906.
18 Donald J. Berthrong. The Southern Cheyennes. Norman, Oklahoma: University Press, 1963, page 199.
19 George Bent Testimony: Estate of Slow Smoking. Washita County, Oklahoma. March 23, 1914. Bent states Slow Smoking married Peg Leg prior to the allotments and was still married to him at the time of her death in1914.

Chapter 11
1 *The Southern Cheyennes.,* page 241.
2 Lavender in *Bent's Fort* identifies the woman slain as Yellow Woman. Halaas and Masich in *Halfbreed* state it was Island.
3 George Bird Grinnell. *The Fighting Cheyennes.* Norman, Oklahoma: University of Oklahoma Press, 1956, page 208.
4 *The Peace Chiefs of the Cheyenne,* pages 112-113.
5 Indian Affairs. Laws and Treaties. Vol. 11. Compiled and Edited by Charles J. Kappler. Washington, D. C., Government Printing Office, 1904.
6 *Edmund Gasseau Chouteau Guerrier.*
7 *The Southern Cheyennes,* page 68. The Dog Soldiers were a large group of Cheyenne and Cheyenne-Sioux warriors who formed a band within the tribe and had their own chiefs. In a position of military leadership and privilege, they camped in the tribal center. They were an aggressive group that recognized their fellow band members for success in battle, the rescue of friends from the battlefields and for scalping live enemies.
8 *Bent's Fort,* pages 389-390.
9 John A. Sierra, S.F. 1910-1960*: A Church of the Plains: Jubilee History of St. Mary's Parish.* Las Animas, Colorado.
10 Bent's Fort, page 392. The year of Bent's marriage to Adalina Harvey was listed as 1867. In Halfbreed, page 249, the year of the marriage was listed as 1868.
11 *Halfbreed,* page 249.
12 *Life of George Bent,* page 260.
13 *Edmund Gasseau Chouteau Guerrier,* page 370.
14 *Halfbreed*, pages 221-222.
15 *Edmund Gasseau Chouteau Guerrier,* pages 371-372.
16 David Dixon. "A Scout with Custer: Edmund Guerrier on the Hancock Expedition of 1867." Article. Kansas History: Vol. 4, #3, page 160.
17 *The Fighting Cheyennes,* pages 252-253.
18 *A Scout with Custer ...*, page 160.
19 *A Scout with Custer ...*, page 162.
20 Ibid, page 162.
21 Blaine Burkey. Custer, Come at Once. Hays, Kansas: Thomas More Prep, 1976, page 12. This was not the only time Custer shot his horse during a buffalo hunt. It happened again two weeks after the April 15, 1867 departure from Hancock's camp in his pursuit of the Cheyenne. This next time was on a two-day hunt on May 4 and 5 scheduled for the personnel of Fort Hays as an amusement, in which teams were chosen, the winning team to be that which killed the most buffalo. Although on the winning team, Custer was not reported to have killed a buffalo.
22 Ibid, pages 4, 5.
23 Ibid, page 20. William "Medicine Bill" Comstock was esteemed by the Arapaho and given his nickname after he cut off the finger of a tribal member who had been bitten by a rattlesnake, thus saving the man's life. Comstock was the grandnephew of James Fenimore Cooper. He was called by Myles Keogh "an eccentric genius and admirer of everything reckless and daring." Comstock was shot in the back by Cheyenne while leaving a camp on the Solomon in August 1868. Page 40.
24 *A Scout with Custer ...*, page 164.
25 *Custer, Come at Once*, page 20.
26 Ibid, page 23.
27 Ibid.
28 Ibid, page 29.
29 *Edmund Gasseau Chouteau Guerrier,* page 272.

30 *Custer, Come at Once,* pages 32,33.
31 *Bent's Fort*, page 449.

Chapter 12
1 *Hawk: The Life and Times ...*, page 95.
2 *The Peace Chiefs of the Cheyennes,* page 116.
3 Ibid, page 93.
4 Ibid, page 97.
5 *Hawk: The Life and Times of ...*, page 72.
6 *The Peace Chiefs of the Cheyennes,* page 92.
7 Ibid, page 7.
8 *Life of George Bent,* page 285.
9 Douglas C. Jones. *The Treaty of Medicine Lodge.* Norman, Oklahoma, University of Oklahoma Press, 1966, pages 111-112.
10 *Halfbreed,* pages 237-238.

Chapter 13
1 Boggsville was named for Thomas A. Boggs, son of Lilburn Boggs and Panthea Boone. Thomas Boggs received a 2,040-acre land grant from the Vigil and St. Vrain land grant, and built a large adobe house on his sheep ranch. Thomas later became territorial governor of New Mexico, just as his father Lilburn had become governor of Missouri in his day. *Boggsville: Cradle of the Colorado Cattle Industry,* pages 4, 5, 6.
2 Tom Dunlay. *Kit Carson and the Indians.* Lincoln, Nebraska: University of Nebraska Press, 2000, page 414.
3 *Life of George Bent,* pages 292-293. The horse wandered from George Bent's herd, was found by a soldier and presented to an army wife at Camp Supply. George then wrote to the army wife, identified the horse as his, but said she could keep it if she wished. She did. George's gift exemplified the generous Cheyenne spirit.
4 *Kit Carson and the Indians,* page 414.
5 *Boggsville: Cradle of ...*, page 14.
6 *Kit Carson and the Indians,* page 415. Kit and Josefa Carson's bodies were moved and reburied at Taos in 1869.

Chapter 14
1 *Halfbreed,* page 261. George Bent moved out of Magpie's lodge and married 18-year-old Kiowa Woman in 1868, who had his daughter Julia in 1869.
2 *Boggsville: Cradle of ...*, pages 17-19. Robert Bent filed a depredations claim against the government for the loss of his stock but it was not until 1902 that the claim was paid. Robert by that time had died.
3 *Halfbreed,* page 256. Robert Bent signed on as scout with Captain William H. Penrose's 7th Cavalry to track the war party that killed the beef herd at Boggsville.
4 *Dee Cordry. True Heart: The Story of Edmund Guerrier.* Printed on the Internet: April 18, 2001. Guerrier's sworn statement was sent to General Sherman in Sheridan's November 1, 1869 report on military operations. Page 6.
5 Wilbur Sturtevant Nye. *Plains Indians Raiders.* Norman, Oklahoma: University of Oklahoma Press, 1968, page 20.
6 *Halfbreed,* pages 243-248.
7 George Bent Affidavit in the estate of Slow Smoking. Washita County, Oklahoma. March 23, 1914. George reported Charlie died in 1867, although sometimes he was in error on his dates.
8 *The Southern Cheyennes*, pages 328-329.
9 Ibid.
10 Ibid.
11 *Custer, Come at Once,* pages 64-68. Major Benteen wrote that Custer and the Seventh Cavalry officers selected Cheyenne women as sexual consorts following the Washita massacre, and that Custer chose Mo-nah-see-tah, a particularly lovely woman and the daughter of chief Little Rock. The accusations were corroborated by writers Thomas Marquis, Charles J. Brill and Mari Sandoz who had heard this story from their interviews with several Indians and other informants. Other material disputes the accusations that Custer had a dalliance with Mo-nah-see-tah.
12 *Custer, Come at Once,* pages 96, 97. Lt. Thomas Ward Custer, George Custer's brother, was a heavy drinker and a trickster whom his brother and commanding officer once had to place under arrest. Tom Custer won the Congressional Medal of Honor twice. He died with his brother at the Battle of the Little Big Horn.
13 Morris F. Taylor. "The Carr-Penrose Expedition." *Article. Chronicles of Oklahoma.* Oklahoma City, Oklahoma: Oklahoma Historical Society, Vol. L1 #2, Summer 1975, pages 160-161.
14 "Edmond Gasseau Chouteau Guerrier," page 374.
15 *Hawk: The Life and Times of ...*, Page 107
16 "Edmund Gasseau Chouteau Guerrier," page 374.
17 Ibid.
18 Ibid, page 375.
19 Ibid, page 375.
20 *Bent's Fort,* page 393.
21 *The Santa Fe Trail Revisited,* page 43.
22 *Halfbreed*, pages 267-268. Rancher John Prowers eventually bought the Colorado land grants belonging to the Bent children and to Edmund Guerrier.

Chapter 15
1 *The Southern Cheyenne*, p. 333.
2 The prophecy that Medicine Arrows made to Custer in the event of his treachery came to fruition at the Battle of the Little Big Horn when Custer and his entire command were killed on June 25, 1876, by the Cheyenne and Sioux.
3 *The Southern Cheyenne,* page 337.
4 Ibid, page 338.
5 *Custer, Come at Once*, pages 68-69. George Bent identified those men killed as Curly Head (or Big Head) and Lean Face (or Dull Knife), the wounded man as Fat Bear.
6 United States 1870 Census of Bent County, Colorado. Julia Bent was listed, with her age given as twenty-six. If George Bent was correct in giving her birth date as 1847, she was actually twenty-three in 1870.
7 *Hawk: The Life and Times ...*, page 112.
8 Ibid, pages 112-113.
9 Ibid, pages 114-115.
10 "Ed. Guerrier, Interpreter in Washington," Letter. Kiowa Federal Relations. June 15, 1871. Oklahoma City, Oklahoma: Oklahoma Historical Society.
11 "Belle Balenti Martin Died Suddenly Mon. Night," Article. Geary Newspaper, May 4, 1939. Courtesy of Merle Rinehart, Geary, Oklahoma.
12 *Life of George Bent*, page 355.

13 *The Southern Cheyennes*, page 370.
14 Ed. Guerrier. C&A Depredations, CAA24. 6-14-1874. Oklahoma City, Oklahoma: Oklahoma Historical Society.
15 *The Southern Cheyennes*, pages 391-395.
16 Harvey Pratt, Cheyenne Chief, Interview. August 29, 2011.
17 While in the Florida prison, Oakerhater fell under the sway of the Episcopalian religion, was trained in New York, then returned to the reservation to minister to the Cheyenne as a deacon at Whirlwind Mission in Fay, Oklahoma. In 1985, he was added to the Calendar of Episcopal saints.
18 John H. Seger. *Early Days Among the Cheyenne and Arapaho Indians.* Norman, Oklahoma: University of Oklahoma Press, 1934, page 81.
19 Dan Peery. "The Indians' Friend, John H. Seger." Article, *Chronicles of Oklahoma.* Oklahoma City, Oklahoma: Oklahoma Historical Society, March 1933. Volume II, #1, page 724.

Chapter 16
1 Pratt, Harvey. Interview with author, June 10, 2004, Oklahoma City, Oklahoma. Pratt is the great-great nephew of Robert Bent, and a chief of the Cheyenne tribe.
2 Ibid.
3 Fort Reno was the Army post set up by the government in 1875, located a few miles west of the city of El Reno, the easternmost settlement on the reservation, for the purpose of keeping the peace on the reservation.
4 United States 1900 Census. Edmund listed his age as sixty, and that of Julia as forty-five, although she was fifty-three. They had been married twenty-five years, children William born April 1881 and Annie born October 1885, with two children deceased.
5 Shadlow, Ann Guerrier. Interview with author, April 24, 1989. Family legend recounts Julia's arranged marriage and her ample dowry, but reveals no date of the wedding ceremony in 1875. No additional documents could be located regarding the date and place of the marriage.
6 Ibid.
7 Cheyenne Census. Cheyenne Indian Archives, Oklahoma Historical Society, Oklahoma City, Oklahoma.
8 Cheyenne-Arapaho Records. Volume 20, Letter of December 30, 1887. Archives, Oklahoma Historical Society, Oklahoma City, Oklahoma.
9 Grinnell, George Bird. *The Fighting Cheyennes.* University of Oklahoma Press, Norman, Oklahoma, 1955, page 403.
10 Ibid.
11 *Halfbreed,* pages 299-301.
12 *Hawk: The Life and Times of* ..., page 127.
13 *Boggsville: Cradle of* ..., pages 63-66. Prowers, a former employee at Bent's Fort, was an early settler in Boggsville, manager of the stage station at Bent's Fort, and later a store owner in Boggsville, as well as a farmer and rancher.
14 Three-fourths of the Indian families continued to live in tepees.
15 *Hawk: The Life and Times of* ..., page 142.
16 Berthrong, Donald J. *The Cheyenne and Arapaho Ordeal,* University of Oklahoma Press: Norman, Oklahoma, 1976, page 109.
17 Ibid, page 115.
18 *Hawk: The Life and Times of* ..., pages 129-130.
19 *Webster's Collegiate Dictionary.* G. and C. Merriam Co., Publishers: Springfield, Massachusetts, 1946. Barouche: a four-wheeled carriage with a driver's seat in front, two double seats inside facing each other, and folding top.
20 *Hawk: The Life and Times of* ..., page 130.
21 *The Cheyenne and Arapaho Ordeal,* Illustration.
22 United States Census 1900. It listed that Anna Guerrier was born in the year 1885, October.
23 Ann Guerrier Shadlow. Interview with author, March 13, 1997. As Ann recalled the story, Rosa died on "the high seas," but was buried on the land north of El Reno that was awarded to Edmund Guerrier in appreciation and payment for his service to the government. This was the site where many Indians were buried, according to Shadlow.
24 Cheyenne-Arapaho Records, Volume 20. Letter of December 30, 1887. Archives, Oklahoma Historical Society, Oklahoma City, Oklahoma.
25 Merle Rinehart. Interview with author. February 7, 2003, Geary, Oklahoma.
26 *Their Story: A Pioneer Days Album of the Blaine County Area.* Heritage Book Committee: Oklahoma City, 1977, page 16.
27 Dee Cordry. *True Heart.* Article, Internet. April 18, 2001. The Guerrier allotment was SW/4, Section 20, T14N, R10E, Canadian County, bounded on the east by the North Canadian River. Their allotment numbers were: Edmund, #366; Julia, #367; William, #368, Anna, #369.
28 *The Cheyenne and Arapaho Ordeal,* page 196.
29 Harvey Pratt. Interview with author. June 10, 2004, Oklahoma City, Oklahoma. Pratt is the grandson of William Guerrier and is a chief of the Cheyenne.
30 Ibid.
31 *The Cheyenne and Arapaho Ordeal.* Donalf J. Berthrong. University of Oklahoma Press: Norman, Oklahoma, 1976, pages 221-224.
32 Blaine County Court. Territory of Oklahoma. Copy of document provided courtesy of Ruth Burch, Docent, National Cowboy Museum, September 13, 2001, Oklahoma City, Oklahoma.

Chapter 17
1 Cordry, Dee. *True Heart,* page 8. Also, "Geary: The First 25 Years." Article, n.d.,n.a.,n.p.
2 Harvey Pratt. Interview with author. Oklahoma City, Oklahoma, June 10, 2004. Pratt is the grandson of William Guerrier.
3 *The Cheyenne and Arapaho Ordeal,* page 303.
4 *The Cheyenne and Arapaho Ordeal,* pages 306-307.
5 Ibid, page 325.
6 Ann Guerrier Shadlow. Interview with author.
7 Barde, Fred S. *Edmund Gasseau Chouteau Guerrier,* page 361.

Chapter 18
1 Ann Guerrier Shadlow. Interview with author.
2 Cheyenne-Arapaho Records, Concho, Oklahoma.
3 Ibid. In the same year of 1913, William Guerrier sold 80 acres of his land, the west half of the SW/4, Section 29, Township 13, Range 7W in Canadian County, good productive black loam soil. Perhaps with a wife, two children and a step-daughter to feed, and with an income limited to day labor, William was desperate for money. In September, William's property sold for $5,325.

4 Hyde, George. *Life of George Bent.* University of Oklahoma Press: Norman, Oklahoma, 1968, page 192
5 Annie Guerrier's allotment was Lots 7 and 8 in the SE/4 of Township 14, north of Range 10W of the Indian Meridian. Her allotment number was #369, under Act of March 3, 18911. Cheyenne-Arapaho Records.
6 Harvey Pratt. Interview with author. Pratt provided the unpublished report to author.
7 Harvey Pratt. Interview with author.

Chapter 19
1 Harvey Pratt. Interview with author.

Chapter 20
1 Ann Guerrier Shadlow. Interview with author.
2 Cheyenne-Arapaho Records. Concho, Oklahoma. On October 22, 1917, Edward (sp), Julia and Annie's widower Emory Ballou applied to the Cheyenne-Arapaho Agency to sell their shares of Annie's allotment land, or 72.74 acres, and split the proceeds between the three of them. Edmund stated, "My wife and I plan to move to Montana, to purchase grazing land so that we may raise livestock for our living."
3 Ann Guerrier Shadlow. Interview with author.
4 Photograph of marker courtesy of Merle Rinehart of Geary, Executive Director of the Blaine county Historical Society, Geary, Oklahoma.
5 Ann Guerrier Shadlow. Interview with author.
6 Ibid.
7 Law Heirship #113838-16 S.E.B. Department of the Interior, Office of Indian Affairs. Cheyenne-Arapaho Agency, Oklahoma. November 22, 1916. Bear Woman's first husband was a white man name Moran, their child Mary Moran, or Washee. Henry and Bear woman's children: four children died in infancy; daughter Walking Behind married Jerome Bushyhead (Red Belt), their son named Henry. Walking Behind died at age 28. Two other Guerrier children were Yellow Hair, daughter, and Oscar, son. Bear Woman died July 9, 1915 at age 55.
8 Cheyenne-Arapaho Rolls. Concho, Oklahoma. April 22, 2001. Henry Guerrier was listed as enrollee #910 in the Cheyenne-Arapaho census of 1926, widowed, born in 1854.
9 Oscar N. Pratt, or Noble Oscar Pratt, born April 3, 1904. Cheyenne-Arapaho Roll #1695.
10 Ann Guerrier Shadlow. Interview with author.
11 Ibid.
12 Ann Guerrier Shadlow. Interview with author.
13 The gravesite of Julia Bent in the Geary cemetery is Block 3, Lot 11. Information courtesy of Merle Rinehart, president of the Geary Cemetery board.

Chapter 21
1 Charles Edward Pratt, born November 8, 1937.
2 Otto Pratt, born January 8, 1939.
3 Ann Guerrier Shadlow. Interview with author.
4 Anthony Pratt, born January 7, 1943.
5 Ann Guerrier Shadlow. Interview with author.
6 Charles Pratt. Interview with author, August 19, 1988. Santa Fe, New Mexico.
7 Charles Pratt. Interview with author. June 13, 2000. Oklahoma City, Oklahoma

Chapter 22
1 Ann Guerrier Shadlow. Interview with author. January 5, 1990. Oklahoma City, Oklahoma.
2 Merle Rinehart. Interview. Rinehart's cemetery records list William Guerrier's death on June 18, 1967 at Northeast Nursing Home in Oklahoma City, due to prostate cancer. Burial was in Block 3, Lot 10, Geary Cemetery.
3 Laketa Pratt. Interview. October 29, 2011. Oklahoma City, Oklahoma.

Chapter 23
1 A woman must first select the color and type of fabric she wants, then find a coordinating spool of fringe, then design a pattern for the shawl's decoration. Some are plain, but many shawls are adorned with traditional patterns of ribbon-work or beadwork designs. Each piece of fringe is cut to the desired length, holes punched in the edging of the material with an awl, then the process of tying the strands of fringe on the material begins. It is a time-consuming process.
2 Ann instructed both Indian and non-Indian students in the culture, lore, history and dances of the Plains Indians, appearing in full school assemblies, classrooms and small groups. Video and audio tapes were made of her demonstrations for use through the library lending source of the administration.
3 Ann Guerrier Shadlow offered classes on a regular weekly basis for each class of preschool, elementary, junior high and high school students in crafts, storytelling, and culture. Activities included singing, dancing, cooking and sewing.
4 Ann won four awards in Women's Senior Buckskin Dancer category at the Dallas-Fort Worth Powwow from 1979 to 1983. At the 1983 Little Rock Powwow, she placed first in her shell dress, and received a second place award in Senior Cloth Dancer at the 1985 Seminole Nation Powwow.
5 *The Southern Cheyennes*, pages, 62-63.
6 Ann Guerrier Shadlow. Interview with author. August 15, 2001. Oklahoma City, Oklahoma.
7 "The Wisdom Keepers." Anchor, Jennifer Reynolds. CBS Channel 9 evening news. June 9, 1994. Oklahoma City, Oklahoma.
8 "Lullabies of the World." Tom Hunsinger's company of Boulder, Colorado. 1995.
9 Bear Heart. *The Wind is My Mother: The Life and Teachings of a Native American Shaman.* Berkley Publishing: New York, 1968.
10 David Paulides. Sketches by Forensic Artist Harvey Pratt. *The Hoopa Project: Bigfoot Encountered in California.* Hancock House Publishers, Ltd: Blaine, Washington, 2008.
11 David Paulides. Sketches by Forensic Artist Harvey Pratt. *Tribal Bigfoot.* Hancock House Publishers, Ltd., Washington, 2009.

Index

About the Author

An Oklahoma Choctaw Jo Ann Kessel received her Associate of Arts at Christian College in Columbia, Missouri, and Bachelor of Arts and Master of Social Work degrees from the University of Oklahoma. She worked with children and families in adoption, foster care, parenting classes, and school social work as clinical social worker, as well as Consultant with the Indian Education Program at the Oklahoma City Public Schools.

As Clinical Assistant Professor in the School of Social Work at the University of Oklahoma, she managed a child welfare student training program and developed and taught courses in family and Indian Child Welfare.

Her appreciation for Indian and western art, combined with a love of history, has allowed her to showcase her contemporary Indian fashions at the National Cowboy & Western Heritage Museum banquet sponsored by the Cowbelles Auxiliary of the National Cattlemen's Association, on the late Jerome Bushyhead's television program *UNITY*, and at Indian arts shows throughout the southwest.

A docent at the National Cowboy & Western Heritage Museum, Kessel's other hobbies are travel, reading, riding, and breeding and showing smooth standard dachshunds.